Roy Campbell
A Critical Biography

Roy Campbell

A Critical Biography

PETER ALEXANDER

DAVID PHILIP
Cape Town

Published in Southern Africa by David Philip, Publisher (Pty) Ltd,
217 Werdmuller Centre, Claremont, Cape Province, South Africa,
and in the rest of the world by Oxford University Press

ISBN 0 908396 49 X

Printed in Great Britain, bound in South Africa

To my parents

ACKNOWLEDGEMENTS

THE need for a biography of Roy Campbell has long been felt by students of his poetry. It has been difficult to unearth from published material even the most basic facts about his life. Standard works of reference give only the vaguest biographical outline, and when they do provide details these are often wrong. Even the year of Campbell's birth is usually given as 1902 (it was 1901). Biographical notes prefacing Campbell's own works are equally untrustworthy. The Penguin edition of his autobiography *Light on a Dark Horse,* for instance, contains a note informing readers that Campbell fought in the Spanish Civil War, and that during the Second World War he 'went with a crack fighting unit to Burma'. These entirely false statements probably originated from Campbell himself, and they illustrate another problem facing the student of his work: Campbell was a great myth-maker. His two autobiographies do not merely distort and conceal the truth; they substitute for it an elaborate and consistent un-truth, a realistic mask which has to be torn aside before an attempt to see Campbell as he was becomes possible.

The task of obtaining accurate biographical information is made more difficult by the fact that Campbell very seldom dated his letters, and few of the original envelopes with postmarks have survived. As a result, the task of dating the Campbell correspondence occupied many months, and in many cases the dates of important events in Campbell's life must remain speculative. This is as Campbell would have wished; he cared nothing for factual precision, and often did not know what day of the week it was, or what month of the year.

In unravelling the confusions and complexities of Campbell's life I have depended at all times on the unfailing generosity of Mrs Mary Campbell, who turned what could have been a nightmarish task into a pleasure. From the start she welcomed and encouraged my research. In spite of her poverty and failing health, she opened her house to me for extended periods. She spent many days answering my questions and reliving her life for my tape-recorder; she sorted through hundreds of letters and thousands of news-clippings, and she put her extensive collection of photographs at my disposal. She endured my probings into the deepest secrets of her life, reacting to my questions sometimes with laughter and often with pain, but never protesting. When she was reticent, it was always to protect someone other than herself; not once did she ask me to suppress a fact likely to be damaging to herself. Although it is too early to tell the full story of Campbell's last decade, it was not Mary Campbell who placed constraints on my work. I read her the completed manuscript; she made no objection to any part of it. She told me that she longed to hold the finished book in her hands, and it is a source of deep regret to me that she did not live to see its publication.

Campbell's elder daughter Teresa gave me help which was second only to that of her mother. She allowed me to pick her brains, giving me vital information I could have got nowhere else; she let me read her unpublished memoir of her father, on which I have drawn largely; and she gave me much valuable advice. Above all, her calm faith gave me a practical insight into the nature of her father's Christianity.

I have been immeasurably helped in writing this book by the labours of two previous scholars: the late Professor W. H. Gardner of Natal University, and Mr Alan Paton. Professor Gardner planned a biography of Campbell, and although he was never to write it, his work in interviewing Campbell's friends or acquaintances while their memories were fresh, and his energetic search for Campbelliana, have saved me both time and labour, and greatly enriched this book. His painstaking scholarship has served as an example and as a reproach. My debts to him have been recorded in detail in the notes.

To Alan Paton I am indebted for his selfless generosity in handing over to my keeping the notebooks he was using to prepare his own biography of Campbell, as well as Professor Gardner's collection of Campbell papers. Throughout the writing of this book he has supported me with advice and encouragement. He put his home, his time, and his matchless knowledge of South African literature at my disposal, and I am grateful.

Sir Laurens van der Post endured long hours of questioning, allowed me to see many of Campbell's letters to him, and put me in the way of much information I should otherwise have overlooked. Others who generously put their memories at my disposal include Campbell's younger daughter, Dona Anna Cavero de Carondelet; the late Dr George Campbell, his wife Agnes and their son, Dr Hamish Campbell; Mr Edgell Rickword; Professor Guy Butler; Lady Kathleen Epstein; Mr Stephen Spender; the Marquess of Aberdeen (formerly Archie Gordon); Mrs Daphne Collins (Campbell's BBC secretary); Mrs Martin of Aberdaron, who shared with me her memories of the Campbells' stay in Wales; Mr Basil Holt, who allowed me to read his unpublished biography of Campbell, *Outrageous Poet*; Mr David Wright; Sir Sacheverell Sitwell; Mrs Violet Tschiffely; Sir William Walton; Mr Michael Wishart; and Mr Geoffrey Dutton.

Others who have provided information and assistance include Mr Geoffrey Grigson; Professor F. T. Prince; Mr. F. J. Temple; Mr George Watson; Mrs Vernon Watkins; Mr Francis Bywater; Mrs Clover de Pertinez; Mr Alister Kershaw; Mr Peter Eaton; Mr John Green; Mme Catherine Aldington-Guillaume; Dr J. R. de S. Honey; Mr Michael Holroyd; Mr Laurie Lee; Mrs Eileen Moloney; Dr Alan Munton; Professor Ian Gordon; and Mr Howard Newby. Professor D. S. J. Parsons helped me to gain access to important material in the University of Saskatchewan Library. Mrs Valerie Eliot kindly allowed me to copy Campbell's letters to her husband, T. S. Eliot; Mr Rob Lyle allowed me to read his unpublished memoir, *Horseman of Apollo*.

I wish to thank the following for permission to quote from Roy Campbell's writings: The Bodley Head for poems from *Flowering Reeds* (1933) and *Mithraic Emblems* (1936) and for lines from *The Georgiad* (1931) (from *Collected Poems*), and for passages from *Broken Record* (1934) and *Light on a Dark Horse* (1951); Curtis Brown Ltd. on behalf of The Estate of Roy Campbell for poems from *Adamastor* (Faber & Faber, 1930); Faber & Faber Ltd. for poems from *Talking Bronco* (1946); Jonathon Cape Ltd. for lines from *The Flaming Terrapin* (1924) and *The Wayzgoose* (1928); and Hughes Massie Ltd. for poems from *The Poems of St John of the Cross* (Harvill Press, 1951) and *A Translation of Les Fleurs du Mal* by Baudelaire (Harvill Press, 1952). I also wish to thank Mrs T. S. Eliot for permission to quote from T. S. Eliot's letter of 26 March 1945 to Roy Campbell; Uys Krige, for permission to quote from his article 'A Meeting with Roy Campbell'; Curtis Brown Ltd., London, on behalf of the Estate of Victoria Sackville-West for permission to quote lines from *King's Daughter* and *The Land* (The Hogarth Press 1929, 1933); André Deutsch Ltd., for permission to quote from Laurie Lee's *As I Walked Out One Midsummer Morning* (1969); and Romilly John, for permission to quote from *The Seventh Child* (William Heinemann, 1932). For permission to quote from Wyndham Lewis's *One Way Song* (Faber & Faber, 1932), *Snooty Baronet* (Cassells, 1932), *Blasting and Bombardiering* (Eyre & Spottiswoode, 1937), and letters from

Lewis to Campbell, dated 6 April 1930 and 13 April 1936, I thank the Estate of the late Mrs G. A. Wyndham Lewis, by permission of the Wyndham Lewis Memorial Trust.

Dr John Rathmell of Christ's College, Cambridge, and Mr John Bell of Oxford University Press kindly read an earlier draft of this book, and made many valuable criticisms and suggestions.

My sincere thanks are due to the staff of the following institutions, which gave me prompt and courteous assistance: The BBC (Archives Division); The British Library; The University of Chicago Library; Cornell University Library; The Olin Library, Cornell University; The University Library, Durham; The Cambridge University Library; The University of Iowa Library; The Johannesburg City Library; The Durban City Library; The Killie Campbell Africana Library; The Witwatersrand University Library; The South African National Library; The Corey Library, Rhodes University; The Lockwood Memorial Library, University of Buffalo; The University of Saskatchewan Library; The Washington University Library; and the Humanities Research Center Library, University of Texas at Austin.

I have been greatly helped in the gathering of information by generous financial help from Christ's College and Darwin College, Cambridge, from The British Academy, and from the Human Sciences Research Council, Pretoria. A Research Fellowship from Darwin College, Cambridge, gave me the opportunity to rewrite the book in its present form. A grant from the University of New South Wales covered part of the cost of typing the manuscript, with other related expenses.

Finally, I owe more than I can say to my wife, whose work on this manuscript considerably delayed her own writing on Charlotte Brontë, and without whose unfailing encouragement this book would have taken much longer to finish.

P.F.A.

University of New South Wales

CONTENTS

ILLUSTRATIONS

I

The Making of a Poet
1901–1918

IN the spring of the year 1850 the brig *Conquering Hero* slipped her
moorings at a Glasgow dock, moved down the Clyde, and, once in the
Atlantic, set sail for the south.[1] Her destination was the African
settlement of Port Natal, and she carried 127 prospective settlers,
most of them Scots. They had been recruited by a man named Joseph
Charles Byrne, who for a small consideration had agreed to arrange
passage for them all to a land where, he promised, they could not fail
to grow rich. Byrne sang the virtues of Natal with great eloquence.
The soil was more fertile than they could imagine, he told them;
anything would grow in such a climate. And there was land for the
taking, thousands of rolling acres for each man, and plentiful cheap
black labour to go with it: how could they fail? There was only one
potential source of danger, and that was the voyage itself; if they
should be shipwrecked on the dangerous coast of West Africa, they
might lose all they owned. But Byrne had provided for every
contingency. If the travellers would take the precaution of depositing
their savings with him before setting out, his agent in Port Natal
would refund the money safely to them as soon as they landed. This
scheme recommended itself to most of the passengers; and as the
Conquering Hero began to pitch and toss in the first of the Atlantic
rollers, many a prudent Scottish emigrant must have congratulated
himself on his foresight in having left his savings in the hands of
Byrne. Among those who had so insured themselves against the perils
of the deep was a twenty-nine-year-old railway manager, sailing for
South Africa with a wife and three young children. He was William
Campbell, future grandfather of the poet.

After a voyage lasting three months, the *Conquering Hero* anchored
off Port Natal in June 1850.[2] The settlers crowding the rail for a first
sight of the paradise Byrne had described must have wondered what
they had come to. The 'harbour' was a broad, shallow lagoon, its
mouth protected by a spit of land known as 'the Bluff', but so choked

with sand that the *Conquering Hero* could not enter it. All around stretched a waste of sand dunes, on which scrubby castor-oil plants and an occasional palm clung to life. There was no jetty; the only signs of human habitation were a few mud huts, one of them dignified with a flagpole, and a fragile-looking 'fort', armed with a couple of cannon and manned by a small platoon of soldiers. A sandy track wound into the bush across the flat towards the town, which lay somewhere between the lagoon and the long, jungle-covered hill which overlooked it.[3] No one, gazing with sinking heart at that wild scene, could have foretold that on this site would rise the city of Durban, or that that unpromising lagoon would become the greatest port in southern Africa, and that it was these settlers and their descendants who would work the transformation.

The passengers were transferred into heaving flat-bottomed lighters, their hatches battened against the Indian Ocean surf, and towed perilously across the bar into the calm of the lagoon. There they were met by teams of naked Zulu labourers, who waded into the water and carried the passengers on their backs to land. In this singular way William Campbell and his family found themselves standing on a South African beach on 29 June 1850.

A greater shock came when the settlers went to reclaim their savings from Byrne's agent. The man was solemn; he had terrible news for them – Mr Byrne had been declared bankrupt! There was nothing to be done about it; poor Mr Byrne was ruined. If they would only wait patiently, they might in due time receive a portion of their savings once Mr Byrne's affairs had been wound up. . . Too late the settlers realized that Byrne was a confidence trickster on a big scale; he made a good living out of pocketing the savings of those for whom he arranged passages to the colonies. Bankruptcy was his favourite refuge, and he operated under many aliases; on at least two occasions he 'died', to reappear in Mauritius or Australia under a different name. The newly landed passengers of the *Conquering Hero* were forced to resign themselves to their losses. William Campbell was luckier than most of his fellows. He was saved from complete destitution by his wife who, more sensible than her husband, had before leaving Glasgow sewed into the lining of her clothing 120 gold sovereigns.

William Campbell made good use of this material advantage and he did not remain poor for long. He was a man of driving ambition, with great reserves of energy and practical ability. It was he who, with another settler, built the breakwater that still forms the foundation of the great North Pier in Durban harbour. To transport the stones for it, he built the first railway in Natal, a mile of wooden rails on which ran wooden, ox-drawn carriages. He was also among the pioneers[4] of large-scale sugar-cane cultivation, which rapidly became – and has remained – Natal's most important crop. In doing so, he also established the basis of his own fortune.

He reared nine children. One of them, another William, became a chief magistrate in Natal; another became Sir Marshall Campbell, the wealthy head of Natal Sugar Estates, a Senator in the first Union Parliament in 1910 and a friend of the Prime Minister, Louis Botha.[5] Yet another son, Archie, became a District Native Commissioner in Rhodesia, and pioneered farming techniques in that country.

The poet's father, Samuel George Campbell, was born in 1861. Borrowing the money from his brother Marshall, he went in 1878 to Edinburgh to study medicine. Sam Campbell was academically brilliant. He took three prizes at Edinburgh (for surgery, clinical surgery, and botany) and graduated with honours in 1882, at the age of twenty-one. After doing postgraduate work in Paris, at the Pasteur Institute, he went to Vienna to specialize in the treatment of ear, nose, and throat ailments, in 1883. Back in Natal, he spent three years in practice before returning to Scotland in 1886 to take his MD and become a Fellow of the Royal College of Surgeons. A fine athlete, he performed remarkable feats of long-distance swimming, and he played rugby for Edinburgh University. It was in Scotland that he met Margaret Wylie Dunnachie, the daughter of James Dunnachie, a self-made businessman of great wealth, who, towards the end of his life, brought himself to the brink of ruin by filling his house with expensive paintings of dubious merit. Sam Campbell married Margaret in February 1886,[6] and in 1889 took her to South Africa.

The young doctor had all his father's energies and abilities. He would go any distance, at any hour of the night, to attend a patient. He treated black and white alike, a colour-blindness so rare in early Natal that it earned him the undying love of the Zulu people. The poor seldom had to pay him. His acts of generosity were renowned and stories such as that told by his son, Roy, of his swimming a raging river and then walking miles to see a patient contain more than a grain of truth.[7] Sam Campbell quickly became one of the town's most respected citizens. Despite his generosity, his large practice enabled him to build up a considerable fortune.[8] He founded the town's Technical College (which was to give birth in turn to Natal University); he established the town's social services. He was intellectually, financially, and socially successful.

In the carefully posed photographs of this period, he looks at first glance very much the small-town doctor. There is about him an air of plump prosperity. A watch-chain glitters on the dark, rotund waistcoat; the hair is thinning, and a walrus moustache spreads itself as if in compensation. It is the eyes that mark him out as something different. In their level stare one catches a hint of the iron will of the man. His sons admired him enormously, and longed to be like him.

The fourth child of this distinguished man was born in Durban on 2 October 1901. The Boer War was moving wearily to its close. Sam Campbell, serving with great distinction in the Natal Volunteer Medical Corps, had survived the siege of Ladysmith, and was once more on active service; it was many days before he knew of the birth of his third son. The boy was christened Royston Dunnachie Campbell, 'Royston' after an uncle by marriage, Colonel 'Galloping Jack' Royston, whose legendary martial exploits were ended about this time by his death from enteric fever. Grandfather Dunnachie wrote from Scotland to his daughter,

> So Royston Dunnachie Campbell has got his name at last, and I am sure from all accounts of him that have reached us that he will do honour to all three. There is something in a name, either of an individual or of a family, if the record is an honourable one. If we bear the name, it gives us an ideal and a motive to follow in the same lines, and it is ideas and ideals, not physical forces, that lie at the foundation of things, and rule the world of human effort and aspiration. May every blessing descend on little Roy.[9]

The assumption of the importance of family traditions which lies behind this letter was strongly shared by the poet's parents and, in time, by their children. They measured themselves continually against their forebears. It was a sign of the strength of tradition that in this steamy African town the Campbell boys, second-generation South Africans, were dressed for church in Eton collars one Sunday, and in kilts the next.[10] It was tradition (and reaction against a persistent streak of alcoholism in the family) that made the Campbells strict Presbyterians and teetotallers. Tradition dictated that the boys should learn Highland dances, and be able to play the bagpipes; Sam Campbell brought out from Scotland a coachman, Dooglie, who could teach them both arts.[11] It was in accordance with tradition again (but an African one this time) that each of the boys shot his first buck at the age of eight.

Young Roy Campbell's spiritual inheritance was a rich but curiously divided one. Many of the 'ideas and ideals' which Grandfather Dunnachie affirmed lay at the foundation of things, were part of the baggage which old William Campbell had brought from Scotland: traditions and codes of behaviour which drew their vitality from Europe and lived on in Natal despite being as inappropriate as Eton collars on this sweltering coast of the Indian Ocean. The folk-songs Campbell's mother sang at the piano, the poems his father recited after dinner, were songs and poems of Scotland, evoking visions of clansmen clashing on an icy moor, while the Campbells' Zulu servants listened uncomprehendingly, and the African night panted outside. The sensitive boy grew up with a deep sense of the contrast between the ideal world of poetry and song, with its heroic figures and Nordic landscape, and the equally exciting world of reality: the darkness of the African bush pressing in all around, full of game and mystery. And since he belonged to both these worlds, the division in his background became a division in himself. The child was cared for by a devoted Zulu nurse, Catherine Mgadi, and from her he learnt Zulu at the same time, and in the same way, as he was learning English. The division between Africa and Europe was carried through even into his mother tongues.

When the boy was five years old, he saw his father ride away to war once again; the Zulus had risen in rebellion all over Natal, and were slaughtering whites. Despite his youth at this unsettled time, Campbell's recollections of the great Rebellion of 1906 were vivid.[12] Thus some of his earliest memories were of war in a colony which still had much of the frontier spirit about it. Durban in 1906 was a little town of scattered, tin-roofed houses and wide, sandy streets; it was bounded on three sides by dense, subtropical bush, and on the fourth side by the Indian Ocean. The town asserted itself against the bush by a law requiring the Zulus to wear trousers once they passed the city limits, and against the sea by William Campbell's breakwater. It was still a society in which the man who did not stand up for himself went under. The Campbells, quick-witted and quick-fisted, fine soldiers, great hunters and fishermen, stood up for themselves very well. In three generations they had built up a tradition of remarkable success in a society which placed great emphasis on personal achievement, on the worth of the individual.

It is worth stressing the values and achievements of the poet's family, because they help to explain his deep unhappiness when he felt he was failing to live up to them. For though his brothers, Archie,

George, Neil, and Bruce, loved nothing better than violent physical activity, and spent their days riding bucking calves, staggering along the beach under bent fishing-rods, or taking rifles into the bush to kill anything that moved, Roy seemed to have been born out of place. As a boy he appeared to have little interest in riding, shooting, or fishing. Somehow he never seemed to apply himself to the problem of staying on a moving horse; the buck heard him coming miles away when he went out stalking; he was always a poor shot; and though he was big for his age he took little pleasure in punching other boys.[13]

It was not ability he lacked in these practical matters, but interest. What attracted him was art. He early showed great skill in drawing and painting. From the age of four he would sit underneath his mother's piano as she played, while he doodled and sketched. This situation, an habitual one in Campbell's childhood, was in several ways symbolic.* His mother's unwavering love provided the boy throughout his nervous, delicate childhood (he suffered much from asthma) with the security he needed. His love for her was as great as his admiration of his father. Her unshakeable calm provided the still centre around which the family moved. Campbell thought of her always as a haven from the storm; for him she was surrounded by images of warmth and harmony, as his published references to her show:

Quite as memorable as any of our jaunts on the lagoon or into the forests were the long winter evenings at Peace Cottage when my mother would play the piano for us and we would sing the old Gaelic, Highland, or Border songs she had learnt from her grandparents in Scotland . . . [She] knew a thousand ways of amusing us on these long evenings . . .[14]

Her gifts of stillness complemented her husband's ceaseless energy. Campbell knew he could always turn to her when he had angered his father; she never failed him.

His mother encouraged Campbell's artistic abilities from their earliest manifestations – the beautiful sketches of African buck, which he drew upside down, starting with their hoofs at the top, and finishing their horns at the bottom.[15] By the age of six he was producing panoramic pictures of land and sea battles.[16] When he was fourteen he and his sister Ethel wrote and illustrated a book for the amusement of their Dunnachie grandfather. In thanking them for it

---

* All his life Campbell seems to have needed the security of a dominant woman's love in order to produce his best work. The childhood experience, and its lifelong significance, seem to have been shared by at least one other artist, D. H. Lawrence.

the old gentleman wrote, 'Now, my dear Roy, I must thank you for your splendid letter to me; I think your literary talent is going to be equal to your artistic ability.'[17]

The letter was prophetic, for though Campbell never lost his interest in sketching (he was to illustrate several of his own books with considerable skill) his attention turned increasingly to verse. He read voraciously, encouraged by his father, who opened accounts for him at the three Durban bookshops and allowed him to buy anything except novels. Dabbling in letters was also something of a tradition in the Campbell family. Old William Campbell had been a prolific writer of doggerel; so was Ethel, Roy's only sister. His Uncle Archie had produced an unsuccessful book called *The Mlimo*, and even Sam Campbell had written a 'satire', *The Blister*, in doggerel couplets; he seems to have regarded writing as a harmless and even respectable hobby.

Campbell attended a kindergarten run by a local spinster until he was eight, when he was sent to the Durban Boys' High School. He quickly became known to his schoolmates as a reclusive bookworm. Sent to collect a younger brother from the railway station, he would be found hours later immersed in a book in a wayside café, heedless of his brother who had returned home crying and alone.[18] An older brother, George, remembers him at this period strolling along the beach reading a book of verse, with his rod over his shoulder, and the fish he had somehow hooked trailing forgotten in the sand behind him. He was, in fact, a dreamer in a world that required men of action.

Schoolboys neither like nor pardon eccentricity in their fellows. The Japanese proverb, 'Protruding nails will be hammered', expresses their attitude aptly, and boys who do not wholeheartedly share the rougher interests of their schoolmates quickly learn to dissimulate. There are letters from Campbell, telling of his prowess as a hunter or rider, but they are always to people he wanted to impress: his cousin Dora or, as he grew older, a girlfriend. For another of his characteristics came to light at an early age: his innate showmanship. From his earliest youth he loved to tell a good story, and he records significantly that even in kindergarten he disliked the word 'impossible'.[19] Part of the attraction which the wild and free life of the bush undoubtedly had for him may well have lain in the fact that his experiences made very good stories. There was never, for him, a wide gulf between art and life.

He had plenty of stories to tell. Provided with guns and horses, an experienced Zulu to guide him when he needed guidance, and huge tracts of wild country to roam in, his was a childhood such as most children only dream about. Even in Natal at this period his upbringing was an extraordinarily fortunate one. There were no strains in his home, for his parents were happily married, comfortably off, and indulgent almost to a fault with their children. Their big house in Musgrave Road on the hill known as the Berea, overlooking the city and the sea, stood in huge, beautifully kept grounds, and Campbell later remembered counting thirty different kinds of fruit growing in that garden. Holidays were spent at Peace Cottage, a spacious seaside bungalow belonging to Sam Campbell's brother Marshall, set in virgin bush on a beach so little visited that the Campbells had it to themselves for days on end. At other times they would travel inland to the foothills of the Drakensberg to spend a week trout fishing in the icy mountain streams, an activity Sam Campbell loved.

The Campbell boys were encouraged to become good hunters; they were given the run of the buck-filled cane fields on Uncle Marshall's huge farm, where they shot bush-buck or exotic Javan deer. Later they would be packed off by train and ox-waggon to Belingwe, in what was then Southern Rhodesia, where their Uncle Archie lived. Here they would be allowed to go off for weeks at a time into the bush on long, lazy voyages of discovery. Campbell never forgot them:

This leisurely method of travel is surely the best in the world. It leaves the traveller free to make expeditions into the adjoining country, to follow honey-guides and take hives, or to make a hunting detour, yet never get left behind by his bed and kitchen. He treks during the cool of the morning and afternoon, outspanning during the heat of the day to let the oxen graze and drink, and to pass a pleasant siesta under some great shady fig, mahogany, or marula tree. About twenty miles a day is the average trek. The ox-waggon is the traveller's house, or his ship, with bunks and table complete.

I found it a delight when the lions began to roar and shake the darkness with their voices: I felt then that pleasant and awe-stricken sensation that I was able to experience in the pre-Disney days. . . The cattle were all enclosed in their corral of newly-lopped golden mimosa boughs with their terrible two-sworded lion-proof thorns. We stacked the fires higher and lay on our backs under the stars singing with the natives for the sheer joy of being alive, singing all through the night, falling asleep and then waking to pick up the song again. . .[20]

Every childhood seems magical to the adult looking back on it; no wonder that, with such a childhood as this to recall, Campbell ever afterwards thought of the Africa of his youth as a Paradise Lost.

The serpent in this paradise was the headmaster of the Durban Boys' High School, A. S. Langley. Campbell first came into contact with him in 1910 and he was to prove scarcely less of an influence on Campbell than his own father. There seems little doubt that Langley was not only a stern disciplinarian but a bully. Campbell described him years later in a chapter entitled 'The Surly Tutor of my Youth';[21] the allusion is to one of Campbell's own lines of verse: 'Hate was the surly tutor of our youth'.[22] Campbell believed Langley was actuated by hatred of Sam Campbell, who had founded the Technical College, rival of Langley's own school. Whatever his reasons, Langley persecuted the boy relentlessly. Campbell was lazy at his work, Campbell did not excel in games – Langley would flog some sense into him.

The poet, in common with other boys at Langley's school, admired the headmaster's tremendous strength of character, for it was in many ways like that of his father:

He [Langley] was the queerest mixture of a sensitive artist and a stern disciplinarian. More than half the school would have died for him: and even I (who abominated him) was always elated for days if I could accidentally earn a word of praise from him.[23]

Campbell may have exaggerated Langley's treatment of himself, but his schooldays became a misery to him when it became clear that this man whom he so respected was attacking his beloved father:

If . . . I made a mistake in Latin grammar, I was never allowed to forget the fact that I was associated in the mind of the whole school with the Tech. At close range in class he could see from my expression that he drove a knife right through me every time he mentioned the Tech ('Get along with you to the Tech! What are you doing at my school?') and raised the scornful sniggers of the whole class. He revelled and gloated in the misery he inflicted on me. That was his roundabout way of getting at my father whom he feared and respected.[24]

The boy was torn: one of his idols was blaspheming against the other. The short-term result was to increase his love for his father, and give him a fierce hatred of Langley – a hatred that he nursed for the rest of his life. In the long term, however, this conflict of loyalties gave rise to a deep-rooted contradiction in his character; hatred of one father-figure and love of another made him both hate authority and long to be subjected to it. This dual love and hatred came to centre itself on his father alone after Campbell left Langley's school, and an understanding of its roots goes far towards explaining much of Campbell's seemingly contradictory behaviour in later years.*

The boy came to associate academic discipline with his hatred of Langley; all his life he professed a contempt for 'book-learning', while venerating writers. By contrast, the free life of the wild seemed ever more attractive to him. It became a refuge from the drudgery of unpleasant duty, a dream-world to which he fled in juvenile verse:†

> I am sitting in a classroom with a problem in my brain
> And a dozen impositions to my name:
> But my heart is in the splendour of Belingwe's mountain chain,
> My soul is on the ridges with the game!
> . . .I gaze upon the blackboard – then there floats across the scene
> A vision of some lonely, lost lagoon,
> I hear the rushes whisper, and above the wild ravine,
> I see the virgin glory of the moon.[25]

Curiously, then, his hatred of Langley contributed to what became a lifelong habit of mind for Campbell: the idealization of a life of freedom and action, in contrast to the bookish inactivity for which he was fitted by temperament and inclination. It was the origin of yet another of the seeming contradictions that characterized this complex man.

But the boy was by no means incapable of sharing in a practical way in the life he preferred to dream about. He was a close observer of wildlife, an amateur naturalist of surprisingly wide knowledge. Numerous sketches survive to prove that the markings of many African antelopes were imprinted on his memory in the most minute detail. He was a great lover of birds and trees and fish, and something of an authority on them, and he was particularly fond of impressing his father's many foreign visitors with stories of the wild. The traveller Evelyn Wrench, for instance, visited the Campbells in 1913, and wrote of Roy (then aged eleven) in the London *Daily Mail*,

. . . [He] entertained us the whole evening with snake and sporting stories. He is quite a naturalist and born sportsman and goes out shooting buck within a few miles of the town. The number of deadly snakes here is horrible . . . 'But you can kill any snake by putting tobacco juice on his tongue,' Roy assured us! Roy draws and keeps nature-notes. . .[26]

---

* It helps to explain, for example, his natural anarchy and his attraction, during the early 1930s, to the orderliness of the European dictatorships. It explains both his early anti-clericalism, and his later adherence to the authoritative teachings of Roman Catholicism. And it explains both his hatred of 'regimented' modern life, and his happiness in the British Army.

† In this respect Campbell's juvenile writings have much in common with those of Charlotte Brontë: Belingwe was to him the haven Verdopolis and Angria were to her.

Campbell's accounts of childhood hunting expeditions in his autobiographies are not far from the truth; the active life was, after all, as much a tradition of his family as the wearing of kilts, and he was a great follower of family tradition. Moreover, physical activity gave him an opportunity to emulate his father in being a leader of his fellows. He organized a group of other boys into a gang, and led them on hunting and fruit-stealing trips. The 'Fezelas' (Scorpions) as they called themselves, proved a seditious influence in the school and drew down Langley's wrath on Campbell.[27]

By 1916 Campbell had begun to think that another kind of active life offered him an escape from school, with its drudgery and its floggings. The Great War, two years old, was bogged down in the mud of Flanders, and Campbell's older brothers, Archie and George, on active service, wrote home optimistic accounts of the action. The school magazine for December 1916 was full of thrilling tales of valour. Campbell determined to run away and join up: could a Campbell stand on the sidelines when there was a war on? Besides, he would get away from Langley. It was almost certainly at this time that he wrote the unpublished poem 'Shadows', which ends,

> With the fierce legions I must cross the sea:
> Dust into dust, our proud platoons will roll!
> And I will die. And God will smile to see
> The peace of many shadows on my soul.[28]

He told the recruiting sergeant that he was Roy MacKenzie, from Rhodesia, and he produced a forged letter of permission from his father. Though he was only fifteen, he was already tall and broadly built; he had no difficulty in being taken on. But a neighbour had seen him going in to sign up; she told his mother, and before he could get on to the troop-train he was dragged back to school and to another beating from Langley.[29]

He was writing more and more at this time – most of it, predictably, very derivative verse. The evident influences on him are an interesting reflection of his own divided attitudes towards the active life. On the one hand he loved poems of action, poems of simple passions – the ballads of Scott and Burns (two of his father's favourite writers) and of the Anglo-Canadian poet Robert Service. On the other hand he was much influenced by the dreamy, world-weary verse of the early Yeats, the Yeats of 'The Wanderings of Oisin' and 'The Rose'.

In 'Eclogue', probably written in 1916, Scott's influence is unmistakable, though Campbell's own vigorous imagination asserts itself in the last lines:

> Enid: Dawne, silver-footed o'er the ruddled reles,
>   Her snowy bosom in the east reveals.
> Ellayne: Ah, woe is me, that I have lived to see
>   This dernie daye, that brings not backe to me
>   The sail of my Lord Hugh, who truly said
>   I shall be backe by Sabbath, or be dead.
>   . . . All yesternight in anguishement I lay
>   For I could see the ugsome lightnings play
>   Across the ocean, into ruddy flakes,
>   Or like in aspect unto twisted snakes . . .[30]

He was about fourteen when he discovered the work of R. W. Service, perhaps the first 'Colonial' poet to achieve wide popularity. Service's *Rhymes of a Rolling Stone* went through thirteen editions during the years of the Great War alone, and his celebration of natural beauty and the tough men who conquered the Yukon made a great impression on Campbell. One of his schoolboy poems is dedicated to Service, and is a fair imitation of him:

> I have roved the hush of the soundless snows
> In the spell of thy magic lines;
> I have heard the rune of the lonely loon
> and the moan of the Arctic pines.
> It seems I have camped on thy blazoned peaks
> By the flickering camp-fire's glow
> When the Northern Glories shot their streaks
> O'er the shuddering ribs of snow;
> When the wild winds wafted their frosty spice
> And the west was a crimson dye,
> And the ranges lifted their tusks of ice
> To rip at the frenzied sky. . .[31]

But running counter to these poems of vigorous action (that vigour which was to become Campbell's most obvious characteristic) is the influence of Wordsworth, Shelley, and the early Yeats. This is the other side of his nature, which has been largely ignored. Campbell never lost his admiration for the Romantic writers, and their influence was felt very early. Again and again the juvenile poems picture Campbell as a solitary dreamer lost in reverie, not conquering nature but being acted on by it. In an early untitled poem there is a characteristic interplay of Wordsworthian passivity and Shelleyan fervour:

Calm is the hour: the night is still
And sprayed with stars, and splashed with dew:
Cool night-winds breathe about the hill,
And trailing mists perplex the view.

Till a mysterious ecstacy,
Born of the night of stars and wind,
Awakens in the heart of me:
Forth leaps my spirit unconfined!

And with a fervour nothing mars
I leave the silence of the woods
And plunge through shoals of sleepy stars
To scour the skies' infinitudes.

And out beyond the swirling suns,
Beyond the tides of time and space,
To find, more far than fancy runs,
The white dream-splendour of your face.

And then in dreamy rapture roll
Our trembling spirits, pale and high,
And heart to heart, and soul to soul,
Are blown about the midnight sky![32]

The same mood of *fin de siècle* reverie is found in another early poem
which, like the one just quoted, confirms that Campbell very early
began his lifelong habit of writing almost entirely during the hours of
darkness:

Now, like a ghost in shadow lands,
The lamp-light fades away:
My fumbled pen, in weary hands,
Hath written all it may.

And yet remains superb, unsung,
A thought which is not mine,
A song to tuneless numbers rung,
Half human, half divine!

A second pausing, dream-beguiled,
I heard it swell and sway:
Till unattainable and wild
The echoes died away. . .

The morning woods are slumbering,
And drenched in silver dew:
Ah! that the song I could not sing
Might stir my breast anew.[33]

These poems are worth quoting, not for their intrinsic merit (they have little) but for the light they shed on the conflicts in the young poet. The influence of Europe, acting on him through family traditions and through the reading that occupied so much of his time, affected his poetry strongly once he began writing seriously from the age of fourteen. Only occasionally does Africa obtrude into the juvenile verse, as in the early poem 'Dreams', in which Campbell is clearly recalling his Rhodesian holidays –

> I remember dreamy evenings beside the dim camp-fire
> By those mighty, mottled oxen that I love . . .[34]

but the remembered experience is followed in the next line by a vision of snow-capped peaks of the sort Robert Service is fond of describing. Campbell's earliest verse is predominantly 'literary', in the sense that it draws on what he had read rather than on what he had experienced.

Even the finest of these juvenile poems, 'The Theology of Bongwi the Baboon', the first to be published in England and the only one he cared to retain in later years, shows the continuing influence of Yeats (and incidentally shows him beginning to react against his parents' orthodox Christianity). In Yeats's poem 'An Indian Upon God', a meditative Indian hears a moorfowl proclaiming that God is 'an undying moorfowl', a lotus announcing that 'He hangeth upon a stalk', and a roebuck and peacock countering that He is made in their images.* Pleased with this idea, Campbell elaborated on it, giving it a deliberately absurd and subversive edge:

> This is the wisdom of the Ape
> Who yelps beneath the Moon –
> 'Tis God who made me in His shape
> He is a Great Baboon.
> 'Tis He who tilts the moon askew
> And fans the forest trees,
> The heavens which are broad and blue
> Provide him his trapeze;
> He swings with tail divinely bent
> Around those azure bars
> And munches to his Soul's content
> The kernels of the stars;
> And when I die, His loving care
> Will raise me from the sod
> To learn the perfect Mischief there,
> The Nimbleness of God.

---

* Rupert Brooke used much the same idea – of fish – in his poem 'Heaven'.

For some time Campbell had been concentrating a good deal more on verse than on his schoolwork. Late in 1917 he left Durban Boys' High School with a third-class matriculation pass. It was the lowest possible pass mark, but at least he was free of Langley's tyranny. He was still keen to join up, and he intended now to go to Sandhurst.[35] But he was still only just sixteen; to fill in time until he was old enough to be accepted by the Army, he registered at Natal University College, as it was then, to read English, Physics, and Botany.[36] He lived in the YMCA in Longmarket Street, Pietermaritzburg. He did a good deal of reading, though not of the prescribed books, and very much enjoyed his first extended period of living away from his parents' home. He spent much of his time playing elaborate practical jokes (as he had at school) on Authority wherever he saw it. In an unpublished chapter of his autobiography *Light on a Dark Horse*, he records secreting pieces of filter-paper soaked in ammonium chloride (which, when dry, explodes if disturbed) in the YMCA hall, where a meeting of the South African Socialist Party was due to take place. The resulting panic in the meeting, which was to have been addressed by a prominent politician, delighted Campbell, who sat on the roof to watch the spectacle through a skylight:

The crowd started turning up, and as soon as an Indian waiter set a big tea-cannister down, there was a fairly good bang which sent the tea flying: then another from the hinges of the cloakroom door. People started shouting in loud voices about 'Sinn Feiners', 'Germans', 'Hertzogites', and 'Rebels' . . . Pops and bangs were going off, a smell of singed cloth stole up to our eyrie, and some people started leaving. Others, before going, began surreptitiously filling their pockets with cakes, vegetarian demaroids, buns and foodpills . . . Many were too honest to fill their pockets so they lingered nervously snatching at the buns and pills as if they had been chestnuts in the embers, and were liable to explode at any minute . . .[37]

Campbell's schoolboyish pleasure in such jokes was a symptom of a desire to disrupt the society he increasingly disliked. He seems to have been partly responsible for encouraging a strike of tramway workers in Durban on Armistice Day:

As bad luck would have it, my father had to be sent for as the only man who could persuade the Tramway men to go on with their work. He was on the spot in a few minutes and had them all back to work at once. He was very angry at having to come all the way down to the post office: he said he wanted to get hold of the man who had started the mischief. The mayor, who was just as angry at having his Armistice Day spoilt, told him that that would be quite easy as the ringleader lived in his own house!

I was very sorry indeed to give my father the idea that I was a sort of left-wing agitator . . .[38]

He was beginning to break away from the public-spirited attitudes of his father, with their emphasis on service to the community and success – material success – in it. He began to chafe, too, against his father's teetotalism, and his views on morality. It was during his last year in South Africa that he believed he had fallen in love with the girl he calls 'Blackstockings' in *Light on a Dark Horse*: she was Joan Tatham, daughter of a local judge. He tried to teach her to ride and shoot, and wrote her tremulous letters to persuade her to spend part of her holidays with him at the Campbells' beach house, or at Peace Cottage. In several of these letters one catches perfectly the blend of nervous schoolboy and daring flouter of conventions that he was late in 1918:

I have to get to Sandhurst by November 8, so I will very likely be here [in Durban] for a good time yet. I will come up and see you after your term of office has expired . . .

Look here, we simply *must* have another holiday at the Beach before I clear off. I am going to approach Mother on the subject and I think it will come off all right.

It will be out of season for buck, but we'll forget that, only we will not be able to shoot quite so many as we do in season. Anyway we'll make up for that in sandlice fights, which are just as good . . . I gave Wonky [his horse] your love and told him of our intended stay at the Beach, whereupon he swooned.[39]

And a month later he is importuning,

You simply *must* chuck up this schoolmarm stunt in time to come to Natalie's place before I go. Natalie doesn't mind your leaving it undecided in the least. We can just walk in whenever we like. But you will come, won't you? I am going about the middle of the month (next) unless you can't get down till after that. But you MUST come!

We will have a ripping time. I promise you it'll be better than at the Beach.[40]

He seems to have suffered from impotence at this time – what he later called 'my awful physical shyness of girls, which had been the bugbear of my existence'.[41] Though he soon overcame it, his reaction to this 'bugbear' may well have contributed to the aggressive masculinity of his verse.

He was growing rapidly away from the conventions of his family and the traditions in which he had grown up. Increasingly he fixed his eyes on the world beyond Durban's horizon. His reading had given him a keen anticipation of the delights he hoped Britain had to offer. He lived in the world of his reading-matter, and that world had a Nordic landscape; he seemed, to himself, to know the Scottish Highlands or the Yukon as well as he knew Belingwe. The frost and ice which he had never seen, but of which he had read so much, had for him a mysterious fascination. They feature frequently in his early verse.[42] Natal has always been the most 'English' part of South Africa, and Campbell, more than most Natalians of his day, felt himself to be not wholly of Africa. What had Africa to offer an artist? He used at this time to quarrel angrily with his father, who held that it was quite as possible to immortalize the sakabula (a long-tailed, irridescent South African bird) as the nightingale.[43] Though he was deeply imbued with his South African background, he felt himself culturally bound to Europe. By going to England he might be able to bridge, as every artist must, the gulf between himself and his cultural heritage.[44]

The foundations of Campbell's character were already firmly laid. His family's sense of tradition, despite his growing alienation from it, made him identify strongly with their code of honour, their martial prowess, their ability to lead men and make money: in fact, with their very evident material success. Everywhere around him he could see

marks of what members of my family of ex-Irish bogtrotters* have done to decorate, enliven, or deface the landscape; monuments of their energy, fantasy, or eccentricity, were visible in the shape of universities, colleges, hospitals, gardens, statues, and plantations.[45]

Yet already he must have been conscious of a sense that his destiny was bearing him away from all this; that his dedication to a life of art was going to require a break from much of what his family stood for. The pain of that break was yet to come. But already there was fixed in him the rebellious streak which Langley's harsh discipline had engendered. It combined with a love of individuality and freedom, a vigour of temperament and violence of expression which his free-ranging childhood had fostered. He had become a very complex person indeed. There was fixed in him a hatred of discipline, and a keen need for it; a delight in solitude, and a desire to be recognized by his fellows; a contempt for 'bookishness' and an addiction to poetry. There was a deep-rooted respect for his puritannical upbringing, constantly undermined by a growing amorality. Finally, there was pride in his African background and alienation from it.

---

* Grandfather William Campbell's forebears, originating in Scotland, had for several generations been transplanted to Ireland.

The war had ended by the time he was about to leave for Sandhurst, a month after his birthday in October. He announced his intention of going to Oxford instead. Getting a berth on any sort of ship immediately after the war was difficult; it was through the influence of one of his father's friends that he was eventually able to sail for London on a tramp-steamer, the SS *Inkonka*, late in December 1918. He had a little money, some drawing-materials, a good many books, and letters of introduction from his father to Sir Walter Raleigh and several other Oxford dons. Seeking adventure he was to find, in addition, a way of reconciling the conflicting elements in his personality. He was just seventeen.

Mrs Sam Campbell with Roy, aged six months,
in April 1902

Dr Sam Campbell, the poet's father

The Campbell family home, Musgrave Road, Durban, about 1908

Campbell in his last year at Durban Boys' High School

II
Oxford and After
1918–1924

CAMPBELL loved the voyage from Durban to London, though on the first day at sea the ship's mate, a man with strong views on the danger of knowledge, had pushed most of his poetry books out of the porthole into the sea.[1] Campbell was a good sailor, and to pit himself against the natural forces of wind and wave produced in him an exhilaration like that he had felt at night in the Rhodesian bush.

Standing up at the fo'c'sle head and ducking under the cross-plate at the vortex of the bows when the ship dove her nose into the great Cape rollers forty feet high with a quarter of a mile between their marbled summits, one shouted and sang with joy and elation in the movement of the ship and in one's own immunity, as the spate of water rushed overhead and one emerged from the safety of the cross-plate to see the next great hill of water approaching as the ship tobogganed down the slope of the last one, to meet it.[2]

The *Inkonka* called at Dakar ('It was the first time I had seen whites philandering with blacks')[3] and Las Palmas, and in mid-February, in the bitter winter of 1919, slid quietly up the Thames. Campbell walked wide-eyed about the streets of London marvelling at the first snow he had ever seen, wondering at the vitality of Cockney children who had never known the countryside, exulting to find himself in Trafalgar Square. Too timid to call a taxi when he needed one, he hired instead a man with a donkey-cart. He was always more at home with animals than machinery; even the simplest mechanical device baffled him.

He paid a short visit to his Dunnachie grandfather in Scotland (the old gentleman gave him £10, with which he was able to replace his lost books), and then went south to Oxford. His hope was to learn enough Greek to pass Responsions (in effect, an entrance examination, requiring a basic knowledge of classical languages) and then to enter Merton College. Oxford early in 1919 was crammed with returned servicemen; Campbell was lucky to find a single attic room in a house in Walton Street.[4] Nervous and painfully shy, for weeks he spoke to no one but South Africans whom he already knew. One of these, the eccentric Izaak Rousseau,[5] who lived in the same house as Campbell, offered him the use of his sitting-room. Here Campbell sat day after day, plunged in a big armchair by the fire, reading voraciously. As he later wrote, 'Never before, or since, have I done such an amount of reading as I did at Oxford: had I taken an ordinary course in English for three years, I would not have read a quarter as much.'[6] He had 'discovered' T. S. Eliot, and began writing poems in imitation of him; the subjects seem mainly to have been the huge and gloomy railway stations he had seen on the way to and from Scotland.[7] None of these poems survives, for after reading them to Rousseau or some other friend, Campbell would put them on the fire.[8]

He began trying to learn Greek, though rather half-heartedly, from a tutor, G. W. Young. Attending the same classes, also with the aim of passing Responsions, was another student even younger than himself: William Walton. Campbell and Walton soon found that they shared an enthusiasm for the poetry of Eliot and the Sitwells (whose anthology *Wheels* had just appeared), and for the prose of Wyndham Lewis. Although Campbell was later to feel that they were temperamentally different, and that Oxford had forced them together 'like travellers on a dark night'[9], he and Walton grew very close indeed. This intimate friendship had several important effects on Campbell's life, for the two young men met at a moment when Campbell was ready to strike out along quite new paths. He was impressed to find that this pale sharp-featured youth with the strong north-country accent was already a well-known composer. From Walton he learned to dedicate himself completely to his art. The artist must be prepared to accept every privation in order to devote himself to his work, Campbell came to believe; he must throw aside any constraints of morality, any convention of society which might prevent him from living fully for his craft. This idea, so foreign to his family's scale of values, was a revelation to Campbell; once he had accepted it, he never deviated from it. Money, fame, the respect of others: he was prepared to sacrifice them all to the strict demands of his art. This total dedication was to cost him dear, but he never lost his sense of indebtedness to Walton.[10]

The two young men soon gave up studying Greek. Campbell discovered that if he poured a good deal of alcohol down his throat he could throw aside his terrible shyness and don conviviality like a mask. He took to beer in a big way. The influence of his parents had made Campbell completely teetotal up till now, but from this point he was never to lose his reliance on alcohol. He and Walton went out drinking night after night.[11] They paid court to two Irish waitresses at Buol's Restaurant.[12] Campbell seems also at this period to have had at least two short-lived homosexual affairs.[13] His bisexuality was yet another facet of his divided nature, its roots deep in his background. These seem to have been his first homosexual attachments, and they illustrate the degree to which the hold of his family's values and traditions on him was slackening.

Walton was able to introduce Campbell to many people he might not otherwise have met: among them were Wyndham Lewis, and the composer Philip Heseltine, who used the name 'Peter Warlock'. One Saturday Walton took Campbell to one of Edith Sitwell's 'bun'-parties at Pembridge Mansions. That memorable afternoon he also met Edith's two brothers Osbert and Sacheverell,[14] and T. S. Eliot. His friendship with the Sitwells was broken off shortly after, when Campbell arrived at one of their dinner-parties only to be denied admission by Osbert because he was not wearing evening-dress.[15] Campbell slunk away in rage and shame, and it was ten years before the friendship was renewed. His acquaintance with Eliot, on the other hand, developed into a distant but continuing friendship, which was to last all Campbell's life.

He was also meeting new people at Oxford. One of the most important of these was T. W. Earp, then president of the Oxford Union. In later life Earp (the son of a wealthy brewer) published several volumes of literary criticism and art history, though he never quite lived up to the promise of his Oxford years. But he impressed Campbell as a thoroughly polished man of the world – witty, rich, and experienced. Earp was attracted to Campbell not only by his evident dedication to poetry, and his quick wit, but by his physical beauty. By the age of seventeen Campbell was tall (six feet two), slim and well-muscled, his figure graceful and freely moving, with the broad shoulders that denote great strength. His fair hair was already beginning to recede at the temples, so that he looked older than he was. His face was strong but sensitive, his mouth thin-lipped and constantly curling in amusement; but it was his eyes that impressed themselves on the memories of those who met him. They were blue-green, large, wide-set and slanted like a cat's; and they were change-able as the sea. When he was alarmed or angry they seemed to grow pale; when he was elated by conversation or moved by some piece of writing, they flushed with colour. He lived every experience with a nervous intensity that seemed impossible to sustain. In conversation he was so shy that in large groups he would sit silent for hours, but warmed by alcohol he would talk with tumbling energy, impressing his friends with his already encylopaedic knowledge of literature, natural history, and painting. He was a fine raconteur and a superb mimic, with a seemingly endless fund of stories of the African bush. He played up his African 'wildness' to good effect, flaunting a strong Natal accent and sprinkling his speech with Zulu words and phrases. As a result, Marie Beerbohm about this time nicknamed him 'Zulu', and he appears as 'Zulu Blades' in Wyndham Lewis's satirical novel *The Apes of God.*

Earp took this phenomenon under his wing, introducing him to everyone who was anyone at Oxford: Robert Graves, Louis Golding, Russell Green, and Aldous Huxley.* Campbell had great admiration for Earp, who with his elegance and lightning wit was the centre of undergraduate life at this time.[16] Campbell later wrote of him,

He is still, to my mind, the finest wit and the most exquisite literary critic alive. The miraculous feeling of walking into a famous University from the Bush and being accepted on a much higher level than one was accepted at home, was very exhilarating.[17]

He gradually drifted away from Walton and attached himself, still more closely, to Earp. Earp's influence over him was at first very strong, for he was an assured, experienced man of the world, while Campbell was still a rather timid colonial. L. A. G. Strong, the future poet and novelist, who was then working as a schoolmaster near Oxford, described meeting Campbell as 'a pale and scared looking slender boy of nineteen, emerging from a cupboard at Tommy Earp's, in which he had been hiding from some tradesman to whom he owed money.'[18] Earp was a man of considerable wealth and Campbell made weekend trips with him to Berlin or London, where they stayed in the best hotels,[19] (Edgell Rickword† occasionally met them for lunch at the Savoy in London, where they were staying together)[20] or to Paris, where they stayed in the Latin Quarter. Campbell was soon writing

---

*Robert Graves was recuperating from a severe wound sustained in the First World War; Aldous Huxley had already written several novels and was shortly to produce the book that brought him to the public eye, *Crome Yellow.* Louis Golding, novelist, essayist, traveller, and lecturer, is perhaps best remembered for such novels as *The Sorrow of War* and *The Day of Atonement.* Russell Green, at this time a talented student, was later to become a noted critic and editor of *Coterie.*

†Poet, biographer, and critic; editor of *The Calendar of Modern Letters,* and subsequently of *Left Review* and of *Our Time.*

home for an increase in his allowance, though the £3̄50 a year his father gave him was a considerable sum in 1920.[21]

Earp influenced Campbell in several ways. He encouraged Campbell's tendency to reject his family's ideas of 'getting on', and temporarily converted him to a Marxist hatred of the 'bourgeois'. Earp seems to have believed that capitalism had, for gain, caused the war which had killed off the flower of his own generation; Campbell accepted Earp's views because he liked Earp.[22] Campbell became a regular attender at Union meetings, and a firm supporter of the Left in student politics. He was turning against everything that had led to the war, and the values he was rejecting were the values of his own family. Drink and homosexuality were the banners of his revolt against the militarism of his father.

His anarchic spirit also made him a supporter of Sinn Fein:

The best night [at the Union] was when Esmond, the youngest and most brilliant of the Sinn Fein leaders, spoke. He had the house in tears of laughter over the British policy towards Ireland. It was very courageous of him to speak in the way he did in a hostile country. I was surprised to find that Sinn Fein won in the voting . . . Esmond says he can give me a job for the vacation, i.e., to deposit a bomb under Lord French's bed. I wouldn't mind the job, but I firmly object to the penalties that might come.[23]

Earp's chief significance, however, lies in his effect on Campbell's tastes in literature. He steered Campbell away from the influence of the Romantic poets and of Service, Tennyson, and Thompson, and introduced him to the French symbolists. On an extended trip to Paris together, in the summer of 1919 (a trip on which they met several members of the Dôme and Montparnasse groups, including Utrillo and Diaghilev),[24] they 'discovered' Valéry:

Here Earp first saw three Odes by Valery: and he and I ferretted through every old magazine until I had collected all his printed work up-to-date. I came back to Oxford with six typed copies containing nearly all that is found in *Charmes*. . . They were, I am ready to bet, the first collection of Valery's poems that ever came to England.[25]

Valéry, Laforgue, Rimbaud, Baudelaire, and Mallarmé now became his models.

Earp and Edgell Rickword, another of Campbell's closest friends at this time, used to read and criticize Campbell's verse. With Rickword (who had already published his first volume of verse), and A. E. Coppard, the short-story writer and poet, Campbell and others inaugurated a literary club, 'The Jolly Farmers':

We rented a small parlour in the pub of that name where we used to read plays, and put away quantities of beer, every Thursday night. I was all for the Elizabethans: but we read Otway and even Beddoes . . . It was by far the most spontaneous literary gathering I ever knew.[26]

In Earp's company Campbell's natural wildness grew. He drank more and more heavily; he affected soft ties and floppy hats; he gave up any thought of taking a degree. During the next two years he seems to have had many casual affairs, a number of them with women, and he used an acquaintance, who had many friends among the shop-girls of Oxford, as a pander, giving him small sums of money for his services.[27] Wyndham Lewis's description of Campbell as 'Zulu Blades', put into the mouth of another character in *The Apes of God*, provides a contemporary portrait:

Blades was the 'black beast', an evil neighbour: what with his upstart disrespect as well for his metropolitan betters, since he had brought the hearty habits of the African out-stations into their midst, here. His skill with women was natural, it was true he roped them in like steers, he must be working off ten years' solitary confinement in the Veldt.[28]

There were wild literary parties, such as the 'Death Dinner' organized when Campbell announced that his doctor had diagnosed in him an incurable disease. He had, he said, only a few months more to live. In fact, he was continuously diagnosing dreadful ailments in himself; his childhood asthma was the first of a lifelong series of psychosomatic illnesses. He was an incurable hypochondriac, and his friends seem to have realized this. Coppard, Louis Golding, Alan Porter (poet and future literary editor of the *Spectator*) and others made up a party of thirteen who assembled at Buol's, ghoulishly, to celebrate Campbell's approaching demise. It was at this party that Campbell wrote the first and last lines of a sonnet to which each of the other members of the party contributed a line.[29]

Campbell became an enthusiastic supporter of Futurism, with its exaltation of colour, violence, and speed.[30] He saw it as an antidote to the milk-and-water poetry of the then-fashionable 'Georgian' poets. He wrote to his father:

We have passed the ages of Romanticism, Parnassianism and Symbolism. We have come to the age of psycho-analysis – futurism. Art is not developed by a lot of long-haired fools in velvet jackets. It develops itself and pulls those fools wherever it wants them to go. It reacts more thoroughly and easily than the most sensitive artist in the world. Futurism is the reaction caused by the faintness, the morbid wistfulness of the symbolists. It is hard, cruel and glaring, but always robust and healthy. It is Art pulling itself together for another tremendous fight against annihilation. It is wild, distorted, and ugly, like a wrestler coming back for a last tussle against his opponent. The muscles are contorted and rugged, the eyes bulge, and the legs stagger. But there it is and it has won the victory. . .

Let us examine the other schools of art existing at the present day. The New English School imitates the Pre-Raphaelites and yet is not a tenth as good as they were. They are stagnating. They do not advance: but mark time on the old ground.

The Georgians, those who in the reign of George V. (in the age of machinery, and probably one of the most important stages in the history of our evolution) persist in groping amongst the dust of ancient folios for what they write. They are treading the same ground that was trodden by the Elizabethans, 400 years ago. . . . So it is pretty certain that our Georgian friends will fizzle out pretty soon.

The last school is that of very young people like Rickword and myself. We have had the shell broken for us by futurism. We accept *Wheels* as a very necessary but badly-written hypothesis on which to work our theorems. We apply our work closely to the life that goes on around us. We read the French symbolists, modern futurists, the Elizabethans, modern scientists, the Roman poets and as much as we can of the Greeks. No one can say we are not as widely read as any of the Georgians or Futurists, most of whom turn their backs on science. I have now read about three-quarters of Darwin and Freud, a good deal of Huxley, and seven volumes of Nietzsche. . .[31]

As the tone of this letter suggests, Campbell was growing in confidence. He was no longer the timid colonial of nine months before; he was no longer impressed by all he saw. It became clear to him and to Walton that they were not going to pass their exams; they left Oxford, and Campbell went to London to live with Earp, in a flat in Regent Square which they shared for a time with Aldous Huxley and Russell Green. Campbell was deeply disappointed at his academic failure, though in writing to his angry father he attempted to carry off the situation with a show of bravado:

With regard to a degree, I find that Oxford with its lectures etc, interferes very much with my work. I cannot conscientiously apply valuable time to such a subject, for instance, as Anglo-Saxon . . .[32]

It was in London at about this time, early in 1920, that Earp introduced Campbell to Augustus John. John later wrote of the poet,

He was certainly a fine, tall young fellow with a careless buccaneer air about him which contrasted sharply with Tommy's cultivated precision of speech and manner. I took to him at once . . . being professionally an opportunist, I

seized my chance and without any difficulty got him to sit for me at Mallord
street . . .[33]

John's fine portrait of Campbell now hangs in the Carnegie Art
Gallery, Pittsburgh.

During 1920 Campbell's relationship with Earp became increasingly troubled. He was beginning to react against Earp's excessive
polish, and their liaison was in several respects coming to resemble
that of Rimbaud and Verlaine. And, despite his efforts, Campbell
could never shake off entirely his puritanical upbringing. He became
more and more uncomfortable. Augustus John was later to suggest,
shrewdly, that Campbell had taken to drink 'as a means of counteracting the almost pathological condition of moral discomfort' with which
he had been troubled at Oxford.[34]

He disliked sharing the flat with Huxley, whom he described as
'this pedant who leeringly gloated over his knowledge of how crayfish
copulated . . . but could never have caught or cooked one.'[35] He was
irritated, too, when the police called to say they were receiving
complaints about Huxley and a friend who made love in front of a
window from which they were clearly visible to passers-by.[36] The
truth was that Campbell was feeling in need of a change of air. He had
heard from Augustus John of the beauties of Provence and in the
company of a friend, Geoffrey Nelson,[37] he travelled there in 1920.

The northern Europe he had so avidly read about, and so eagerly
looked forward to, had proved a disappointment. It was true that he
had met a great many interesting people, and had had the thrill of
being accepted by them as an equal. He had loved Oxford, and
resented having to leave it without ever having become a member of
the University. His bitter disappointment can be heard through his
attempts to be light-hearted about it:

My one ambition was to be a Don and live in a mouldy old tower with a
salary, so that I should never have to do any uncongenial work. I wanted to
read and write in front of a big fire with good college beer to drink. But the
great barrier of Greek intervened, and I could only be my own private Don
in a back-street.
    Whenever I think of Oxford it is with regret . . .[38]

If he were to forget this disappointment, he must get away from his
Oxford friends completely. In addition, England itself had been a
disappointment to him. He disliked the ordered, calm landscape:
'English scenery to me is like those pictures one sees on chocolate

boxes', he wrote.[39] He had begun to long for the brilliant light and vigorous life of Africa. In England he felt an alien: 'The old colleges . . . seemed to resist me and push me out, as someone born under corrugated iron', he wrote.[40] His attempt to bridge the gulf between his cultural heritage and his experience seemed to have failed.

Provence, by contrast, delighted him. With its wide, empty landscapes, its sunshine and its dryness, it reminded him of South Africa. 'I was ravished by the beauty of the country,' he wrote later; 'my eyes were able to rest on sober dry colours and drink real sunlight once more.'[41] Its wildness impressed him; it was the nearest thing to Africa-in-Europe he had found. Parting company with Geoffrey Nelson ('a lugubrious parasite')[42] at Cassis, he took a job on an Italian barque plying between Marseilles and Naples, with side-trips to Algiers. Between voyages he would do a little grape-picking, or painting, or fishing. He seems to have had several further casual affairs at this time, one of them with a gypsy girl, Imperio, a seventeen-year-old widow.[43] He wrote a good deal of verse and tore it up; apart from what he had written before leaving South Africa, little of the work of his long apprenticeship has survived.

He was to spend eighteen months in this apparently leisurely fashion, with occasional brief visits to London, where he took odd jobs at the docks or as an extra in a film. He lived on the allowance his mother continued to send him. The holiday atmosphere of these months is conveyed in his letters home:

Please excuse my not writing for so long, but I have been on board since my last letter – I got an ordinary working job on an Italian Schooner in Marseilles as they were shorthanded. We went to Corsica and Genoa and I got off here at Cassis, where I am going to take a rest. I feel very fit.

After a few days I'm going to look out for something that will take me over to North Africa. I want to get into the interior for a few days. It is very amusing down there: this time I'm going to Tangier or Tunis as I know Algiers more or less . . .[44]

I'm doing a good deal of work, but I'm in the middle of one of those periods when nothing works out rightly, so I just hammer away using about one writing-pad per day and then having to throw everything away. I wish I could think of some news.[45]

He tramped about southern France, a bearded, long-haired figure in shabby clothes who was several times mistaken for an escaped convict; he travelled for a time with three exiled Russians, earning money at fairs; he sailed down the Rhône from Lyons in a barge; and always he drank. But this rootless existence, pleasant at first, gradually got him down; his work seemed to be getting nowhere. He began to feel that his life had lost direction. He injured his back working as a dock-labourer in Cassis, and had to lie up for some time to recover; he ate less and less and became painfully thin. In late September 1921, he decided to return to London.[46]

He stayed for a time with Rowley Smart, and with Geoffrey Nelson, and it was at this time, in October 1921,[47] that he met Mary Garman, the girl he was to marry.[48] She was one of nine children (seven daughters and two sons) of a wealthy doctor from Wednesbury, near Birmingham. Her mother had been the illegitimate daughter of Lord Grey of Falloden by his housekeeper, an Irish beauty with hair so long that she could stand on it. Lord Grey seems to have provided for his mistress until she married a disreputable doctor named McGill, who ill-treated her for years before stumbling drunk into a ditch and drowning himself.[49] Mary's paternal grandfather was more respect-able, if less romantic; like her father, he was a doctor, and had made a good deal of money by investing in a local foundry. Mary's father was a very handsome man, but it is not clear from whom she inherited her strikingly un-English beauty. With her pale olive skin, dark eyes, thick black hair (so unmanageable that it seemed alive with electric-ity), arched nostrils, full lips, and a bone structure that seemed to give her face vivacity even in repose, she looked more like a high-born Spaniard than the eldest daughter of a doctor from Birmingham.

She had a devoutly Anglican upbringing. In her early teens she fell hopelessly in love with the local priest, decided to become a mission-ary, and preached to the local mine boys; she and her brothers and sisters held religious services complete with an altar and vestments, and Mary would lead the children in prayer. When she fell out of love with the priest, the spell of his teaching wore off too, and it was years before Christianity had any meaning for her again.[50]

In 1919, in their early twenties, she and one of her sisters, Kathleen, 'fed up with the curates our parents wanted us to marry',[51] ran away to London together, against their parents' wishes, deter-mined to study Art and learn about Life. They earned a little money at first by driving a Lyons van delivering bread, and when their father relented and began giving them an allowance, they rented a studio in Regent Square,[52] and drifted about on the fringes of the artistic world, much as Campbell himself was doing. Mary studied painting, and Kathleen music. Their freshness and their striking beauty soon gained them many admirers. Jacob Epstein, the sculptor, laid siege to

Kathleen, while Bernard van Dieren, a composer, middle-aged and married, followed Mary about for nearly a year until she invited him home to the studio-room. Van Dieren used to cook wonderful meals for the girls on their gas stove, and he composed several songs for Mary. His scores were all but illegible even for a good musician, but Mary, with more confidence than skill, would sit down at Kathleen's piano, saying, 'I'll just give you an idea of what this sounds like', and launch into song. Van Dieren would stand behind her, wincing at her mistakes, but adoring. When she finished he would say, with careful irony, 'Mary, you attacked that like a master.'[53]

The two girls knew nothing about housekeeping, not even that they should put mantles on the gas jets, so that their studio was lit by naked gas flames, picturesque but dangerous. At one crowded Bohemian party Kathleen noticed with horror that the tall Jewish artist Jacob Kramer's long hair was alight. 'Kramer, you're on fire!' she shrieked across the room, and Kramer's initial amusement at what he took to be a joke turned to sudden panic.

Mary and Kathleen had seen Campbell one day from the top of a bus and, attracted by his appearance, had jumped off and followed him to the Eiffel Tower restaurant. But it was not until two weeks later, on 10 October 1921, that they met on the doorstep of 13 Regent Square.[54] Campbell thought Mary 'the most beautiful young woman I have ever seen'[55] and she found him equally attractive. He was just twenty and she was twenty-three. Neither was inhibited by consider-ations of morality; within three days of meeting them, he moved into the girls' studio-room. He had been living almost solely on beer, and the two girls undertook to feed him up. Mary, Kathleen and he would lie arm in arm in front of the fire, while he read them fragments of the first draft of *The Flaming Terrapin* and told them tall stories by the hour.[56] An unfounded rumour soon spread that he had become the lover of both girls. Van Dieren (who had been in the habit of writing Mary long, stilted letters beginning 'Dolcissima, carissima Maria') for a long time resented his displacement by Campbell. He would sit, in his perfectly cut suits, staring disapprovingly at Campbell, who squatted by the fire, grubby, bearded, and very much the lover-in-possession. Van Dieren tried to call Mary's attention to Campbell's defects. 'You don't wear shoes Campbell', he would observe coldly to his grinning rival. 'You prefer to go about barefoot.'[57]. Eventually, however, he had to acknowledge defeat, and bowed out sadly. But Epstein, whose model Kathleen had become, was violently jealous.

The two girls invited Campbell home to Oakswell Hall to meet

their parents in December 1921. 'Father, this is Roy, who's going to
marry Mary,' said Kathleen. The old gentleman looked Campbell up
and down: 'My eldest daughter? To a complete stranger?' He thawed,
however, on finding that Campbell's father, like himself, was a doctor
trained in Edinburgh; they even had friends in common, and cordial
telegrams were soon passing between Durban and Birmingham.
Campbell took care to conceal his drinking from his future father-in-
law by refusing all wine during meals, but afterwards he would take
Mary's unsuitably young sister Helen to a local pub and spend the
evening there with her. Dr Garman was soon warning Mary, 'You are
marrying a dipsomaniac'.[58] Mary, however, enjoyed drinking with
Campbell in London, and the two of them would go out every night
to a pub, rolling home late at night to tell Kathleen of the quarrels
Roy had had, and laughing uproariously as he embroidered the
anecdotes.

From Oakswell Hall, immediately after Christmas, Campbell and
Mary went on to spend some days at Augustus John's Dorset house,
Alderney Manor. Here, one evening, a 'marriage ceremony' was
organized. A gypsy wedding-ring was procured, and Trelawney
Reed, a poetaster, archaeologist, and John's chief jester, took the part
of the priest, with John dressed as an acolyte and Earp as a choirboy.
When the cermony, the drinking, and the speeches were over, the
couple were ceremoniously conducted to a nearby cottage and put to
bed. 'It was good fun and I thought wanted very little to make it a true
and valid ceremony,' wrote John later. 'As a matter of fact, there
could have existed no closer union in the world than that of Roy and
Mary Campbell.'[59]

The couple were more conventionally united in an Anglican
ceremony in Wednesbury on 11 February 1922, with a ring bought by
Kathleen at a local market. The bridegroom arrived from London in a
shiny second-hand suit and a yellow collar, with his long hair
plastered down, so that he looked like an undertaker. The bride wore
black and red velvet. 'And I always thought Miss Mary would marry a
gentleman with a park!' lamented the Garmans' old housekeeper.[60]
After a sedate wedding-breakfast at Oakswell Hall, Campbell and his
wife returned to London for a wild party at the Harlequin Restaurant
in Beak Street. Campbell's elder brother George, who had just
finished his medical studies at Edinburgh, turned up at this party to
sit in wondering respectability among 'the howling dervishes of
London Bohemia'. With the party still in full swing, Campbell and his
bride retired to bed in a nearby room. The guests proceeded to

quarrel. In his autobiography, *Blasting and Bombardiering*, Wyndham Lewis has left a vivid record of the scene:

Jacob Kramer and Augustus John were neighbours at table and I noticed that they were bickering. Kramer was a gigantic Polish Jew (and still is, I believe) and he was showing John his left bicep. It was between John and himself. It expanded convulsively under his coat sleeve, and he kept drawing John's attention to this fact.

John did not seem interested. But Kramer would not be put off or have his bicep high-hatted like that. It went on moving about under his sleeve in an alarming fashion, and Kramer looked at it as if irresistibly attracted. It was such a funny thing to have in your sleeve, a sort of symbol, he seemed to feel, of Power. He tapped it as a prosperous person taps his pocket.

'I'm just as strong as you are John!' he kept vociferating, screwing his neck round till his nose stuck in John's face.

'You've said that before,' John answered gruffly.

'Why should I put up with your rudeness, John – *why*! Tell me that, John! You're a clever man. Why should I?'

John shrugged his shoulders, and looked down rather huffly [*sic*] at his spoons. He sought to indicate to his neighbour that philosophically interesting as the question might be, it was not time to discuss it, when we were convivially assembled to celebrate the marriage of a mutual friend.

At this moment Roy Campbell entered in his pyjamas. There was a horrid hush. Someone had slipped out to acquaint Campbell with the fact of this threat to the peace. In a dead silence the bridegroom, with catlike steps, approached the back of Kramer's chair. That gentleman screwed round, his bicep still held up for exhibition and metaphysical examination. He was a very supple giant, and by this time he was sitting one way but facing another, having as it were followed the bicep round behind himself.

'What's this, Kramer?' barked Roy, fierce and thick, in his best back-veldt. 'What are you doing, Kramer!' Roy Campbell pointed his hand at his guest and began wagging it about in a suggestive way as if he might box his ears or chop him on the neck with it.

'Nothing, Roy! I'm not doing anything, Roy!' the guest answered, in a tone of surprise and injured innocence.

'Well you let John alone, Kramer! Do you hear!'

'I'm doing nothing to John, Roy, I was talking about painting,' Kramer said.

'Never mind painting, Jacob. Is that how you talk about painting, Jacob?'

'Yes, Roy,' said Kramer, in an eager and conciliatory voice. 'I get worked up when I talk about painting, Roy.'

'Look. Could I throw you out of that window if I wanted to Jacob?'

'Yes, Roy, you could,' said Kramer humbly. 'You could, Roy.'

'You know I could, Jacob?'

'I know you could Roy.' Kramer nodded his head, his eyes screwed up.

'Well then let my guests alone, Jacob. You let my guests alone. Don't let me hear you've interfered with John again. Mind I'm only just upstairs, Jacob. I'll come down to you!'

A strangled protest and assent at once came from Kramer; and stiffly and slowly, his shoulders drawn up, his head thrust out, in apache bellicosity, Campbell withdrew, all of us completely silent. When the door had closed, Kramer got up, came round the table and sat down at my side. He'd put his biceps away. He continued with me the conversation about painting which had taken such a personal turn on the other side of the marriage board.[61]

Campbell's indulgent father was at last moved to cut off his son's allowance. For some months the Campbells lived in London by pawning their wedding presents; Campbell did a little reviewing. In the early stages of their married life Campbell suffered a good deal from jealousy about friendships Mary had had in the past. On one occasion, in their rented rooms above the Harlequin Restaurant, when Mary was stretching and saying 'Oh, how lovely she was!'[62] Campbell rushed at her in a fury and, crying 'Don't you *ever* say that again!' caught her up and held her out of the window, in his arms, so that she found herself lying, face-downward, gazing at the traffic two storeys below.*

To their financial and emotional difficulties, however, were added the strains caused by Epstein's continuing jealousy. He still believed, mistakenly, that Campbell was the lover of both sisters, and he enlisted the co-operation of waiters at the Harlequin to gather evidence of the orgies he believed to be taking place. Campbell eventually resorted to fighting Epstein – one of the few confirmed times he seems actually to have struck anyone.[63] One evening when Kathleen and Epstein were dining at the Harlequin, Campbell sent Mary out with Augustus John, and then got a waiter to deliver a message to Epstein's table: 'Mr Campbell would like a word upstairs with Mr Epstein.' With a set face Epstein rose and went up the stairs to the Campbells' room, while the diners in the small restaurant fell silent. There was a foreboding pause, and then suddenly thunderous sounds of two men fighting above. All eyes turned to where Kathleen sat alone. Feeling that she must do something, she rose from her table, rushed upstairs and flung open the door to find Campbell and Epstein rolling about among upturned furniture. 'Stop it. *Stop* it! You're behaving like animals – you *can't* behave like that here,' cried Kathleen, and the two men rather sheepishly got to their feet.

---

* Campbell tells this story in *Light on a Dark Horse*, p. 248, where he improves it by claiming to have held Mary out by her ankles, to the horror of a passing policeman.

Without a word to either of them Campbell went out to find Mary and John and tell them about his victory.[64] (In his autobiography, *Light on a Dark Horse*, in which he calls Epstein 'Sennacheribs', Campbell inflates this fight into an epic battle.) The artistic world, of course, was delighted with this incident, and the stories surrounding the Campbells intensified. A rumour was soon put about that Campbell was complaisantly allowing Mary to be with Van Dieren.[65] The Campbells accordingly decided to look for somewhere quieter – and cheaper – to live. With a gift of £5 from Mary's old nurse, they travelled to the isolated Welsh village of Aberdaron, on the coast opposite Bardsey Island in Caernarvonshire. Mary had been there on holiday several times as a child and knew the area well.

They camped out for a time, then after brief stays in two cottages they rented a converted cowshed, Ty Corn, about three miles out of the village. Augustus John's son Romilly, who was staying with them at the time, having run away from home, later recalled his dismay at the prospect of moving into this hovel:

The floor was earth stamped unevenly down, and in some places the mud had fallen from between the rocks of which the walls were built, so that the wind came whistling in. Mary and I both fell prey to unspeakable gloom. . . . But it was astonishing how quickly we cheered up under the influence of Roy's indomitable spirit. I really think it had never crossed his mind that the cottage in any way fell short of a desirable country residence; nor did it, when the holes had been stuffed up and a great fire was roaring up the chimney.[66]

In this shanty, which stands today much as they found it, the Campbells were to live 'on the continual intoxication of poetry'[67] for the next eighteen months. They acquired some notoriety among the villagers for the flowing, brightly coloured clothes they wore, for the length of Roy's hair, and for their habit of making love on the clifftops in broad daylight.[68] They covered the walls of their cottage with charcoal sketches of each other in the nude and one day, when the door was opened to the coalman by Mary and her sister, both naked, the man forgot what he was going to ask, and went away in confusion.[69] 'We were the first hippies,' Mary Campbell has said.[70] Campbell's father had resumed his allowance (at George's urging); the couple spent the greater part of it on books, and on beer which Campbell would carry up from the village in a gallon-jar. The poet supplemented their diet by growing vegetables, by collecting seabirds' eggs, and by poaching rabbits and pheasants with a small shot-gun he had bought. It was at Ty Corn, on 26 November 1922, that their first daughter, Teresa, was delivered during a violent storm by a young midwife, by the light of a single oil-lamp that swung crazily from the rafters as the wind rose. Campbell, unable to be present, sheltered behind a piece of corrugated iron on the beach, and suffered fearful sympathetic pain. At dawn, as the storm abated, he went out and shot a snipe, and grilled it on a spit for Mary's breakfast.[71]

It was at Ty Corn too that Campbell completed the first draft of the long poem he called *The Flaming Terrapin*, writing night after night in a tiny loft, while Mary slept below. He wrote lying on his back on a mattress with the notebook propped on his knees, the rafters just above his head, two or three candles wavering in a saucer by his side. In the morning he would emerge, triumphant or despondent, to read Mary what he had written before going to sleep for the rest of the morning. With the industry of narcissism he made five copies of *The Flaming Terrapin* in a beautiful, printed hand and sent them early in September 1922 to his closest friends. Edgell Rickword was the first to respond:

I have waited three days and three nights to be able to tell you quite coolly that the poem is magnificent. One doesn't often find anything to overwhelm one's expectations but this did completely . . . I know of *no-one living* who could write in such a sustained and intense poetical manner . . . Lots of things might have weighed against my liking it (particularly your philosophy of sweat) but the sheer fecundity of images ravished my lady-like prejudices . . . Good luck and ten thousand thanks for such a poem.[72]

Sending this letter to his mother, Campbell wrote,

He is the one man among the younger poets whose opinion I revere at all and I only expected rather a cold-blooded criticism from him. I simply fell down on my bed and howled like a baby when I got it.[73]

Rickword's letter was to prove typical of the general reaction to *The Flaming Terrapin*. Desmond MacCarthy, to whom Rickword showed it, was so impressed that he planned to review it before its acceptance by a publisher – a very unusual occurrence. As it happened, Campbell had little difficulty in finding a publisher for it, though it was rejected by Chatto. Augustus John was one of the friends to whom he had sent a copy. John showed it to T. E. Lawrence who, much excited, sent a postcard to Jonathan Cape urging him to 'get it – it's great stuff'.[74]

The Campbells had by this time (mid-1923) moved back to London – partly because Mary's mother had decided that Ty Corn was no place in which to rear a child, and partly because of the need to find a publisher. They took a room at 90 Charlotte Street; and it was while they were staying here that Cape wrote to Campbell, who brought the manuscript in to be read the next day. Cape was delighted with it. He gave the overwhelmed young poet an immediate £10 advance. *The Flaming Terrapin* was published in May 1924.

III

The Flaming Terrapin

1924

THE critics gave the new poet an unexpectedly warm reception. Both in Britain and in America, where *The Flaming Terrapin* was published almost simultaneously,[1] it was hailed as a remarkable work. By contrast with the banalities of the Georgian poets popular at the time, Campbell's vigour was, as the *Spectator* put it, 'like a breath of new youth, like a love-affair to a lady in her fifties'.[2] *The Flaming Terrapin* was praised by critics ranging from Edward Garnett to Desmond MacCarthy. The sheer energy of the poem seemed to them overwhelming:

> It is something, after all, to have the courage to be damnably poetical. It is something to be unafraid of the ample gesture, the upswung arm, and the frenzied eye, of the cloaked figure standing prophetically out against the horizon and wind-driven clouds, of lone defiance flung shatteringly up to Heaven and downwards to the ruck of the groundlings. It is still (1924) something to be shameless in one's rank superbity of spirit, to have no urbane shrinking from the preposterous eloquence of trumpets or thunder or hurricanes . . . [3]

And many critics contrasted Campbell's work with that of more established poets:

> . . . in this extraordinary poem we are far from the mimble-mamble of the slim-volumed Georgians, as far too from the elegant nervosities of pseudo-Eliots and pseudo-Cocteaus. Full circle! We have spun back . . . back to an exuberant relish of the sheer sonority and clangour of words, words enjoyed for their own gust, and flung down to fit each other with an easy rapture of phrase.[4]

There is no doubt that the enthusiastic reception Campbell got owed something to the general polarization into literary camps that was typical of the Twenties. He was welcomed by supporters of the full-blooded romantics as an antidote to the dry scepticism of Eliot's followers and to the mushy trivialities of Squire and Marsh. Consequently many of the reviews he got are marked by the enthusiasm with which adherents to a cause greet a powerful new ally. Although several critics, including MacCarthy and Garnett, thought Campbell needed to learn to moderate his voice and curb his 'extravagance of manner', they agreed that it was better to have too much energy than to have none at all.

Philip Heseltine had written to Campbell,

the buoyancy and exhilaration of the whole thing are immense, and practically unique (unique at any rate in conjunction with a really intellectual imagination) in this dispirited and half-hearted generation that knows not youth. Bravo![5]

And 'AE' (George Russell), in the *Irish Statesman*, wrote:

Among a crowd of poets writing delicate verses he moves like a mastodon with shaggy sides pushing through a herd of lightfoot antelopes . . . . No poet I have read for many years excites me to more speculation about his future, for I do not know of any new poet who has such a savage splendour of epithet or who can marry the wild word so fittingly to the wild thought.

Campbell, thrust so suddenly into literary prominence, had like Byron awakened one morning to find himself famous.

It is perhaps surprising, considering the amount of attention *The Flaming Terrapin* received, that no critic commented on the allegory that gives the poem what unity it has. Campbell's 'plot' is simple. A great flood has drowned the world; Noah and his sons, threatened by the raging water, are saved by the appearance of a gigantic turtle. The deluge, Campbell wrote to his parents, was representative of 'the war and its subsequent hopelessness'; the Terrapin is 'the symbol for masculine energy', and in the triumph of the Noah family he was showing 'the survival of the fittest'. And, he wrote,

in a world suffering from shell-shock, with most of its finest breeding-stock lost, and the rest rather demoralised, it is interesting to conjecture whether a certain portion of the race may not have become sufficiently ennobled by its sufferings to reinstate and even improve on the prewar standard, and in the end to supplant the descendants of those who have become demoralized and stagnant, like the Russians for instance. I have taken this more cheerful view . . .[6]

Noah, the helmsman, presumably represents guiding intelligence; he puts an end to the Ark's aimless wanderings by attaching it to the Terrapin. In passages reminiscent of *Moby Dick* and of Coleridge's 'Rime of the Ancient Mariner', the Ark is towed south, round the

Horn and into the Antarctic wastes, and then on from there until it reaches 'a nameless cape', where it is beset by terrible storms. This is the nadir of the journey. From here the Ark is towed northward again, and the crew revive. Their ordeal has purified them, so that they have become heroes, fit to inherit the earth. They are towed back to Europe, where the Terrapin prepared the world for reconquest by defeating Satan. The animals are released to go forth and multiply, the Terrapin disappears into the sea, and Noah is left at the end of the poem standing dramatically against the sunset,

> The Man, clear-cut against the last horizon!

Despite this clear narrative line, Campbell's method of composition made a certain amount of the fragmentation critics have highlighted inevitable.[7] He composed the poem over a period of at least two years, writing in notebooks or on odd scraps of paper,[8] and a good deal of confusion also arises because Campbell's attitudes changed during the poem's composition. He was, in *The Flaming Terrapin*, finding his own voice; and he was shaking off some of the ideas he had adopted at Oxford. He had begun to assert his Africanness in his poetry; symptomatic of this was his introduction of African animals, and his glorification of the natural life he had known in Africa. But this change came when the composition of *The Flaming Terrapin* was well advanced. It is surely no accident that his invocation of the virgin 'Muse of the Berg' comes not at the beginning of the poem, but in Part Four. Even in that section, with its wild natural imagery, one finds a typically Futurist celebration of the power of the Machine.[9] And the Terrapin himself is seen at one point as 'a great machine'.[10] Campbell had adopted the ideas of Marinetti,[11] arch-priest of Futurism, under Earp's influence, and that influence was only gradually waning. But increasingly he was connecting life with the 'natural' world in which he had grown up, and death with the mechanized world he was coming to hate.[12]

His use of African elements early in the poem lacks confidence. He resorts to the introduction of such lifeless abstractions as 'mambas of deceit', and 'Tyranny, vulture-beaked'.[13] Even his assertion of his African origins has the aggressiveness of the man who is not quite sure of himself:

> Far be the bookish Muses! let them find
> Poets more spruce, and with pale fingers wind
> The bays in garlands for their northern kind.
> My task demands a virgin muse to string
> A lyre of savage thunder as I sing . . .

Choose me some lonely hilltop in the range
To be my Helicon, and let me change
This too-frequented Hippocrene for one
That thunders flashing to my native sun . . .
                    (CP, I, 77–8)

In this early poem he was still searching for a literary persona; the mask is not yet a perfect fit. His sense of being a colonial and an academic failure remained very fresh. In later years, by contrast, he was to boast of his foreignness, in *Broken Record*, his first autobiography:

I am presenting an outsider's point of view: you may take it as that of the pre-victorian man, or of a pagan who never was put through any mill except that of the pre-industrial European culture of an equestrian, slightly feudal type, a sort of inhabitant of the moon, a foreign being . . .[14]

For all the poem's limitations – its derivativeness, its confusion, and its fragmentariness (it is full of echoes of Milton, Coleridge, Shelley, Yeats, Rimbaud, and even of Vachel Lindsay and Edith Sitwell, while Campbell himself criticized it for having three climaxes)[15] – it remains a remarkable achievement for a poet who was only twenty when he sent the first copies to his friends. The poem is not simply an allegory of the world's redemption through the suffering of the First World War. It is also a picture of Campbell's struggle to find himself. Campbell hints at its personal applications in his explanatory letter to his parents, when, after setting out his optimistic belief that the war may have ennobled men, he applies his theory to himself: 'I have taken this more cheerful view, as I would much sooner feel that I was a Simian in the state of evolution into something higher, than a fallen angel in a state of decline.'[16] Now Campbell had not passed through the fire of war himself, despite his attempt to join up; in what sense had he 'survived the Flood'? Campbell never quite decided what the Ark, the Terrapin, and the Flood were to represent. Why was it necessary to have a Terrapin at all? Why should the Ark not merely drift, as in the biblical story? Part of the answer is clear. The Noah family are purified and ennobled not simply by tossing on the waves, but by being taken on a journey – a journey south, to an 'unnamed' Cape of Storms. 'Cape of Storms' was the original Portuguese name for the Cape of Good Hope. Campbell, who felt bitterly his alienation from Europe, gives the Noah family greatness through contact with South Africa's primeval wildness. They are drawn there by the unthinking God, as Campbell had been born there; and under the wild influence of the South, Noah's guiding intellect is compounded with savage vigour:

> Like moonlight the new splendour of their minds
> Flushed their clean limbs: beauty ran all aflare
> Through nerve and bone . . .
>
> (CP, I, 74)

The intellect of Europe is combined with the riotous life of Africa, a combination that was the goal of Campbell's own ambition. And yet, the way he chooses to conceal his glorification of South Africa shows the depth of his divided feelings for his homeland.

It is worth mentioning at this point the contrast between Campbell's 'more cheerful' view of the post-war world and that of Eliot. Campbell's attitude to the dominant new poetry of the time was highly ambiguous. He admired Eliot's work immensely, and never ceased to admire it, but he never sought to imitate it after he left Oxford. As a colonial, he had the advantage of remaining unaffected by the coterie values of the *Criterion* and the *Adelphi*, and he makes less accommodation to the spare modern idiom even than Yeats, thirty years his senior. Campbell's striking and unwavering sense of his place in the poetic tradition owes a good deal to the accident of his African birth. It is part of the African strength he celebrates in *The Flaming Terrapin*.

But there is still more to the poem. The Terrapin is for Campbell a symbol of creativity, of Art – it is the Being who called both Man and Pegasus from the dust. It has both the energy and the tension that Campbell sought in his own work, and as Campbell tried to unify the incompatible elements in himself, he makes the Terrapin – a water-reptile – flame. Poetry, he hoped, would give his life the direction and purpose it so signally lacked during his aimless wanderings in France. It is significant that Noah attaches the Ark to the Terrapin not by a lasso or a harpoon, but by throwing 'his blunt stone anchor' at it.[17] Campbell sought stability as much as direction.

For the time being, poetry gave him both. *The Flaming Terrapin* had immediate popular success; the first edition sold out so quickly that the poem had to be reprinted that same year.[18] Campbell pretended to be indifferent to the adulation. Some months earlier, when his mother had praised the first draft he sent her, he had written, 'I am very pleased you like my poem. I am more pleased that you like it at home than if every paper in England went mad about it.'[19] But in fact he cared very much what the critics said about him; all his life he carefully kept reviews of his work. The fact that he was being universally praised did wonders for his self-confidence. When his proud parents offered to pay his passage home, he jumped at the chance. In England, despite the money he was getting in royalties from his poem,[20] he was still finding it very difficult to live. Campbell's cousin Natalie, who visited Roy and Mary at this time in Charlotte Street, was taken aback to see how poor and hungry they were, and she at once took them out for a huge meal in a nearby restaurant. Worry about his responsibilities for a wife and child made Campbell drink more heavily still. It was a vicious circle, for the more he drank the faster their money went, and the more he worried. One evening Mary came back to Charlotte Street to find that Campbell had locked up and gone off to a pub. She sat for hours on the doorstep in the raw cold of a snowy March evening, comforting the crying baby, until Campbell appeared drunk and contrite. For the first time she wondered if her father had been right in disapproving of the marriage.[21] But most of the time Campbell did his best to share the burden of looking after Tess. Wearing a wide-brimmed straw hat and a scarlet bandanna, he would strap the baby to his back in a blanket, Zulu-style, and walk with her for hours through the London crowds.

It was becoming clear to both of them that poetry was at best an uncertain way of earning a living. They were forced to stay for a time with Campbell's now-widowed mother-in-law, who had moved to Leominster after Dr Garman's death. The thought of returning to Durban was very attractive to Campbell; he would surely be able to earn his living in South Africa, where he would be a big fish in a very small pool – and where he had rich relatives who could be expected to look after him. Leaving his wife and child temporarily with his mother-in-law, he sailed in May 1924 on the SS *Umtata* for South Africa. He was full of hope. Off Cape Finisterre he wrote to Mary,

There has been a very good omen today!! As I was looking over the side of the ship suddenly I saw something like a piece of floating rubbish and lo and behold, it was a huge Terrapin covered with barnacles . . . . How I wished you had been there to see it with me. I'm sure you would have felt it meant good luck.[22]

The world, wide and inviting, seemed all before him.

IV

Voorslag

1924–1926

IF Campbell had high expectations of South Africa, South Africa expected much of him too. A SOUTH AFRICAN POET: AUTHOR VISITS HIS HOME AT DURBAN, trumpeted the headline in the *Natal Advertiser* of 14 June 1924. Newspapers in Johannesburg and Cape Town featured the 'local boy makes good' story. *The Flaming Terrapin*, published only a month before in London, had not yet reached South African booksellers, but the fact that English critics had acclaimed him meant he could safely be labelled 'a genius' and described as 'brilliant' by the papers of his home town. Because so little was known of his activities in Europe, the potted biographies that appeared in the papers ascribed to him the most astonishing experiences and the most diverse accomplishments.

The object of this adulation was delighted by it. He wrote to Mary,

It is wonderful, kid, the way they are fussing about me here. My name has been in almost every paper in S,A. The Johannesburg Star had a huge notice and in the Durban Advertiser . . . they put it in the headlines of the paper, before the political news.[1]

He was full of confident dreams. He would be joyfully welcomed home by his family; money and offers of work would be showered on him; his wife and child would join him; he would build a house by the sea and live by his writing, an honoured recluse; he would be able to give up the humiliating allowance from his parents and support his family himself. At last he would lead the life he had always wanted.

With such expectations on both sides, disappointment was perhaps inevitable. Disappointment for the poet began almost as soon as he had unpacked his bags. Dr Sam Campbell, though only sixty-three, was in poor health, his mental powers waning. He had a little over eighteen months to live, and his steady decline formed the tragic background to the poet's stay in South Africa. Although Campbell had renounced many of the family values which his father embodied for him, he still felt challenged by his failure to live up to them. He felt his father's public-spiritedness, his support of middle-class values and middle-class morality, as a reproach to his own rebellious attitudes, and yet he admired his father's strength and his achievements. In these last years of Sam Campbell's life, the poet's need for and hatred of authority grew steadily, focussing themselves ever more clearly on his father. The two disagreed angrily.

One of their first clashes brought home to Campbell how powerless he was. He had promised Mary that as soon as he arrived in Durban he would wire her some money. Having none of his own, he asked his father to cable some; his father refused on the grounds that cabling was an unnecessary extravagance. He offered to post the cheque instead. Campbell raged and sulked like a schoolboy, without effect, and he had to resort to refusing to eat his meals before his father agreed to wire the money.[2] His weakness is very clear in his letters to Mary:

Beloved,
It is a weary boy that is writing you this letter. Darling, your last letter nearly broke my heart. I am dreading the next. Sweetheart, I tried to get Father to send you a wire when I arrived, but he said no. Darling I cannot sleep for thinking that you are cross with me . . . .
You said in one letter that you just wanted to live with me away in the forest, and that will soon come true. Mother says that if I only wait, things will be all right. But Oh how sick & tired I am of it all. I just mope around the house – waiting, waiting, waiting. It just seems as if my whole life has stopped like a clock.[3]

Sam Campbell had been successful in all the fields in which his poet son had failed, and he wanted to see Roy 'make his way' in life. He was proud of his son's literary fame, but he wanted to see it translated into hard cash: Roy must get a job. Tremendously active himself, he could not understand how a young man could lie about scribbling all day. If he was going to write, let him become a journalist; if he was interested in literature, let him teach it at his father's Technical College. Above all, Roy must stop drinking. Both Marshall and Colin Campbell, Roy's uncle and cousin, had been alcoholics; so had the poet's paternal grandfather. 'Poor old father is worrying as to whether I can remain a total abstainer if I stay out here,' Campbell wrote to Mary. 'They all dread that I'm a budding toper.'[4]

Unable to live up to his father's values, he began to react against them, affecting an open and aggressive contempt for them which his

divided feelings could not fully support. Unable to 'get on', he turned
his nose up at the idea of doing so; all that was beneath a true artist.
He emphasized his youth and his poverty. He labelled the wealthy
Natalians among whom other members of his family found a natural
place 'grocers' and 'bourgeois'. He passed most of his first six months
in Durban, while he waited for Mary to join him, as if on holiday,
lazing, taking trips on whalers, riding his brother's horses inexpertly,
and fishing. He made one leisurely trip inland to the Drakensberg.[5]

That he longed to be at one with his hard-working, hard-playing
family is clear from the literary mask he built up for himself in both
his autobiographies and many of his poems. With a persistence that
became almost obsessive he presented himself as a man of action,
fighting, sailing, riding, shooting, fishing, and farming. He longed to
be seen as the Yeatsian all-round man:

> Soldier, scholar, horseman he,
> And all he did done perfectly . . .[6]

The growing rift between his father and himself placed an increasing strain on him. By the time Mary and little Tess joined him, in
December 1924, it was clear that he could not continue to live with
his parents in Musgrave Road. Early in 1925 he accepted Natalie
Campbell's offer to move his family to Peace Cottage, the bungalow
north of the Umthlanga lagoon where he had spent holidays as a boy.
He later wrote of this lovely place, which Natalie had inherited from
her father, Marshall,

It was connected to the lagoon by two buck-paths and an unmetalled road.
At night it was lit up by a sort of Morse code of electric blue thunderflashes
from the inrolling breakers which shook the house and made the candles
tremble with every crash, as they cascaded into phosphorescence, illuminat-
ing the twisted boughs of a giant milkwood tree which over-arched the
house.[7]

The Campbells covered the walls of Peace Cottage, as they had Ty
Corn, with drawings, so that one visitor remarked that it looked like a
paleolithic cave. The bush behind the cottage was full of silver-furred
vervet monkeys which would play round the house during the day,
and at night the darkness was alive with fireflies, which Campbell
sometimes wove into Mary's hair as they rowed on the warm waters of
the lagoon. But though it was an idyllic weekend bungalow, Peace
Cottage was not equipped to be a permanent home, and because it
belonged to his cousin, Campbell still felt he was dependent on his

relatives. Within a month, he was looking about again. Help came from an unexpected source.

In an attempt to earn some money, he had begun contributing articles, on literature in general and his own work in particular, to Durban papers such as the *Natal Mercury* and the *Natal Advertiser*; the editor of the *Advertiser*, Harold Wodson, had for years been a friend of the Campbell family. Campbell had also begun writing a long love-poem, 'The Golden Shower', which he hoped to have published in Durban by another of his father's acquaintances, Maurice Webb, a local businessman. (Webb's sole publishing experience had been the production of a Commercial Directory, and Campbell used to tell a story of how Webb once found a manuscript of Bernard Shaw's being used for wrapping fish. 'That's the closest Webb ever came to literature!' Campbell would say gleefully.)[8] It was Webb who, in March 1925, introduced the poet to Lewis Reynolds, the wealthy son of a local sugar-baron, Sir Frank Reynolds. Campbell had no hesitation in begging for help. Edward Roworth, then a popular South African painter, who was present at this meeting, wrote of it,

[Campbell] talked of his desperate poverty and what a mental strain it was to have himself, his wife and child entirely supported by his mother and that unless he could get away and have a place of his own it was utterly impossible to do a line of work and that he had written nothing since he came to Durban. Lewis and I were seriously perturbed by all this ɪ . .[9]

Lewis Reynolds, a generous patron of the arts, had left Oxford only shortly before Campbell arrived there, and he had read and been greatly impressed by *The Flaming Terrapin*. He invited the Campbells to occupy a seaside bungalow at Sezela, on one of his estates, Umdoni Park. Set, like Peace Cottage, in thick bush by the edge of the sea, it was a simple rectangular structure of corrugated iron lined inside with wood for protection against the fierce sun; but it was well-constructed and spacious, and on three sides it had a deep cool verandah where the Campbells could sit during the day. The surrounding bush was romantically wild. Soon after moving in the Campbells killed a cobra on the path near the bungalow, and they also killed a deadly mamba just as it was going in at their front door. On another occasion Mary was pursued by a large and threatening monkey.[10] Near the bungalow stood a large *rondavel*, a circular thatched hut which Roworth, who with his wife had occupied Sezela before the Campbells moved in, had used as a studio.[11] The bungalow was full of the Roworths' antique furniture (including a beautiful four-poster bed) and their books. The Campbells were delighted with it when they moved in in mid-April 1925. 'Mary and I are in clover – thanks to you,' Campbell wrote to Roworth, 'and I'm working better than I've done for years.'[12]

In fact, he was not working well; his long poem, 'The Golden Shower', was going very slowly indeed. He wrote to Edward Garnett,

> The truth is that I have come to a very difficult time: I am beginning to grow up and I am trying to sort out my ideas and bring more discipline into my work, which costs me so much time and energy that I have hardly any time to devote even to Mary and Tess. However things are slowly beginning to emerge from chaos . . . . The love-poem that I was writing had to be reconstructed altogether: it has cost me much trouble . . .[13]

To satisfy his father and increase his income, he continued to contribute occasional articles to the Durban papers, and he also agreed to deliver a public lecture in the Arthur Smith Hall in Durban. All his life Campbell hated public speaking, and he was never at ease in large gatherings. The audience that night (4 May 1925) was unusually large, drawn as much by the popularity of Campbell's father, who stood beaming with pride at the door to welcome them, as by the poet's own reputation. Mary Campbell, splendid in a vivid red dress, with her long black hair wild and loose, drew much attention. Campbell's first action on reaching the podium was to upset the water-jug, which rolled gurgling across the table. But his nervousness seemed to disappear as he stood up to speak. He launched at once into a discussion of the lack of 'intellectual communication' between his father's generation and his own, and proceeded, in a tone of irritating superiority, to savage the poets his audience was likely to know and hold dear. He was particularly scathing about Kipling,* who at this time was very popular in South Africa (he had lived for a period near Cape Town, and had written several poems and stories about South Africa). Tennyson, and the Pre-Raphaelites, were scarcely mentioned. Campbell managed to imply, in attacking the late-Victorian writers, that his father's generation had been poetically barren, and lacking in literary taste as well. Since the greater part of his audience was made up of his father's contemporaries, this criticism was not enthusiastically received. When he passed on to praise such writers as Owen, Sassoon, and D. H. Lawrence, the temperature dropped further. Those of his audience who had heard of these writers knew that they had failed to glorify the sacrifices made in the Great War;

---

* The *Natal Advertiser's* headline the next day was KIPLING CRITICISED: POETS UNDER THE LASH.

and the war, six years after its conclusion, was still a live issue in Natal, where many regarded it as having been a struggle by heroes for the maintenance of civilization. Campbell dismissed the war years as a period of 'sentimental hysteria'.

But he reserved his sharpest barbs for the end, closing his lecture with an appeal to Natal:

It is not enough to have made a grocer's paradise of half the earth; we must have a culture of our own if we intend to keep our place, especially where we come so much into contact with races who have not the advantages of a long civilization behind them. We must have a deeper and less ostentatious pride in ourselves than that which is born of our richness and power. While commerce must remain as the mainstay of our social existence, let us not think of it as such a high form of self-expression that it will keep our supremacy out of range of the lower races . . .[14]

This was much too close to home to be comfortable. Natal 'a grocer's paradise'! The sugar-barons shifted uneasily in their seats. But what was most provoking was his veiled remarks about the 'lower races': was he implying that they would not remain lower for ever? No; they would not do a son of Dr Campbell an injustice; they must have mistaken the drift of his remarks. And so the lecture ended in tolerant applause, and the papers next day reported that it had been a great success. But many prosperous citizens of Durban must have gone home that night thinking that Dr Campbell's son had picked up some very strange ideas during his travels.

Campbell did not risk any further public lectures of this sort, but for a small salary he began a series of weekly talks as part of the adult education classes his father was organizing. He used these lectures, ostensibly on English literature, to air his views on anything from Communism to the scandalous lack of recognition accorded literary genius in Natal. His class dropped from fifty to less than a dozen in a week. He was fitted to be neither a teacher nor a journalist; and poetic inspiration seemed to have left him. He began to suffer from depression. He sought solace in beer.

He mixed very little in Natal society, partly because he so disliked his family's circle of friends. At dinners which his father gave to bring Campbell and wealthy Natalians together, the poet's embarrassment showed itself in irritability and assumed arrogance, so that it took all Sam Campbell's tact to prevent open quarrels.[15] One of the few people the Campbells did befriend was Anna von Schubert, the cultured and beautiful wife of a wealthy expatriate Estonian. She was greatly attracted by Campbell (Laurens van der Post was later to describe her as 'emotionally unemployed' at this time)[16] while in turn both he and Mary were drawn by her vivacity and intelligence. She was a keen amateur painter, and the owner of several fine Impressionist pictures. It was she who introduced them to the avant-garde German artistic magazine *Der Querschnitt* – illustrations from which the Campbells stuck on the walls of Reynolds's bungalow. They saw a great deal of her and of Roworth during 1925.

It was in May that the idea of starting a literary journal, on the lines of the *Dial* or the *Adelphi*, was mooted. Reynolds, who would finance it, had for some time been considering such a project. Campbell, he thought, would be an ideal editor, lending his name and his talent to the magazine. Webb would handle the business side of the publishing, and Roworth would be Art Editor. Reynolds had been General Smuts's secretary at the Paris Peace Conference in 1919, and he was on good terms with General Hertzog (the Prime Minister) and with Cresswell (leader of the South African Labour Party). The new magazine would be assured of the support of the country's political leaders. Campbell was delighted with the scheme: here was his chance to make money pleasantly and influence South African literature at the same time. He suggested that the name of the new publication be *Voorslag*: 'Whiplash'. Reynolds and Webb agreed. They were to regret their decision.

While preparations for the new magazine were going ahead, in June 1925, Campbell met William Plomer for the first time. Plomer and his parents were running a trading station in Zululand. He had just finished writing his first novel, *Turbott Wolfe*, which was to be published in London in March 1926. Hearing of him through a mutual acquaintance, Plomer invited Campbell to lunch at a Durban hotel, Twine's. After lunch, since it was low tide, they walked on the sand of the beach, and talked for several hours. Despite differences in background, temperament, and upbringing, they were attracted to each other at once, as Plomer later wrote, 'by propinquity, isolation, some community of interest, possibly an attraction of opposites, mutual liking, mutual (I feel sure) admiration, and youthful high spirits and playfulness.'[17] Campbell was delighted to have found a kindred spirit in 'the grocer's paradise'. Plomer, tall, spectacled, and intense, had spent part of his education in England, and he shared Campbell's open contempt for Durban society, as well as his conviction that Art was what really mattered in life. His book, *Turbott Wolfe*, was a revolutionary examination of a subject which had been until recently taboo in Southern Africa: love and marriage between black and white. Campbell, sympathetic to the blacks and desirous of disrupting white society, admired the book immensely. He had already decided to dedicate his own work in South Africa to the task of bettering the lot of the African, as his letters at this time show:

I don't expect very much of my poetry for some time yet – I don't want to be rewarded with the faintly ornamental immortality that is usually the lot of minor poets. I would far sooner, even at the risk of ruining any artistic qualities that I possess, load my work with some moral purpose and direct all the knowledge I possess towards counteracting the evils of race-hatred and colour-hatred that cause so much misery out here.[18]

With characteristic generosity, Campbell urged Plomer to move into the bungalow at Sezela and become a joint editor of *Voorslag*:

We . . . can put you up for good if you can only get away. I think I'll be earning from £20 to £30 a month for editing 'Voorslag': so we'll live like millionaires, man![19]

Plomer accepted, moving into what had been Roworth's studio in May 1926, two months after the birth at Sezela of Campbell's second daughter, named Anna after Frau von Schubert. The two men settled down to an intense period of writing, turning out articles for *Voorslag*. They also seem to have planned to write, in collaboration, a series of poems describing and satirizing the course of white settlement in southern Africa. The series was to have been called *The Conquistadors*. It is not clear how far the work proceeded or why the project was abandoned. Campbell subsequently published one poem, 'Solo and Chorus from "The Conquistador"', in his volume *Adamastor* (1930), and Plomer retained a poem entitled 'Conquistador' in his *Collected Poems*. These two surviving poems are enough to show how closely the two men were collaborating at this point.

It was a delightful existence, almost exactly what Campbell had dreamed of. Every morning a basket of fresh milk, fruit, and vegetables was sent down to them from the Reynolds' great house, Lynton Hall, together with frequent gifts of venison, which their Zulu servant cooked. Their material needs supplied, they worked and planned for their magazine, writing feverishly when the mood took them, or talking animatedly for hours on the verandah, while the surf crashed and boomed on the beach. Campbell seemed to give a vividness to life that was tremendously uplifting – and exhausting – to other people. At night he loved to drag up all the driftwood he could find and make great bonfires that would burn for hours, while he danced and sang in wild elation.[20] Mary and Plomer tried, with little success, to husband and channel his energy.

Something of his vitality, and his delight in the hard sunshine, the violence, and vigour of Africa burns through two of the poems he almost certainly wrote at about this time: 'The Zebras' and 'The Sisters'.[21] 'The Zebras' is the first of Campbell's mature nature poems. Among the most obviously 'African' of his lyrics, this tightly control-led sonnet shows many of the characteristics that became his trademarks: driving speed and violence of movement that is the more impressive for being restrained by the most demanding of all stanza-forms, and visual images vivid as flames:

> From the dark woods that breathe of fallen showers,
> Harnessed with level rays in golden reins,
> The zebras draw the dawn across the plains
> Wading knee-keep among the scarlet flowers.
> The sunlight, zithering their flanks with fire,
> Flashes between the shadows as they pass
> Barred with electric tremors through the grass
> Like wind along the gold strings of a lyre.
> Into the flushed air snorting rosy plumes
> That smoulder round their feet in drifting fumes,
> With dove-like voices call the distant fillies,
> While round the herds the stallion wheels his flight,
> Engine of beauty volted with delight,
> To roll his mare among the trampled lilies.
>
> (CP, I, 40)

'The Zebras' is a poem of creation, a young man's poem, brilliant and sensual. The animals burst from the dark 'as if they had just sprung from the hand of the Maker'; through Campbell's eyes we see them as the first man might have seen them. The freshness of the imagery is reinforced by the sheer speed of the poem, spurred through its three sentences by the use of energetic rhythm, insistent alliteration, and daring verbs: 'zithering their flanks with fire', 'volted with delight'. With the boldness of an imagination that could conceive of sunlight striking plangent notes on the beasts' striped flanks, Campbell brought acute observation to this remarkable poem. Thus he photo-graphs the zebras' breath in the dawn light, and captures their curious melodious whinnying.

The poem is largely free of any attempt by Campbell to impose on it a burden of allegory; the animals are simply animals, without serving as symbols for anything except their own vigorous life. But

Campbell and Mary in 1921

Above. Ty Corn, the Welsh cow shed in which Campbell wrote *The Flaming Terrapin*, photographed in 1977. *Right.* Wyndham Lewis in the 1930s

From the left: William Plomer, Roy Campbell, and Laurens van der Post on the beach at Sezela, August 1926

their very vigour raises an interesting point. In the last, sexual image of the sonnet, Campbell sees the stallion wheeling his flight 'to roll his mare among the trampled lilies'. But while human lovers might roll among lilies, zebras would not: Campbell sees the animals' sexuality in human terms.* There is no doubt that horses and bulls had for him a sexual significance which went beyond the traditional symbolism associated with them.

'The Sisters' reinforces this view. Campbell wrote that the poem was inspired by the chance sight of two naked girls, his boyhood love Joan Tatham and her sister: 'I wrote it years afterwards, when I remembered having seen the two girls just before sunrise, ride out their horses into a cove at low tide.'[22] There is in this memory nothing of the frustrated sexuality with which Campbell opens his poem:

> After hot loveless nights, when cold winds stream
> Sprinkling the frost and dew, before the light,
> Bored with the foolish things that girls must dream
> Because their beds are empty of delight,
>
> Two sisters rise and strip . . .

Though Campbell goes on to tell us that the night is very cold (the frost of which he speaks is unknown in subtropical Durban) the sisters undress as if to meet their lovers. And the horses come, not to commands, but 'to their low-whistled pleas'. The description of the animals echoes that of the zebras in the earlier poem: they are 'vast phantom shapes . . . that sneeze a fiery stream about their knees'. The girls mount them, and the imagery becomes overtly sexual:

> Through the crisp manes their stealthy prowling hands,
> Stronger than curbs, in slow caresses rove,
> They gallop down across the milk-white sands
> And wade far out into the sleeping cove:
>
> The frost stings sweetly with a burning kiss
> As intimate as love, as cold as death:
> Their lips, whereon delicious tremors hiss,
> Fume with the ghostly pollen of their breath.

The sensuality of the lines unites girl and beast, frost, beach and sea[23] in an act that is climaxed by the sunrise:

* They are partly 'humanized' earlier in the poem too, when they are seen as having 'knees' and 'feet'.

Far out on the grey silence of the flood
They watch the dawn in smouldering gyres expand
Beyond them: and the day burns through their blood
Like a white candle through a shuttered hand.

(CP, I, 43–4)

The mood at the end of both these poems is one of fulfilment, achievement, and peace, of being at one with the life of Africa.

It was during this happy and productive time, late in 1925, that Plomer introduced Campbell to Laurens van der Post, a young Afrikaner who was working on Wodson's newspaper. Though Van der Post had by 1925 produced nothing but journalism, and though he was intensely reserved and tongue-tied, Campbell recognized him immediately as a fellow artist. 'You're one of us,' he told Van der Post: 'Come along.' And Van der Post, who never forgot the generosity of this unreserved, instinctive act of recognition,[24] immediately agreed to become 'Afrikaans Editor' of *Voorslag*, making it one of the first bilingual literary journals in South Africa.

Campbell and Plomer intended that the new magazine should fully live up to its name and 'sting . . . the mental hindquarters . . . of the bovine citizenry of the Union'. Their determination was reinforced by the furore caused by the publication, in March 1926, of Plomer's *Turbott Wolfe*. The novel was greeted in Natal by long, outraged reviews under such headlines as 'A Nasty Book on a Nasty Subject'.[25] Van der Post's editor, Wodson, wrote of it,

From first to last the book pictures rottenness; starting from the point where the white stranger with artistic leanings outrages the sentiments of his neighbours by filling his studio with native 'models', and treating them as though they were white people, and ending with the marriage of the royally beautiful Mabel van der Horst [a white woman] to the full-blooded native Zachary.[26]

And in the same editorial, Wodson noted ironically that Plomer was 'to collaborate with Mr Roy Campbell in a projected magazine soon, to give "uplift" to the intellectual life of this country . . .' Thus challenged even before they had begun publication, the two young men determined to use *Voorslag* to hit back.

The first issue appeared in June 1926. Campbell was disappointed by its appearance, calling it 'a coffee-coloured [magazine] . . . which would have disgraced a tradesman's catalogue'.[27] Mary Campbell described the woodcut on the cover, by a now-admired artist, Pierneef, as 'suitable for the tiles in a ladies' waiting room'.[28] And though South African newspapers greeted it with deference and caution at first, there were soon rumblings in the Press. With the exception of an article on beauty by General Smuts, and one on Cézanne by Roworth, the whole of the first number of *Voorslag* was written by Campbell and Plomer, using their own names and such pseudonyms as Mary Ann Hughes (Campbell) and Pamela Willmore (Plomer).

Three of their contributions in particular excited comment. There was an impassioned defence of *Turbott Wolfe* by Campbell, rounding upon those who had condemned the work, and beginning, 'Literary criticism in South Africa is either in its infancy or in its dotage . . .'[29] There was the first section of a long short-story by Plomer, entitled 'Portraits in the Nude', in which he continued the attack he had launched in his novel on white morality, complacency, and superiority; the story abounds with rapacious whites and long-suffering blacks. The third article was a highly favourable review by Plomer of Dr Norman Leys's book *Kenya*, a vigorous indictment of Britain's treatment of the Africans in that colony. To *Voorslag*'s uneasy readers, these articles seemed all to be tending the same way. The editors began to receive anxious and irritated letters from their public.

What annoyed the readers almost as much as the political questions was Campbell's tone. 'Mocking, blasphemous, unanswerable', [30] he challenged the conventions of 'the sleepy self-satisfaction of middle-age', goading and jeering, flaunting his youth and precocious reputation. In *Broken Record* he was to admit that this was probably the result of the coolness between himself and his father: 'Quarrelling with my father made me generation-conscious: there was an enormous wave of Hogarth-Pressure and I simply surfed it . .,.'[31] This continuing disagreement with his father was to have an unexpectedly profound effect on Campbell. For on 12 March 1926 Sam Campbell died. He had been suffering from trypanosomiasis ('sleeping-sickness') for some time, but his poet son does not seem to have appreciated that he was dying. Dr Campbell was on a fishing holiday on the Little Mooi River when he sank into a coma from which he did not recover. The funeral was one of the biggest ever seen in Durban, the streets thronged for hours by thousands of Zulus who poured into the city to express their respect. His father's death was a tremendous jolt for Campbell. After some days of intense grief, he settled down to brood over his sense of having failed to match up to his father's expectations. All his life he was to be haunted by his profound guilt at the rift between himself and his father – a rift which now could never be healed.[32] Increasingly he saw himself as cut off from other men too, scorning the 'mob' and scorned by it.

His concentration on both the 'colour question' and the 'generation gap' came to a head in one of the articles he wrote for the second issue of *Voorslag*, in July 1926: 'Fetish Worship in South Africa'. In it he asserted that white South Africa was as unthinking and as wrong in its acceptance of the values of 'Western Civilization' as the Africans were in worshipping their animist fetishes. 'I repeat that as a race we are unconscious,' he wrote in a phrase which suggests the influence of D. H. Lawrence. 'There is only the race-mind, the mob-soul.'[33] And the white 'fetish' he attacks most bitterly is the 'Colour Bar', as Apartheid was then called.

When the white people came out here they gave the native the Bible and the native in exchange gave the white man a great black fetish to worship. It is this fetish that rules the country – Colour prejudice.[34]

He wrote as the young, conscious, enlightened artist addressing the middle-aged, prejudiced mob. The 'mob', not surprisingly, was irritated by this attack on all its values, religious, political, social, and financial. Many Natalians regarded his urging them to 'jump the mean little fences' of the colour-bar as dangerous revolutionary talk. Lewis Reynolds, who had already sunk £1,000 into the magazine, became alarmed. He did not want to see the publication which he was widely known to be financing, and for which he had secured the support of the country's leaders, turned into a mouthpiece for Campbell's and Plomer's revolutionary views. In addition, he was intending to stand for Parliament in his father's old seat, South Coast.[35] He could not afford a political controversy.

Accordingly, Roworth, Reynolds, and Webb went, one Sunday morning in July 1926, to tell Campbell that they wanted Webb to have more control over the content of *Voorslag*. They asked Campbell to walk with them to the beach so that they could talk to him alone. While Mary and Van der Post, alarmed, watched from a distance, they sat down on a sand dune, Campbell squatting on his haunches like a Zulu, bearded and truculent.[36] He had for some time been nursing his grievances about Webb. The poet had been finding his job as editor an increasing strain, for he had no organizational ability. He had hated the articles written by Smuts and Roworth for *Voorslag;* Roworth's, he said with justice, was plagiarized word for word from French books on art. Webb, by inserting such articles, by putting in an apologetic 'manifesto' in which he claimed to speak for the other editors, and by printing readers' letters (Campbell described one as 'a bland little chortle of admiration . . . quite beneath the dignity of the substance of *Voorslag*')[37] as well as by allowing the printers to change Campbell's and Plomer's manuscripts, had irritated Campbell. Now came this challenge. Was an artist to be over-ridden by a tradesman? He flared up at once. 'You yourself confided in me in the beginning that we must take care not to let *Voorslag* develop Webbed feet', he told Reynolds, his voice shaking with rage. 'Now you want it to have a Webbed head. I've wasted two years of my life on *Voorslag*. You have my resignation here and now.'[38] He was as good as his word; nothing would induce him to change his mind. The third number of the magazine printed the terse note, 'I have much pleasure in announcing my resignation from "Voorslag". Roy Campbell.'

V
South African Poems
1926

CAMPBELL'S decision to resign from *Voorslag* was a courageous one, for it left him once more without an income, without a settled home, and without prospects. He, Mary, and Plomer stayed on in Reynolds's bungalow for a month, until the end of August 1926. During that month, in a brilliant burst of creativity, he wrote several of the best poems of *Adamastor*: great cries of loneliness, defiance, and despair. 'The Serf', 'The Zulu Girl', 'To a Pet Cobra', 'The Making of a Poet', and 'Tristan da Cunha' were all written in these weeks.[1]

This was undoubtedly the single most fertile period of inspiration in Campbell's life. He was never able to work regularly at his poetry, spending a fixed time at his desk each day, as some writers did; instead, he worked when he felt inspired to and lazed when he did not. When inspiration came, he worked unsparingly. His drinking stopped completely, and he ate very little; for days he would take nothing but endless flasks of tea. He would disappear into his bedroom in the evening, and spend the night lying on his mattress on the floor (he always disliked beds) scribbling furiously. This habit of writing while lying on his back he inherited, like so much else, from his father. He used a steel-nibbed pen which had to be dipped regularly into the ink, though reliable fountain pens had long been available. He consumed paper at a tremendous rate, for if he were dissatisfied with a line he would throw the page on the floor and start again rather than simply elide a word. Hundreds of his manuscript sheets survive with only one or two rejected lines on them. After a few days of concentrated work, his bedroom would be ankle-deep in papers, which no one dared touch; during extended periods of inspiration it would become difficult to open his door at all.[2]

The poems he wrote during these extraordinary few weeks show his divided state of mind at this crucial period in his career. His deep depression at the reception of *Voorslag*, coming so soon after the death of his father, linked most of the poems he wrote with a single theme:

his feelings of failure, frustration, and isolation. Thus in his poem about Mazeppa, the Polish boy is thrust out into the wilderness to die; 'The Making of a Poet' pictures the outcast steer suffering and alone; and the same theme runs through 'To a Pet Cobra', 'The Albatross', 'Poets in Africa', and 'Tristan da Cunha'. It is not surprising that his sense of having been rejected by his country should make him turn against it, railing, in poems like 'A Song for the People', in which he pictures 'the People' as having

> Huge buttock-faces slashed with flabby lips,
> Gouged into eyes, and tortured into ears.
>
> (CP, I, 28)

What is surprising is that he never lost his sense of being part of the community that rejected him, and that this sense emerges almost against his will in the lonely poems of this period, as even a brief examination shows.

'Mazeppa', inspired by Victor Hugo's treatment of the legend rather than by Byron's, was begun in France in 1921. Campbell originally wrote it in quatrains before abandoning it.[3] After his experiences in South Africa he rewrote it completely. The story is of a Polish boy thrust out by his community because of an amorous adventure. He is strapped to the back of a wild Ukrainian horse which is then set free to carry him off into the steppe. When the horse dies Mazeppa is rescued by a Cossack band whom he eventually comes to lead. In time he conquers huge territories, and becomes emperor of west Russia and Poland. This tale of the outcast who eventually triumphs exercised a strong attraction on Campbell's mind. He makes no reference to Mazeppa's crime. Instead he gives us a picture of a powerless, pitiful boy being tormented by a crowd of 'gleeful butchers':

> Helpless, condemned, yet still for mercy croaking
> Like a trussed rooster swinging by the claws,
> They hoisted him: they racked his joints asunder . . .
>
> (CP, I, 19)

Campbell recreates this confrontation between the individual and the mob in poem after poem, and his attitude towards it is interesting. He himself related his hatred of organized groups of his fellows to the shock he suffered on being put to school under Langley after a free-ranging childhood:

The contrast of the entire pagan freedom of my pre-school days with that penitentiary treatment . . . was so great that the first shock of finding myself

in the corral confirmed me as a stampeder . . . I am no reformer; the
limitation of all my early verse is that it is a violent claustrophobiac struggle
to keep my individual being, which is the only kind of 'freedom' that exists at
all . . .⁴

Life in early Natal and the Rhodesian bush had taught him the value
of self-reliance and given him a love of solitude; to the end of his life he
sought out isolated places to live. He got support for his preference for
individuality from an unusual source: the writings of Nietzsche. He
read Nietzsche voraciously at Oxford,⁵ and regarded the philosopher
as a poet of a high order.⁶ All his life he read and quoted *Zarathustra*
with approval, and in many passages in that book one can trace some
origins of his celebration of individuality:

Life is a well-spring of delight; but wheresoever the rabble drink all wells are
poisoned. . . . They have poisoned the sacred waters with their concupis-
cence; and in calling their filthy dreams delight they have poisoned words also
. . . . And many a one that went into the desert and suffered thirst with the
wild beasts, cared only that he should not sit about the cisterns with filthy
camel-drivers.⁷

Such passages provided Campbell with a rationale for his hatred of the
'mob-consciousness' he so fiercely attacked in 'Fetish Worship in
South Africa'. 'Crowds and communities', he wrote, 'are actuated
solely by the most primitive instincts: panic, suspicion, race-feeling,
colour-prejudice, ferocity and patriotism.'⁸ Against the blind hatred
of the mob he balanced, as Nietzsche does in *Zarathustra*, the
individual, clear-sighted, just, worthy to lead the 'rabble' and
rejected by them for that reason. Campbell undoubtedly saw himself
as a Mazeppa, fitted to direct the future course of South African
literature through *Voorslag*, but rejected by those he tried to help. One
would expect to find a very close identification between Campbell and
Mazeppa.

A careful reading of the poem only partly confirms this expectation.
Campbell is certainly sympathetic to Mazeppa, and describes his
sufferings in terms calculated to awaken our sympathy:

So when his last vain struggle had subsided,
His gleeful butchers wearied of the fun:
Looping the knots about his thighs and back,
With lewd guffaws they heard his sinews crack,
And laughed to see his lips with foam divided,
His eyes too glazed with blood to know the sun.

(CP, I, 19)

But whereas Campbell affected to despise the South African public, and made sure that they knew of his contempt for them, Mazeppa has none of the pride and defiance Campbell so admired. On the contrary, he is 'still for mercy croaking', though tormented and condemned. And the qualities we look for in vain in the tortured Mazeppa, we find in another tortured creature: the horse to which he is strapped. It is the horse which is 'tameless', which has 'never felt the bit between its jaws', while its burden is described as a 'trussed rooster swinging by the claws'; and while Mazeppa cries for mercy, it is the horse which smokes with hate.

In Voltaire's *Charles XII*, on which Hugo drew for his treatment of the story, the horse is described as a wild Ukrainian animal which instinctively gallops back to the Ukraine when released. The legend of the untameable horse gaining his freedom hundreds of miles from his native pastures and overcoming every obstacle in order to return home fascinated Campbell. He was to return to it in greater detail in 'Horses on the Camargue', a few years later. The horse has his sympathy as much as Mazeppa has; more, it has his admiration. His identification with the beast is as close as with the man. The deficiencies of Mazeppa are made up for by the horse. If Mazeppa is tortured, so is the horse; each is the other's torment. In the image of beast and man strapped together and plunging blindly over the endless plain towards death, Campbell had found a symbol for himself, divided and tormented, and for his own career. It is perhaps the richest of all the symbols he was to find for his dichotomous being.

That the horse's career was linked in his mind with his own is clear from the fine description he gives us of the racked pair:

> Now the dark sky with gathering ravens hums:
> And vultures, swooping down on his despair,
> Struck at the loose and lolling head whereunder
> The flying coffin sped, the hearse of thunder,
> Whose hoof-beats with the roll of muffled drums
> Led on the black processions of the air.

He was to use the 'muffled drum' image, with all its connotations of horror, in the Futurist poem 'The Festivals of Flight'; the image, which derives from Baudelaire and ultimately from Bishop King,* was always identified in Campbell's mind with his own fear of death.

* But heark! My pulse like a soft Drum
Beats my approch, tells *Thee* I come;
And slow howere my marches be,
I shall at last sit down by *Thee*.
(Henry King's 'The Exequy'.)

Horse and burden, then, are a symbol of Campbell himself, and it
is when the poem reaches its lowest point, with the beast 'crashed in
blood and spume' and the man reduced to a scarecrow or a strip of
leather, that Campbell gives us a vision of Mazeppa in his pride:

> This is that Tartar prince, superbly pearled,
> Whose glory soon on every wind shall fly,
> Whose arm shall wheel the nations into battle,
> Whose warcry, rounding up the tribes like cattle,
> Shall hurl his cossacks rumbling through the world
> As thunder hurls the hail-storm through the sky.

Campbell does not mention the peasants who nursed Mazeppa back to
health; there is no gradual transition between agony and triumph.
Gems flower through the scabs. Transmuted by his sufferings,
Mazeppa has taken to himself the pride and strength of the horse.
Again we have a situation in which an individual opposes a mob, but
how different! Victim has become victor; his brutish tormentors now
are 'rounded up like cattle'. Wish-fulfilment plays a large part in this
poem: Campbell goes on to draw the parallel between prince and
poet, the wild horse becoming Pegasus, the poet staggering up

> . . . to find himself a king
> With truth a silver trumpet at his lips.

'Mazeppa' shows how ambiguous Campbell's attitude was both to
himself and to the 'mob' he affected to despise. The horse-man
symbol is self-tormented. There is no doubt that much of the rejection
Campbell suffered throughout his life was the result of his own
actions. Those who knew and liked him were always puzzled by this
side of his nature – 'It was as if he felt he had to make enemies in order
to see himself as a victim and at the same time a hero – or almost as a
martyr and a saint,' wrote William Plomer.[9] 'Mazeppa' sheds light on
some of the origins of this behaviour.

Campbell implies, in the vision he gives us of Mazeppa 'superbly
pearled' even while we are watching him crawl from the vultures, that
his subsequent rise to power was in some way the fruit of his
sufferings; that he had been purified and ennobled by the experience.
Towards the end of the poem Campbell draws a comparison between
Mazeppa and the artist. And what he implies of Mazeppa he states
overtly of the poet, in lines that echo the close of Browning's 'Childe
Roland to the Dark Tower Came':

> Out of his pain, perhaps, some god-like thing
> Is born. A god has touched him, though with whips:

We only know that, hooted from our walls,
He hurtles on his way, he reels, he falls,
And staggers up to find himself a king
With truth a silver trumpet at his lips.

It is clear that he felt suffering gave birth to song. In one obvious way this was true: it was in 1926, with the death of his father and collapse of his hopes weighing heavy upon him, that he wrote so many of the superb lyrics he published four years later in *Adamastor*.

In such moments of desolation he was strengthened by the example of one of the few South African writers he admired: Olive Schreiner. He defended her vigorously against those who criticized her work and political views after her death in 1920. He wrote of her, 'She makes all other South African writers seem a little tame, because she *feels*, gets angry, and throws her weight about. . . Olive Schreiner is a genius: Plomer, Pauline Smith and myself are talented people.'[10] Reading her husband's account of her unhappy life[11] gave Campbell great sympathy and admiration for her, though it is difficult to believe he would have had much in common with the nineteenth-century novelist (friend of such solemn killjoys as Havelock Ellis and Edward Carpenter) had he ever met her. 'Buffel's Kop' may have been inspired by a visit to her grave, a hemispherical cairn on a *koppie* in the desolate eastern Cape, near Cradock:

> In after times when strength or courage fail,
> May I recall this lonely hour: the gloom
> Moving one way: all heaven in the gale*
> Roaring: and high above the insulted tomb
> An eagle anchored on full spread of sail
> That from its wings let fall a silver plume.
>
> (CP, I , 26)

The final image is taken from a symbolic incident in Schreiner's novel *The Story of an African Farm*[12] in which the eagle is named as 'Truth'.[13] Because of her sufferings, he fancied, she had come to see clearly; like her, he would seek truth through adversity.

It is its ability to triumph in – and through – adversity that draws Campbell to the snake in 'To a Pet Cobra',† written on 31 July 1926.[14] The poem opens with a stanza in which Campbell manages, with extraordinary skill, to evoke his feelings for the deadly reptile on his arm:

* The commonly-found 'pale' is a misprint.
† As far as I can discover, he never owned a cobra.

With breath indrawn and every nerve alert,
As at the brink of some profound abyss,
I love on my bare arm, capricious flirt,
To feel the chilly and incisive kiss
Of your lithe tongue that forks its swift caress
Between the folded slumber of your fangs,
And half reveals the nacreous recess
Where death upon those dainty hinges hangs.

                                          (CP, I, 31)

Campbell's identification with the reptile is complete and overt; he will turn 'the hate of men' to good account. If he cannot lead, he will goad. He has a driving need to be recognized by his fellows. If he cannot win respect, he will inspire fear:

I too can hiss the hair of men erect
Because my lips are venomous with truth.

And in a fine stanza he expresses what by 1926 had become his philosophy of life, a simple romantic assertion of the value of living as fully and generously as possible, whatever the cost:

There is no sea so wide, no waste so steril
But holds a rapture for the sons of strife:
There shines upon the topmost peak of peril
A throne for spirits that abound in life:
There is no joy like theirs who fight alone,
Whom lust or gluttony have never tied,
Who in their purity have built a throne,
And in their solitude a tower of pride.

                                          (CP, I, 32)

Yet even in this exultant poem Campbell's divided nature shows itself, and not only in his equivocal attitude to the snake. He says he loves to think of the men at whom the snake and he will strike, but he does not – cannot – cut himself off from them entirely. They are 'men of *my* dull nation'. In just the same way, in 'Mazeppa', he pictured the outcast poet being 'hooted from *our* walls' (italics mine).

Despairing loneliness is the prevailing mood of perhaps the finest poem in *Adamastor*, 'Tristan da Cunha'. Campbell wrote it between 5 and 14 August 1926. On 5 August Plomer showed Campbell a translation of the first two verses of a poem on Tristan da Cunha by Johannes Kuhlemann, which J. R. Gillie (a friend of Plomer's) had

done while at Balliol College, Oxford, in 1922,* and had sent to
Plomer from Germany that same year.[15] Campbell wrote to Gillie that
the translation had stirred his own memories of the island.† But the
original inspiration of Campbell's poem was 'Beyond Kerguelen' by
the Australian poet Henry Kendall, a poem which Campbell called
'the father of my *Tristan da Cunha*. He [Kendall] seized first of all in
verse that mystery of the lonely island walking on the sea.'[16] Campbell
described the genesis of 'Tristan da Cunha' in a letter to T. S. Eliot
two years later:

I read in South Africa a letter to my friend William Plomer from a man
named Gillie in Germany who said he was going to translate the poem. He
gave one verse of his translation: I think it was this verse that set me off on
my poem, though I don't think I actually imitated it. I had already done five
verses of my poem in the same metre under the title of *Kerguelen*. But I doubt
if I should have continued or altered them if Plomer had not produced this
letter and suggested *Tristan* as being a better subject than Kerguelen, which
is neither so well known nor so imposing an object.[17]

In some of its imagery the poem is clearly derivative of Tristan
Corbière's 'Au Vieux Roscoff'.[18] But despite all the influences, the
mainspring of the poem is Campbell's anguish at the collapse of all his
hopes:

> My pride has sunk, like your grey fissured crags,
> By its own strength o'ertoppled and betrayed:
> I, too, have burned the wind with fiery flags
> Who now am but a roost for empty words,
> An island of the sea . . .
>
> (CP, I, 41)

What he admires about the island is its strength in isolation, its
triumph through adversity. Yet because he had to recognize that
however much he might want to cut himself off he was not an island,
he goes on at once to imply that Tristan da Cunha suffers too: it is

> . . .a lorn look-out,
> Waving the snowy flutter of your spray
> And gazing back in infinite farewell
> To suns that sink and shores that fade away.

* Gillie sent his translation to T. S. Eliot, who, when Campbell's poem was published,
recognized the influence of Kuhlemann on it, and wrote congratulating Campbell on the quality
of his work. (T. S. Eliot to the *New Statesman*, 22 Oct. 1927.)

† Despite this, it is by no means certain that Campbell had actually seen Tristan da Cunha.
Sketches he made to illustrate his poem bear little resemblance to the island itself.

And at last, in this poem, Campbell can admit to himself that his isolation is his own doing:

> Exiled like you and severed from my race
> By the cold ocean of my own disdain,
> Do I not freeze . . .?

And the final stanza, deeply moving in its resignation to fate, is also an affirmation of the poet's need for others:

> We shall not meet again; over the wave
> Our ways divide, and yours is straight and endless,
> But mine is short and crooked to the grave:
> Yet what of these dark crowds amid whose flow
> I battle like a rock, aloof and friendless,
> Are not their generations vague and endless
> The waves, the strides, the feet on which I go?

Those among whom he lives, rejected and rejecting, are what give meaning to his existence. Of all the poems Campbell wrote in Africa, it is in 'Tristan da Cunha' that he comes closest to accepting himself and his fellows.

The baby, Anna, was teething at the time Campbell finished this poem, and on the evening of 14 August Campbell and Laurens van der Post walked with her along the beach at Sezela, so that Mary could get some rest. They tried to distract the crying child by making a huge fire. A high wind was blowing, so that the fire quickly burned almost out of control, threatening to ignite acres of sugar-cane, before they beat it down. Then Campbell, exhilarated and panting from his exertions, said, 'You know that poem Tristan da Cunha? I finished it today.' And he began to recite it (as he had earlier in the day to Plomer), his deep hoarse voice contending with the roaring of wind and waves:

> Snore in the foam: the night is vast and blind;
> The blanket of the mist about your shoulders,
> Sleep your old sleep of rock, snore in the wind . . .

He recited it through to the end. The wind swept the dying embers along the beach; Anna, lulled by the rhythm of the words, stopped crying. The poet seemed at one with the elements. In that setting of fire and wind, sea and winter stars, the poem moved Van der Post to tears.[19]

Of the remaining poems Campbell wrote during 1926, there are three that attract attention because they are so closely linked by a theme that does not recur in his work: 'The Serf', 'The Zulu Girl', and 'Rounding the Cape'. 'The Serf', written on 28 July 1926,[20] is a picture of a Zulu labourer working the scarlet earth of Natal. In Zulu society it is the women who till the soil; that a man should be ploughing is an indication that he is a hired labourer, on the farm of a white man. Campbell, of course, vividly recalled the days of the Zulu Rebellion when the threat of large-scale black violence was very real.[21] In his mind the peaceful ploughman is a momentarily subjugated warrior, and the contrast gives the poem great dramatic tension. The ploughman's heart may 'lie fallow' now,

>   But as the turf divides
> I see in the slow progress of his strides
> Over the toppled clods and falling flowers,
> The timeless, surly patience of the serf
> That moves the nearest to the naked earth
> And ploughs down palaces, and thrones, and towers.
>
>   (CP, I, 30)

Campbell's sonnet bears an obvious affinity to Thomas Hardy's 'In Time of the Breaking of Nations'. He has the same conviction that the ploughman, because of his closeness to nature, will endure, while the very artificiality of the 'palaces, and thrones, and towers' will bring them down.

Campbell spoke Zulu fluently; he understood and sympathized with African aspirations. In November 1925 he had written to Edward Garnett:

The government [of General Hertzog] is going to segregate the natives as much as possible – that is all right, provided they give them fertile areas and so on. But they have denied them any power of voting whatsoever. This is only procrastinating trouble, instead of settling it . . . It is obvious to everybody that the population will eventually be a coloured one. There is no other standard by which one is entitled to judge races than that of efficiency. If we take it on ourselves to be their lords and masters because they are less civilized, we have no right to oppose their aspirations towards our civilization.[22]

These were extraordinarily advanced views to hold in 1925, in South Africa. Undoubtedly they had their origin in Campbell's natural sympathy with the common people of every country he lived in, a sympathy perhaps strengthened and given definition by his contact with ardent young socialists at Oxford. They were attitudes supported to an extent by his family, for his father had been widely

known as a supporter of the Zulus (the Zulu paper, *Ilanga Lase, Natal,*
frequently paid tribute to him as a friend of the African)[23] while his
Uncle William, who would disappear into Zululand for weeks at a
time to live among the tribesmen, became a Chief of the Zulus; he was
one of very few white men to be accorded this honour. When he fell ill
he would call in a witch-doctor.[24] Certainly Campbell's African
sympathies existed before his meeting with Plomer, whose influence
on him has been exaggerated. But equally certainly his contact with
Plomer strengthened his 'negrophile' sentiments – particularly when
the expression of those sentiments in *Turbott Wolfe* and *Voorslag*
produced such a sensation.

The theme makes another appearance, still more strikingly, in 'The
Zulu Girl', another picture of African labourers at work. Campbell
spirals in on them from above, showing us first the 'sweating gang',
then the girl who flings down her hoe, and finally focusing on the
black child:

> His sleepy mouth plugged by the heavy nipple,
> Tugs like a puppy, grunting as he feeds:
> Through his frail nerves her own deep langours ripple
> Like a broad river sighing through its reeds.
>
> (CP, I, 30)

The suckling child, like the serf at work, is an image of life at its
simplest and most enduring. And as he conveyed in 'The Serf' a sense
of brooding anger, a threat slow of fulfilment but ineluctable, so the
'broad river' of these lines assumes great significance:

> Yet in that drowsy stream his flesh imbibes
> An old unquenched unsmotherable heat –
> The curbed ferocity of beaten tribes,
> The sullen dignity of their defeat.

The underlying violence of the image is unmistakeable: the broad flow
of black development can be temporarily dammed only at the peril of
the dammers. Campbell had used the same image in his letter to
Garnett:

The colonist cannot be brought to see that machine-guns are only a feeble
argument in the long run: that it will make things far easier to meet the
natives half-way than merely to go on damming up colour-hatred until it
breaks out in every corner of the country.[25]

And William Plomer's poem 'The Scorpion', written about this time, uses the image of the flood in the same way, and with the same sense of threat.[26]

With a connection that defies logical analysis, Campbell links three 'streams' in the poem: the great river of black aspirations, the drowsy milk which the child drinks, and the blood that purples the shadow of the thorn-trees.[27] By the speed with which he moves from one to another, Campbell mingles blood, milk, and water in the reader's mind, so that the final stanza, which makes the same connection in its comparison between the girl's breasts and a thunder-cloud, seems natural, even inevitable:

> Her body looms above him like a hill
> Within whose shade a village lies at rest,
> Or the first cloud so terrible and still
> That bears the coming harvest in its breast.
>
> (CP, I, 31)

With its mingled connotations of creation and destruction, the storm-image shows again Campbell's ambiguous attitude to what he saw as the coming triumph of black over white. He welcomed it, as an end to injustice, and he feared it. For however strong his sympathies with the blacks were, he did not want to see the destruction of the society that had nurtured him.

Meanwhile he had again to think about finding a place to live, for Roworth was pressing Lewis Reynolds to evict the Campbells from Sezela, so that he could reoccupy the bungalow. Though Van der Post had a small flat, in which he offered to put the Campbells and Plomer up for a time,[28] the only reasonable alternative was to move back into the Campbells' big family home in Musgrave Road. The house had been standing empty, for Campbell's mother, the one member of his family whom he felt understood him, had gone abroad after his father's death, herself exhausted by the effort of looking after the dying man. Campbell's isolation seemed almost complete. On 29 August Campbell, Mary, their two daughters, and Plomer moved into the house, though it must have been a bitter symbol for Campbell of his failure to support his wife and children independently.

Though Van der Post had prudently retained his job on Wodson's paper, Campbell and Plomer had now no means of support; it was clear that they would have to cast about for employment. At this point came a surprising development. Van der Post had some time before been contacted by a Japanese, Captain Mori, whose ship was in

Durban, and who had been commissioned by his government to offer a free trip to Japan to 'notable South African journalists', apparently as a public relations exercise. Mori offered Van der Post the trip, but Van der Post, feeling he had a duty to stay and help the others through this difficult period, refused. Campbell and Plomer were astonished when he told them: 'My God, Laurie, haven't you any imagination?' said Campbell, appalled that Van der Post could turn down such an offer.[29] Van der Post, mortified, accordingly contacted Mori again, and persuaded him to extend the offer to Campbell and Plomer, if they could join the staff of a newspaper before sailing. Campbell, depressed and ill, refused, for the offer did not include Mary and the children, but Plomer accepted, and Van der Post hastily arranged for him to be signed on as special correspondent for the *Natal Witness*, a paper whose editor, Desmond Young, had strongly supported *Voorslag*.[30] Plomer and Van der Post sailed for Kobe on 2 September 1926. After the excitement of their departure, Campbell was left feeling more alone than ever.

His feelings of frustration, despair, and failure, which had been growing ever since the death of his father, culminated at this time in something very like a nervous breakdown. He had shaved off his beard on the voyage out to South Africa, but now he grew it again, as he had during the disturbed period after he had sent himself down from Oxford. He began to have fits, probably neurasthenic in origin, during which he experienced 'a sort of electric shock in my neck about every half hour'; he believed he could feel his bones grating as he moved, and he would spend his afternoons walking about 'trying to get the terrible noises out of my head'.[31] He believed himself to be an epileptic.[32] South Africa had become intolerable to him. 'The whole of this country has an acid smell, and all the white people have khaki faces,' he said bitterly.[33] He began writing to friends such as Augustus John and C. J. Sibbett (a Cape Town advertising executive whom he had recently met) asking for money to pay his family's passage back to England, pulling out all the stops:

Mary is trying to find work as a lady-help and I have a very bad lesion in my spine which I can only get cured in England. Therefore I am asking you to send me fifty pounds. I shall never be able to repay it. I am asking it as a gift. You are about the only person in the country I have not made enemies with. My mother is in England and I am without any resources whatever. I am too ill to work. We are going to put our children in a crèche . . .[34]

Sibbett, alarmed, wired Campbell £25 at once, and another £25 a month later.

Meanwhile Campbell waged a long battle in the correspondence columns of the South African newspapers against the critics of *Voorslag's* first two numbers. Harold Wodson of the *Natal Advertiser*, Leo François, President of the Natal Society of Artists, and Bernard Lewis (brother-in-law of the novelist Ethelreda Lewis) who wrote on 'Art and Letters' under the *nom de plume* 'ZZ', all felt the lash of his scorn; but though several of his satirical limericks on Webb appeared pseudonomously in the *Advertiser*, most of his letters were so violent that he could not get them into print. Frustration fuelled his rage. He determined to pursue the attack in verse. Early in December 1926, in the space of a few days, he wrote the greater part of a long satire, *The Wayzgoose*.

It is a lightweight, light-hearted poem, written casually and hurriedly by Campbell for the amusement of his friends. He later claimed that his one-time schoolmaster, Bill Payn, who visited him almost daily during November and December 1926, had suggested many of the best lines.[35] 'It is only a farce', he wrote of it.

It is a satire in doggerel heroic couplets making fun of South Africa and my fellow colonials . . . But it is not very ambitious *as poetry*. It is utterly grotesque: and it is slightly modelled on Churchill's Prophecy of Famine and Marvell's Satire against the Dutch.[36]

And, he might have added, on Pope's *Dunciad*: for the competition to find the dullest writer in Natal is clearly drawn from the second book of Pope's poem.

A wayzgoose is a festival or dinner for printers; Campbell makes it a literary picnic to which all his enemies come. They are principally the journalists he had met during his work on *Voorslag*, and his former associates on the magazine. The poem begins with a general view of 'the grocer's paradise':

> South Africa, renowned both far and wide
> For politics and little else beside . . .
> A clime so prosperous to men and kine
> That which were which a sage could scarce define;
> Where fat white sheep upon the mountains bleat
> And fatter politicians in the street;
> Where lemons hang like yellow moons ashine
> And grapes the size of apples load the vine;
> Where apples to the weight of pumpkins go
> And donkeys to the height of statesmen grow . . .
>   (CP, I, 243)

Having mockingly established a link between farm produce and South Africans in general, Campbell focuses on journalists in particular:

> Shut in his shop, the ruined Butcher sighs
> And o'er the hopeless prospect rolls his eyes,
> For journalists are selling tripe too cheap,
> And profiteering on the brains of sheep.
> And Hill, at wholesale price, when all is said,
> Can sell the contents of a whole calf's head.
>
> (CP, I, 249)

Campbell uses the same train of imagery to lead into his attack on Roworth (whom he calls 'Pollio'), whose overcoloured and highly popular work Campbell had condemned from the start:[37]

> Yet when he paints the air is full of flies
> And hungry vultures gather in the skies –
> Rival of Zeuxis! from whose grapes 'tis said
> The disillusioned birds in dudgeon fled:
> But on his landscapes trusting flies remain
> And from his sunsets sip the gory stain:
> Still round his every masterpiece they hum
> And thick as on a butcher's window drum. . .
>
> (CP, I, 257–8)

Campbell pillories the man in lines which have remarkable satirical sting. Although his targets are provincial, the types he attacks are by no means peculiarly South African. Campbell considered that Roworth's popularity was as much the result of his unscrupulousness in copying the work of other men as the public's bad taste:

> How aptly by some journalistic sage
> Was he misnamed the 'Turner' of our age –
> Reversing Midas' gift, who has been known
> To 'Turn' the style of Turner to his own . . .
> 'Turner' and twister of a thousand styles,
> Over his toil the Muse of Business smiles,
> Pictures and public equally are 'sold,'
> And what he turns to dross, *she* turns to *gold*!

Leo François had criticized Campbell and Plomer in a radio broadcast after the latter's departure for Japan.[38] Campbell derided his habit of writing admiringly about his own work in the column he wrote for the *Advertiser* under the name 'Vermilion':

Another 'painter' came as I presume
Wheeled in a bath-chair by his nom-de-plume,
Who weekly praised him (paint whate'er he might)
In the third person – which was only right.
How much he paid himself such tricks to do
Only himself and his own alias knew,
Yet oft he cursed the younger generation
For 'scratching backs' and 'mutual admiration'. . .
Pass, 'painter,' pass, take off that tearful gaze,
And Long live François in 'Vermilion's' praise!

(CP, I, 259)

Campbell also hits at General Smuts, apparently for no better reason than for his contribution of 'Beauty in Nature' to *Voorslag*. Campbell disliked the solemn attempt to analyse beauty rationally. He disliked Smuts's theory of Holism even more when it went beyond rational analysis; he called it 'a hopeless wallow of emotionalism and mysticism'.[39] In his *Voorslag* article Smuts had written, 'the button of scientific thought has no doubt been pressed by quite ordinary means. But behind the button there is a great story, which Science has not yet discovered.' Campbell's mockery of this passage is funny, if not subtle:

Statesman-philosopher! I shake thy hand –
All tailors envy thee throughout the land
Whose BUTTON-HOLISM, without reverse,
Undoes the Trousers of the Universe!
Long be thy wisdom honoured, and thy race
Renowned for flinging smuts in 'Beauty's ' face!

(CP, I, 257)

But it was the refusal of the newspapers to print his letters that provoked Campbell to write *The Wayzgoose*, and it is journalists he is gunning for rather than statesmen or painters. He assembles them at the wayzgoose, and excoriates them at considerable length: Hill, Wodson ('Wod's Godson'), 'ZZ'[40] and various minor columnists on the *Mercury* and the *Advertiser* – 'Early Bird', 'Sundowner', and others. Above all he attacks Webb, whom he labels 'Polybius Jubb'. Webb was 'a copper-bottomed left-wing liberal'[41] associated with the South African Labour Party. He was also extremely wealthy:

A Socialist thou art in thought and act,
And yet thy business flourishes intact:

A Boss in trade, thou art securely placed,
And only art a Bolshevik in taste:
To kill a sheep, too tender is thy heart,
Yet wilt thou massacre a work of art.

(CP, I, 261)

Webb and the journalists, together with Roworth, were prime targets for Campbell's main thrust in this poem: his condemnation of the connection between Art and Money. It makes its appearance again at the end of the competition of Dullness, when the God presents Jubb with the prize: 'The Sacred Carrot with the golden rind'. The strength of Campbell's feeling about journalists and others who 'prostituted their talents' undoubtedly stemmed from his sense that in his connection with Natal papers and *Voorslag* he had sold himself. And, more than that, his editorship of the magazine represented a last attempt to measure up to his father's values and stand on his own feet financially. It was an attempt that had failed utterly. He saw his resignation as much more than an abandonment of a job he disliked; it was a severing of ties between himself and the family values that meant so much to him. 'All my family except my mother would like nothing better than to see us in the gutter begging them to help us,'[42] he wrote bitterly. In fact, his brother George generously offered to give him £20 a month at this time; his isolation was imaginary, though no less real for that.

This terrible depression explains the rancour that every so often breaks the good-natured surface of *The Wayzgoose*. The poem was not simply a denunciation of his enemies, it was also a renunciation of a part of his background and his very being. It is still worth reading, not so much for its poetic merits (though even now it retains its kick) as for what it reveals about the origins of Campbell's interest in satire. Satire allowed him to externalize those aspects of himself he found unacceptable, to step away from them and attack them. It gave him a way of exorcising the ghosts that haunted him.

For all *The Wayzgoose's* attacks on journalism, Campbell hated the thought that he had failed completely as an editor. He toyed for a time with the idea of starting a new literary magazine, to be called *Boomslang* (a deadly tree-snake) – a title even more threatening than *Voorslag*. But he had no way of raising money for another such venture;[43] it was all he could do to raise the fare to take his family back to England. With *Boomslang* in mind, however, he was reading a great deal of South African literature. He was very critical of all South

African writers except Pringle and Olive Schreiner – and, of course, Plomer; but he reserved particular contempt for Sarah Gertrude Millin, who was then a very popular novelist. 'Mrs. Millin's famous "restraint" is like a dog-collar without a dog in it',[44] he wrote to Sibbett, a jibe which Plomer had originated and which was the germ of Campbell's most famous epigram, one which wittily and pungently identifies the inadequacy of much modern writing:

> You praise the firm restraint with which they write –
> I'm with you there, of course:
> They use the snaffle and the curb all right,
> But where's the bloody horse?
>
> (CP, I, 198)

Poor Gertrude Millin recognized that this devastating thrust was aimed at her; she retaliated ineffectually by putting Campbell into her next novel, *An Artist in the Family*,[45] as the protagonist, Theo Bissaker, a young artist who, having wasted his time at Cambridge, returns with his wife and child to South Africa to live on his long-suffering parents. There he paints flamboyant pictures representing the Africans as 'menacing and sorrowful and full of meaning', though he knows them to be fatalistic and carelessly happy; and he eventually blows his hand off and is consigned to obscurity. Campbell's barb had gone deep.

But apart from this witty satirical squib, he was too disturbed during this period to write verse. To calm his nerves he spent much time in pseudo-scientific investigations, such as cutting up chameleons to see what colours they would turn as they died – a sad imitation of his dead father's serious scientific pursuits. His life was at a very low ebb.

Late in December 1926, feeling that his health would improve out of South Africa, and under the influence of Mary Campbell, who disliked the country, he embarked for England. He was never again to live in South Africa. His return to his birthplace had been a chastening experience. Not only had his hopes of an easy life in the subtropical paradise of his childhood been dashed, he had acquired in South Africa a reputation for holding dangerous political views – a reputation which even now has not completely faded. Above all, his sense of being an outsider had been intensified. The experiment had failed; even at home he was a foreigner. Loneliness became his abiding theme.

The Campbells' ship docked briefly at Cape Town at the end of
December 1926. Campbell put some of his complex feelings towards
his native land and her peoples into a poetic valediction called
'Rounding the Cape'. Inspired by a last view of the stark coastal
mountains of the Cape peninsula, the poem has all the bitterness and
longing of the voluntary exile. For the first time Campbell can see
South Africa whole. He personifies the country in Camoens's black
giant Adamastor, whose name was to supply the title for the volume
in which the poem was published four years later:

> The low sun whitens on the flying squalls,
> Against the cliffs the long grey surge is rolled
> Where Adamastor from his marble halls
> Threatens the sons of Lusus as of old.
>
> (CP, I, 27)

Campbell had first read the Portuguese poet Camoens's epic *The
Lusiads* in Mickle's verse-translation,[46] at the suggestion of C. J.
Sibbett, in May 1926. The passage in Canto 5, in which Adamastor
promises the Portuguese explorers 'grim disasters' appealed to him for
several reasons. It referred to South Africa (and *The Lusiads* was the
first poem to do so); it forecast the disasters he himself foresaw; and
finally, Adamastor's misery seemed to have something in common
with his own. Adamastor had had high hopes of finding happiness in
his suit of the Nereid Thetis, who had seemed to promise him her
love. For long he awaited her coming. At last, the poem continues,

I saw the fair Thetis coming from afar, her face as lovely as ever and her body
still more lovely in its nakedness. Beside myself with joy, I ran with open
arms to greet her who was life itself to me, and began to smother her eyes,
her hair, her every feature with kisses. Alas! – I scarce know how to tell it, in
my anger – when I thought I held my loved one in my arms, I realized that
instead I was clasping a rocky cliff bristling with thickets, its summit what
had been her angelic face. Nor was I, for the moment, any longer human.
Struck dumb and motionless, I might have been a second cliff.[47]

The giant's disappointment may well have struck Campbell as a
parallel to the blighting of his own hopes in South Africa. At any rate,
his sympathy for the 'dauntless' Titan is clear:

> Across his back, unheeded, we have broken
> Whole forests; heedless of the blood we've spilled,
> In thunder still his prophecies are spoken,
> In silence, by the centuries, fulfilled.

But as in 'The Serf' and 'The Zulu Girl', mixed with the sympathy is a brooding fear. Although the poet goes free to Europe, South Africa, with all that he has 'hated or adored', remains subject to the Lord of Darkness:

> The land lies dark beneath the rising crescent,
> And Night, the Negro, murmurs in his sleep.

VI

England

1927–1928

THE Campbells' voyage back to England was not a happy one. The poet was plunged in depression throughout the trip by the contrast between his confident voyage out to Durban just two years before, and his ignominious retreat. All his promises to Mary, all his assurances of the easy living to be made in a new and welcoming land, had come to nothing; his father was dead, and his family and country seemed dead to him too. He was tormented by the problem of how he was to earn a living. The obvious solution seemed to be to live with his mother-in-law and write reviews for magazines such as the *Calendar of Modern Letters*, which his Oxford friend Edgell Rickword and Mary's brother Douglas were running. But it seemed such a retrograde step: journalism and life with his family were just what he was fleeing from in South Africa. And so he brooded on the same questions day after day, as the Atlantic slid by; and finding no answer, he began drinking again – the glum methodical drinking of the escapist.

For Mary, too, the voyage seemed endless. She was seasick for much of the trip, and coping with two small children in the confines of a third-class cabin proved very trying. She could not trust Campbell with the children any more than his mother had been able to trust him to fetch his younger brothers from the station. Asked to take the baby Anna out for some air, he would tie her pram to the mast with his belt and go off for a beer and a chat with two Jewish card-sharps whom he had befriended,[1] leaving the baby to be rocked by the waves or by fellow passengers. The boat was beset by storm after tropical storm, one of them so violent that an Irish stewardess assembled the terrified third-class passengers on deck to say the rosary to stave off disaster.[2] Campbell left their porthole open one day, and they came back from lunch to find the cabin inches deep in sea-water. Several of Campbell's manuscripts were ruined, including his only copy of 'The Golden Shower', the long love-poem on which he had spent so many months and so much effort. Years later with the help of C. J. Sibbett he recovered the only section which had been printed in South Africa, recast it and published it in the second volume of his *Collected Poems*. But the greater part of the poem was lost, a terrible blow to Campbell.

When at length they steamed into Southampton Mary found her old governess, Miss Thomas, standing on the quay to receive the children. 'Thank God! At last I'm home!' she exulted.[3] For Campbell, exiled again, her pleasure must have been a bitter reminder of defeat. Mary's words were also the beginning of a difference of opinion between them, who had previously been united in nearly everything: in future, when Campbell proposed a return to South Africa, Mary opposed him steadfastly and successfully. Even before leaving South Africa, Campbell had written to Plomer, 'I think that as soon as our nerves have had a rest, we *must* begin again out here . . . I think we ought to start a press of our own, out here, preferably in Cape Town.'[4]

Mary's influence, however, prevailed.[5] Campbell had been badly hurt by his experiences in Durban, and he brooded on his hurt. For the first time real bitterness and vindictiveness, at first directed against his fellow countrymen, creep into his letters. In May 1927, for instance, he wrote to Plomer:

Whenever I get the chance of snubbing a S. African I always take it now. You do the same and we will soon be generally loved & respected in our native land. I get invitations to preside at Burns nights or rather nichts and I send the letter straight back instead of ignoring it as I used to. It tickles me. . .[6]

But this virulent writing was never translated into deeds. On the contrary, when Campbell subsequently met fellow South Africans such as Enslin du Plessis or Laurens van der Post in London, he went out of his way to shower them with kindness. His hatreds (and this was only the first of many) seem almost always to have been purely theoretical.

The Campbells spent a fortnight in London and then went to stay for a time with Mary's mother at King's Pyon, near Leominster; but Campbell could not bear to be dependent on his mother-in-law for long. He began receiving £20 a month from his father's large estate, and with this and what he could earn by reviews and occasional poems contributed to magazines, he and Mary began looking about for a cottage in the country, away from his Oxford and London friends.

It was John Squire, editor of the monthly magazine *London Mercury*, who suggested that they should live in the village of Sevenoaks Weald in Kent, where he had a small house.[7] The advantages of country life within easy reach of London attracted the Campbells. They lived in a shanty in the woods, near the poet Edward Thomas's home,[8] for a short time, and then found their own cottage, 'Paris End', late in April 1927. It was small, decidedly ugly, and not very comfortable, but it was their own. Campbell settled down to polishing up *The Wayzgoose*, writing for Rickword's and Garman's journal, and trying to raise money for William Plomer (who was still in Japan) by offering Plomer's short stories to various publishers. Occasionally friends, among them Philip Heseltine and Cecil Gray, the composer and music critic, would come down from London to see them; and very occasionally Campbell would go up to London. But the gossip which had preceded his marriage lingered on, and the sight of his old Oxford friends reminded him of failure; he avoided them as much as possible. 'I have seen none of the old Oxford crowd,' he wrote to L. A. G. Strong. 'I keep away from London and have only spent two days there since I came to England. I find it interferes with my work.'[9]

Meanwhile the Campbells were rapidly forming a new circle of acquaintances. Late in May 1927 they met Vita Sackville-West one morning in the village post office. She had heard of them through Squire,[10] and she had read and admired *The Flaming Terrapin*; they knew of her as a local notable and the author of *The Land*, which had just won the Hawthornden Prize. She invited them to dinner on 23 May 1927,[11] at her beautiful half-timbered house, Long Barn. Here for the first time they met her husband Harold Nicolson, home on leave from his diplomatic post in Persia. The Nicolsons and Campbells seem to have taken to each other at once. Campbell was not only a promising young poet in financial distress; he and his wife were a strikingly handsome pair. The Nicolsons, on the other hand, were intelligent, cultured, and generous. There was thus much in each couple to attract the other, and the Campbells were soon visiting Long Barn regularly.

Harold Nicolson's diary reveals his first, ambivalent response to the poet, describing him as 'an ugly and uncouth creature with fine eyes and brow and a certain charm'.[12] But their relationship warmed. One evening Campbell, his tongue loosened and his imagination fired by the Nicolsons' port, told Harold his life story, embroidering it with the freedom that became one of his characteristics. Amused but impressed, Harold Nicolson compared him to 'another Rimbaud'[13] – a comment which indicates that Campbell had told not only of his wilder adventures in France and Africa, but also of his homosexuality.

Campbell was unimpressed by Vita's poetry, though he was flattered by her high opinion of his. He wrote to a South African friend, 'Vita Sackville-West . . . won the Hawthornden this year with her long poem, The Land. It isn't much of a poem, but she is very nice and has a wonderful library . . .'[14] It was her library, her friends, and her generosity that reconciled Campbell temporarily to the domineering, masterful Vita. A large number of the most important literary figures of the day visited Long Barn frequently, and through the contacts he made there Campbell was able to find work; he did a number of reviews and articles at this time for the *New Statesman* and other left-wing magazines. But the strong sense of isolation which had resulted from his failure at Oxford and his subsequent *Voorslag* experience was growing rather than diminishing in Kent. In South Africa he had distinguished himself from those around him by assuming the mask of a sophisticated and famous man of letters, spurning the colonial Yahoos. In Weald he quickly abandoned this pose, and became the muscular, down-to-earth South African (just as he had been the 'Zulu' at Oxford), exposing with his sound common-sense the affectations of the effete Britons. Thus he wrote of his articles in the *New Statesman:*

I get up the backs of the readers fairly often. But so far I have always managed to have the last word. I am always having shots at vegetarianism, 'liberty', and Fabianism. Of course as my reviews come under the literary section, I am able to say what I like. [15]

'Saying what he liked' included writing very favourable reviews of Wyndham Lewis's books *Time and Western Man* and *Paleface*. He associated increasingly with Lewis during this period, and with Heseltine and Augustus John. Lewis, who was working on an early draft of his long satirical novel *The Apes of God*, was scathing in his criticism of Campbell's new friends, and Campbell agreed with him more and more. A holiday in Provence with Augustus John and Mary in June 1927 brought home to the poet how much he missed the sunshine and his former gypsy existence – and how he was becoming increasingly tied to his benefactors, the Nicolsons. Their continued generosity, which he could never repay, produced in him a sense of gratitude that was increasingly resentful. He compressed his dislike of them and their clever wealthy friends, before whose assurance he shrank into silence, into an epigram he called 'Home Thoughts in Bloomsbury':

> Of all the clever people round me here
> I most delight in Me –
> Mine is the only voice I care to hear,
> And mine the only face I like to see.   (CP, I, 196)

Mary Campbell felt none of her husband's growing dislike of England and the Nicolsons. On the contrary, her stay in South Africa had given her a new love for England. She wrote to William Plomer, 'The English countryside is too gorgeously lovely. We are in a most English village – the sort I used to imagine I couldn't stand . . .'[16] She enjoyed Vita's company, and the people she met at Long Barn:

When I was talking to Harold . . . Vita Nicolson appeared & in her wake, Virginia Woolf, Richard Aldington and Leonard Woolf. They looked to me rather like intellectual Wolves in sheep's clothing. Virginia's hand felt like the claw of a hawk. She has black eyes, light hair & very pale face. He [Leonard] is weary and slightly distinguished. They are not very human.[17]

Campbell was quite unimpressed by the Nicolsons' friends, wealth, or family connections. But for Mary, an inveterate snob, it was not the least of Vita's attractions to know that she was the daughter of Lord Sackville, that her ancestral home was Knole, the huge Elizabethan house two miles from Long Barn, that she was rich and well-travelled, that she surrounded herself with clever and famous people, and that she managed silver, spaniels, and servants with equal facility. As Campbell's dislike of England and the Nicolsons grew, Mary's love for both increased. The poet felt this growing gulf between them very keenly. The Nicholsons' wealth and generosity seemed a reproach to his own poverty. At the dinners they gave he sat silent and downcast among their friends, all his old shyness returning as they talked about people he did not know and countries he had not visited. 'I did not notice that he felt any resentment,' wrote Harold Nicolson later. 'He just felt out of it.'[18] One particular literary dinner-party, in the great hall at Knole, at which Raymond Mortimer, Edward Sackville-West, Clive Bell, and Desmond MacCarthy were present, seems to have stuck in his memory – 'that fatal dinner', Harold Nicolson was ruefully to call it.[19] Campbell was to describe his feelings later, in *The Georgiad*:

> . . . I have sat like Job among the guests,
> Sandwiched between two bores, a hapless prey,
> Chained to my chair, and cannot get away,
> Longing, without the appetite to eat,
> To fill my ears, more than my mouth, with meat . . .

When I have watched each mouthful that they poke
Between their jaws, and praying they might choke,
Found the descending lump but cleared the way
For further anecdotes and more to say.

(CP, I, 231)

And as Campbell had turned to beer to rid him of his shyness at
Oxford, so now his growing discomfort drove him to drink again.
With increasing frequency Mary Campbell would return from the
village shop to find the children alone in an empty house, doors and
windows flung wide, and Campbell gone up to London to get drunk
with John or Heseltine. It was his drinking that made Mary turn to a
sympathetic Vita for comfort. Vita was only too willing to provide it.
Sympathy rapidly grew into something more powerful.

Mary was an unusually vivacious and beautiful woman; Vita had
been an active lesbian since before her marriage to Harold (who was
himself a homosexual).[20] In later years Vita came to bear a strong
resemblance to a crusty Anglo-Indian colonel, but in 1927 she
seemed to Mary an endlessly fascinating being. The two women met
at first in the lane below Long Barn; Campbell's frequent absences
made such meetings easier. The affair quickly became passionate. Its
course can be traced in the volume of poems Vita subsequently
published. Entitled *King's Daughter*,[21] it might (with its pun on
Campbell's name) more accurately have been called 'King's Wife'.

It is clear from the opening poem of the volume that Vita was from
the start fascinated by Mary though doubtful of her reception. Poem I
wonders whether Mary is what Vita rather coyly calls 'a changeling
soul'; in Poem II Vita pursues her

> . . .when she passes
> Barefoot through daisied grasses

in a successful effort to 'follow and hold her'. Vita soon attained her
object; Mary could not long resist the turbulent demands of a woman
to whom she owed so much gratitude, and whom she so much
admired. And Vita, having made the conquest easily, treated it as a
thing of little consequence, slipping into nursery-rhyme to describe it:

> . . .When she sets her candle
> And the mirror gleams,
> And she before her looking-glass
> Slips her shift, and dreams.

Whiter than the candle-wax,
Whiter than the rose,
Is her young and lovely throat,
As Goosey Gander knows . . .

Goosey, goosey gander,
Will you be my spy?
Let into your lady's room
No-one dare to pry.
                    (*King's Daughter*, pp. 12–13)

This love affair, which all but wrecked the Campbells' marriage, which changed the course of their lives, and scarred the poet's mind and affected his verse to the end of his life, was for Vita merely one of a long series of diversions, and by no means the most memorable. (The nursery-rhyme music returns in Poem V, where one hears the jingle of 'Hark, hark, the dogs do bark';

Where some shall pass in rose-red silks,
And some shall pass in rags,
And some shall ride in scarlet cloaks
Beneath the windy flags.)

Meanwhile Campbell was quite unaware of what was happening. He seems to have been pleased that his wife had found a friend. The problem of earning enough money to keep his family still tormented him; even the small rent the Campbells were paying for their cottage seemed an insupportable burden. He wrote no poetry at this time; all his energies went into earning money through articles and reviews, activity which he despised. He was being reduced to the journalism he had so proudly rejected in South Africa. There seemed no way out of the morass.

It was in mid-September 1927 that Vita offered a partial solution. The Nicolsons owned a small, new house set a little further up the slope from Long Barn. Called 'the gardener's cottage', it actually housed their two children and a nanny. Vita now suggested that the Campbells should move into this cottage, rent free, to stay as long as they liked. To her it must have seemed a masterly combination of beneficence and self-interest. Meeting with Mary would now be not only easy, but inevitable. Campbell accepted the offer with little hesitation; they moved into the cottage on 1 October 1927.[22] He wrote to a South African friend,

We have had a certain amount of luck since we arrived here. We have been given a nice house free of rent and for about the first time in our lives we have

Campbell in 1925

Vita Sackville-West in 1924

Mary Campbell, 1927

really settled down . . . We are on the estate of Knole Palace . . . Knole is the place where Dryden, Pope, Otway and many of my favourite authors used to spend most of their time . . . Vita Nicolson's house is next to ours. It is also an interesting place. Caxton was born there . . .[23]

He was quite unsuspecting.

Mary was by now deeply in love with Vita. Once her feelings had become fully engaged she plunged passionately into the affair caring less and less about secrecy. But Vita, having achieved her desire, began to draw back. In Poem VI she records how Mary brought her flowers and left them in her room 'as a token':

> She cheated in the game
> Sweet rogue, that day she came
> And snared me unawares.
> Now shall I tell her name and shame,
> Or shall I yield me pliant to her snares?
> (*King's Daughter*, pp. 17–18)

Mary had become the pursuer, Vita the pursued.

Early in November Mary told her husband what was happening. The move was less daring and less cruel than it sounds. She knew that in his attitude to sexual aberrations he was very tolerant, and in the past neither had kept any secrets from the other; he had known of her pre-marital affairs as she had known of his. He listened in silence, then questioned her as to the extent of the affair; she kept very little back.[24] He was stunned by the news. He went and sought out Vita and told her that he knew. She was quite unperturbed.[25]

It may be that Mary had hoped to give some permanence to her relationship with Vita by forcing Campbell to recognize and acknowledge it. If so, she miscalculated. Bewildered and hurt, Campbell took the train up to London, intending perhaps to drink himself into a stupor. There, in a pub, he met the author and scholar C. S. Lewis, a man he knew only slightly from his Oxford days. To him Campbell, unable to contain himself, poured out the whole story. Lewis, at first surprised, listened in fascinated silence, and then sat back ruminatively. 'Fancy being cuckolded by a woman!' he mused.[26] The uncharacteristically tactless remark seared itself into Campbell's mind. He was an intensely proud man; the thought of being the butt of innumerable Bloomsbury jokes was unbearable to him. The carefully constructed public image of himself as the powerful 'Zulu', drinking, fighting, and womanizing, would be turned devastatingly against him. He flung out of the pub and went back to Weald in a black rage, his sense of betrayal now compounded with jealousy and wounded pride. That night the Campbell children woke crying to an empty house, the curtains flying from open windows, the furniture flung about. Mary, terrified, took refuge with Vita, and (according to Campbell's imaginative account) Dorothy Wellesley,[27] whom Vita had summoned by telephone to Long Barn, sat up all night with a shot-gun across her knees.[28] The next day Vita's diary laconically records her belief that Roy was half mad.[29]

But Campbell's rage could not be sustained at such a pitch for long. Mary was surprised by the violence of his outburst, and frightened by it, but she refused to leave Vita. For days Campbell argued, cajoled, and threatened. He chased Mary with a kitchen-knife.[30] He demanded a divorce. When even this failed to move Mary, he subsided. He could hardly thrash Vita, and Harold had returned to his post abroad on 23 October. Campbell had no money, no prospects, and now, it seemed, no wife. But once his anger had cooled he began to realize how much his own behaviour had been responsible for Mary's betrayal. He blamed himself as much as he blamed her. In these circumstances, he vacillated agonizingly: he could not bear to leave her and he could not bear to stay.

According to Harold Nicolson's biographer, James Lees-Milne, Campbell was meanwhile himself having a brief affair with a bisexual friend of Vita's, Dorothy Warren, who ran the Warren Galleries. Possibly he hoped to arouse Mary's jealousy by such action.

At this point he fell ill; appendicitis was diagnosed, and in February he was taken to hospital for an operation. His illness, and the period of convalescence that followed, gave him an excuse to stay where he was, still hoping that Mary would take pity on him, or that Vita would tire of Mary. It was during this period, in the bitter winter of 1928, that Laurens van der Post arrived in London from South Africa, and wrote to Campbell. The next day he received a reply:

My dear Laurens,
1. Go to Charing Cross Station at once
2. Buy a ticket for Sevenoaks (2/9 single or 5/– return)
3. Get in the train for Sevenoaks (the porter will do it all for you if you tell him you're a stranger. He'll show you the right train – give him a sixpence.)
4. Get out at Sevenoaks station.
5. When you get out at Sevenoaks you'll see plenty of taxis. Get in one and tell him to drive to Weald Village.

6. When you get to Weald Village ask at the Post Office, the butcher's, the baker's, or any of the shops, and they will tell you where I live. Weald is only a tiny village everybody knows my house there. (The taxi costs about 6/– the only alternative is 3 miles walk)
The whole journey will not take much more than an hour.
Come out at once. I am looking forward to seeing you again. I had no idea you were coming.

Campbell was pathetically pleased to see Van der Post. Mary took advantage of his stay to disappear for three weeks, Vita being away at the same time. Van der Post was horrified at the squalor in which Campbell was living, scarcely stirring from his bed, and at his emaciation. He wrote later,

I could hardly believe that the man who had walked the beach in the dark, comforting a hurt little girl in his arms and reciting a great poem with the voice of a prophet, and this thin, shivering hulk of a human being in torn and tattered clothes, could be one and the same person.[31]

Van der Post could hardly believe that Campbell would recover. Though Campbell did not confide in him, he sensed that this dreadful change had something to do with Mary.[32] Campbell was drinking heavily and continuously, mostly gin and cider because of their cheapness, and he spent his days, half-dressed, in his bed, reading back numbers of the German magazine *Der Querschnitt*. There were very few blankets in the house, and Van der Post found it difficult to sleep because of the cold. Several times he woke to find that Campbell had covered him during the night with his own blanket, and he was astonished that even in this extremity of misery Campbell did not forget his duty to a guest.[33]

It was days before Van der Post was able to persuade Campbell to accompany him to London to meet another South African, the journalist and painter Enslin du Plessis. Although it was a bitingly cold day, Campbell wore neither overcoat nor tie, but clasped a thin jacket over his grey flannel trousers, so torn that the skin of his buttocks was visible; he was unwashed and unshaven. They met Du Plessis in Fleet Street, and went to Grooms', an old coffee-house, for a meal of sausage and bacon, the first food Campbell had had for days. Years later Van der Post was to say that cold though that winter was, Campbell's spirit was bleaker still.[34]

Mary's return brought Campbell no relief. He lingered at Long Barn for a time, as hope faded. At last, in April 1928, he gave up. Unable to endure any longer the daily sight of Vita and Mary together, he sadly packed a small bag and took the train to London. He did not return; he had determined to leave England. To go back to South Africa was inconceivable. Instead he crossed the Channel and made his way to Martigues in Provence, where he and Mary had had such a pleasant holiday the previous summer. In that beautiful sunny village, so full of memories of past happiness, he hoped to find consolation. He was on the run again.

VII
The Georgiad
1929

CAMPBELL arrived in Provence lonely and despairing, his self-confidence shattered. He knew the strength of Vita's hold on Mary; she offered her love, comfort, support, and wealth, and she had the sort of social position which so impressed Mary. By contrast, Campbell could offer only poverty, isolation, hardship, and the prospect of life with a man who was drinking ever more heavily. In England his threats had proved as useless as his appeals; it was most unlikely that he could achieve by letters what he had failed to do face to face.

As so often with Campbell, the emotional crisis brought on a psychosomatic illness;[1] not for the first or last time, he thought he had become an epileptic. He seems to have been able to borrow a little money from literary friends before leaving London, and on arriving in Martigues he took a room in Pascal's Restaurant and put himself to bed. The three canals and the old houses of that beautiful sun-soaked little port had no attractions for him, though even today, with the huge nearby oil-refinery blackening the sky, it is a lovely place. He began writing a stream of desperate, pathetic letters to Mary, begging her to join him. He could not live without her, he wrote; more importantly, he could not write without her. Things would be different, he promised her; he would give up drinking, he would do anything to make her happy, she would see how he had changed . . . And to Campbell's delight, the impossible happened. Mary agreed to return to him. The poet saw this as the surest evidence of her continued love for him. In fact, however, there is clear evidence that she was still deeply in love with Vita. Why did she return to her husband?

The answer seems to be that she was urged to do so by Vita, to whom she had become an embarrassment. Vita's fluid affections had begun ebbing quite early in the relationship. Moreover, she was at the same time carrying on no fewer than five other, separate affairs, one of them with Virginia Woolf. Virginia, engaged in writing *Orlando*, was a frequent visitor to Long Barn; she knew about Vita's affair with Mary, and was intensely jealous.[2] She proved a rival Mary could not hope to match. In *King's Daughter* Vita expresses her increasing frustration and sense of being trapped by Mary's love:

> Between what different moods we alternate,
> Caged, snarling beasts that our poor spirits tear:
> Love, magnanimity, revenge and hate,
> Jealousy and emasculate despair . . .
>
> *(King's Daughter*, p. 37)

Vita's increasing coldness, combined with Campbell's humble and desolate letters, persuaded Mary to return to him. Vita was relieved. The 'Envoi' in *King's Daughter* set a seal on the affair for her, as she looked already towards the next:

> The catkin from the hazel swung
> When you and I and March were young.
>
> The flute-notes dripped from liquid May
> Through silver night and golden day.
>
> The harvest moon rose round and red
> When habit came and wonder fled.
>
> October rusted into gold
> When you and I and love grew old.
>
> Snow lay on hedgerows of December
> Then, when we could no more remember.
>
> But the green flush was on the larch
> When other loves we found in March.
>
> *(King's Daughter*, p. 41)

Mary arrived in Martigues with their two daughters on 12 May 1928,[3] to find Campbell apparently very ill and overjoyed to have her back. They found a cheap little house at 3 Rue St Mitre in Martigues,* and with Mary to look after him Campbell quickly regained his health. He was soon writing to friends (from whom he tried to conceal his marital difficulties): 'I had to come away for a change after my operation [his appendicectomy] and Mary was rather run down too. But the sunlight and the sea are setting us up finely.'[4]

But though he recovered quickly and completely, there is ample evidence that his marriage did not. Mary was still deeply in love with

---

* The street is now named the Avenue Docteur Fleming. The house still stands, virtually unchanged.

Vita, to whom she wrote almost daily: hastily pencilled letters on odd scraps of paper, posted secretly when Campbell was out of the house. Having settled Campbell in the Rue St Mitre, she returned briefly to England to see Vita for ten days in June, and again in November 1928.[5] Each time Campbell must have wondered whether she would return. By December she was once again despairing of living with him, and talking of separating from him and living alone.[6] It was only gradually that they learned once again to live together as man and wife, and it is hardly coincidental that Campbell in several poems referring to this period calls Mary his 'sister'.[7]

Knowing that his own drinking had been responsible for driving Mary into Vita's arms was a burden of guilt that played a large part in his relationship with Mary for the rest of his life. He never lost his sense of gratitude towards her, and his sense of wonder that she stayed with him despite everything. For almost a year, during 1928, he had written no poetry; but in January 1929 he wrote the 'Dedication' to *Adamastor*, celebrating his reunion with his wife.

Something of a pastiche, the poem echoes both 'Mazeppa', and 'The Making of a Poet'. In it, Campbell exults in Mary's having returned to him at a time when 'my spent heart had drummed its own retreat'.[8] She had, he said,

> . . . rallied the red squadron of my dreams,
> Turning the crimson rout of their defeat
> Into a white assault . . .
>
> (CP, I, 16)

But in the last stanza Campbell finds an image for his relationship with Mary which shows his awareness both of its strength (proved by the fact that she had come back to him despite Vita's attractions) and of its weaknesses. He compares Mary to a still lagoon and himself to a reef, implying that she gives him a centre of calm and beauty, compared with the sea of life that rages around him:

> Sweet sister; through all earthly treasons true,
> My life has been the enemy of slumber:
> Bleak are the waves that lash it, but for you
> And your clear faith, I am a locked lagoon
> That circles with its jagged reef of thunder
> The calm blue mirror of the stars and moon.
>
> (CP, I, 16)

But the image, as Campbell may have realized, is ambiguous. It was not Campbell who was the reef, keeping the bleak waves from

disturbing Mary's 'clear faith', but she who protected him from the
buffetings of a life he was not equipped to deal with. Why did he
choose to use this image in this way? The answer, perhaps, lies in his
choice of the word 'locked'. Campbell was a highly sensitive man and
it is quite possible that he realized the extent to which Mary felt
herself trapped by his dependence on her. It was at just this time that
she was writing to Vita of her desire to live apart from him. If
Campbell had to adjust to the idea of a wife who was no longer wholly
his, Mary had to adjust to the idea of a husband who needed her more
than she needed him. Her dominance in their relationship grew
steadily from this period onwards. Henceforward she made all the
important decisions for the family, and Campbell, freed from many of
the responsibilities that had tormented him, entered one of the
happiest periods of his life.

Having begun writing poetry again after the emotional storm of
1928, he planned to take revenge on Vita and all that he associated
with her. Early in 1929 he began a long satire, *The Georgiad*. He had
soothed his hurt after the *Voorslag* débâcle with *The Wayzgoose*; perhaps
the same remedy would give him relief now.

The plot of *The Georgiad* is simple and direct. The attack on the
inhabitants of 'Georgia' is spearheaded by a central, compound
character, 'Androgyno', a powerful, passionate bisexual, in whom

> Both sexes rampantly dispute the field
> And at alternate moments gain or yield . . .
> Unlike our modern homos, who are neither,
> He could be homosexual with either
> And heterosexual with either, too –
> A damn sight more than you or I could do!
> (CP, I, 203–4)

Campbell sends this vigorous hero trudging across country to Long
Barn ('Georgiana's Y. M. hostel') where he is accepted as a weekend
guest. Flirted with by Vita, he accompanies her to bed, but once there
he gets quite out of hand. Having reduced her to insensibility, he flies
from room to room raping Harold (cuttingly called 'Mr Georgiana')
and then the other guests, of both sexes:

> . . . not for long in Georgiana's arms
> Our hero lies; but spreading new alarms,
> As soon as she collapses, to loud cries,
> From bed to bed the amorous fury flies.
> (CP, I, 237)

The next morning the exhausted household calls in a Freudian psychiatrist to prove Androgyno cannot exist; but the heedless hero,

> . . . having cursed the hostel for a sham,
> Punched the hostess, and kicked the poor proprietor,
>   (CP, I, 239)

goes back to London to settle to the 'Georgian' task of editing a 'posh review', labour in which his catholic sexual tastes stand him in good stead, for

> . . . in the subtle strife of heads or tails
> The latter, as by magic, still prevails.
>   (CP, I, 239)

In having his bisexual hero sleep with everyone in Georgiana's Hostel, Campbell implies that everyone who stayed at Long Barn joined, willingly or unwillingly, in the sexual pyrotechnics there. This is obviously an exaggeration, although a remarkable number of the people who knew the Nicolsons were either homosexual or bisexual. Virginia Woolf, Lytton Strachey, Dora Carrington, Edward Sackville-West, and Duncan Grant were regular or occasional visitors, and the general air of 'freedom' which prevailed embraced such flights of whimsy as nude races round the garden.[9]

Campbell, who in his later writings boasted of his love affairs,[10] accepted the situation at Long Barn, apparently without protest, until he learnt of his wife's affair. But he seems always to have hated the sterility and lack of spontaneity of 'Georgian' love. The idea of reading textbooks on love by Marie Stopes, Bertrand Russell, or Havelock Ellis repelled him. It repels Androgyno too; he dislikes

> All who have learned this grim felicity
> And swotted bliss up, like the Rule of Three,
> As if life were a class-examination
> And there were penance in cohabitation . . .
>   (CP, I, 208)

It is this grimness, this pedantry, that Campbell attacks in his vitriolic portrait of Vita, surely one of the most powerful literary onslaughts of modern times:

> Each titled bawd, born under Venus' ban,
> Too gaunt and bony to attract a man
> But proud in love to scavenge what she can,
> Among her peers will set some cult in fashion
> Where pedantry can masquerade as passion . . .
>   (CP, I, 209)

He sees her and her kind

> . . . grieving at the transience of delight*
> Which her own gruff moustaches put to flight.
> For even when the balance hangs in doubt
> Their own poor wittols always cut them out . . .
>   (CP, I, 209)

Vita, Campbell felt, used her grimly enjoyed experiences as fodder for her next book of verse; having terminated another love affair, she

> . . . straight in raptured sonnets will expose
> The bunions of her gnarled iambic toes . . .
>   (CP, I, 209)

There is substance to this charge. *King's Daughter* was published in 1929, only months after Vita made the final break with Mary.

In considering Campbell's treatment of the sexual values of 'Georgia', however, we come upon a central problem: what are we to make of Androgyno? Androgyno is used by Campbell both as the embodiment of Georgian values, and as the representative of Campbell's values; he is of Georgia and yet against it.[11] He is an absurd image of a 'Georgian', hermaphroditic and 'frowsy', and at the end of the poem he is left 'editing a posh review' in London.[12] On the other hand, he is like his creator in his hatred of 'bookish' sex, his vigour, and his sensuality. And when he leaves Long Barn, showering curses and kicks, he is behaving very much as Campbell would have liked to do. Some critics[13] ascribe this apparent confusion to Campbell's inability to organize his poem, but it is likely that the problem lies deeper than that. It is the result of the inherent contradictions in Campbell's own make-up.

At Oxford, in France, and in Africa on his return there he had flaunted his defiance of his family's puritanical morality, and asserted his determination to go his own way. And in Kent, suddenly, he had found himself in a false position. He, who had been so fond of shocking others, was himself shocked. He had always asserted his right to do what he liked; what right had he to stop Mary from doing what she liked? It is this moral dilemma, rather than his appendicitis, which explains why Campbell had not moved from Long Barn for more than four months after he became aware of what was afoot. The confusion in Androgyno is symbolic of a confusion in Campbell's own being. His rejection of the society at Long Barn was inevitable from

---

* This is a reference to Vita's sonnet 'Time Was Our Banker Once', printed in *King's Daughter* and referring to the break-up of her relations with Mary.

the beginning of his stay there (his temperament made that certain) but the main grounds of that rejection might have been quite different had he not learnt of Mary's love for Vita. Because of that discovery, *The Georgiad* became very clearly what *The Flaming Terrapin* is: a personal myth. And in *The Georgiad*, as in so much of his lyrical verse from *Adamastor* onwards, the enemy Campbell fought was a part of himself.

The attack on Bloomsbury immorality, in Bloomsbury and in himself, was the core of *The Georgiad*. But as Campbell wrote the poem, he incorporated other attacks, some of them buttresses of his main theme, others mere accretions. He widened his scope as new targets suggested themselves. He cast about for old scores to settle. The poem grew more and more discursive. 'That is the worst of long poems: they always take the bit in their teeth and bolt away with one in the wrong direction', he wrote to a friend.[14] The reader of *The Georgiad* may have difficulty in distinguishing a 'right' direction to the poem. It is repetitive, digressive, and overlong. Much of it was clearly written in haste. Several sentences in the poem are extended over thirty lines or more,[15] and in the course of them Campbell sometimes loses his grip on both grammar and logic. Some of the rhymes are painfully forced:

> For as all nations have their sacred anibal
> (Excuse my cold) – Christian as well as cannibal . . .
> (CP, I, 210)

Campbell was not above repeating in *The Georgiad* lines or ideas he had used in *The Wayzgoose*,[16] nor does he hesitate to use a line twice in the same poem.[17] Moreover, his coarseness often palls on the reader, and some of his arguments are so insistently and shrilly presented that they provoke sympathy for his opponents.

In spite of these failings, many of his jibes are neat and accurate enough to have a real sting. When Campbell depicts Androgyno as flouncing to his feet newly formed and meeting 'his own approval in the glass', he is hinting wittily at the 'Bloomsberries' habit of praising each other's work in their reviews. Michael Holroyd refers to 'the overblown approbation which members of the élite exchanged among themselves in books and reviews'.[18] (Thus Clive Bell sang the praises of his wife Vanessa, sister of Virginia Woolf.)[19] Besides being influential in their own right, the Nicolsons cultivated such powerful friends as John Squire (whose *London Mercury* frequently lauded their work), Bertrand Russell, and Arnold Bennett. Campbell was being realistic when he wrote to Lewis of the Nicolsons, 'they are more powerful than you would imagine'.[20]

The lavish praises which these writers bestowed on one another lend force to the opening lines in which the Poet addresses his Muse:

> Let us commune together, soul with soul,
> And of our two half-wits compound a whole:
> Swap brains with me 'for better or for worse'
> Till neither knows which writes the other's verse:
> Think all my thoughts, though they be stale and few,
> And when you think I'll think the same as you.
>
> (CP, I, 201)

This praise-singing went further than the mere writing of reviews. When the Hawthornden Prize for literature was instituted in 1919, John Squire was made the chief judge; he exercised considerable influence over the other judges. It was not surprising then that the first recipient was Edward Shanks, a close associate of Squire's on the *London Mercury*, or that Vita should have won it in 1927 for her poem *The Land*. Campbell comments scathingly:

> Sing but of country joys and you shall rise,
> Praised by the world, from prize to golden prize . . .
>
> (CP, I, 229)

Campbell's mockery of the Georgians' bad verse goes hand in hand with his contempt for their mutual praise; the two faults were interlinked. *The Georgiad*'s long digressions are accordingly occupied with stinging parodies of Squire, Vita, and Humbert Wolfe. And there is much justification for Campbell's scorn of their work.

Vita's *The Land* is full of deliberately archaic and 'countrified' words: 'lusk', 'ley', 'shrammed', 'reasty', 'winsel', 'shippen', and 'swere' are examples. There is a constant over-hearty celebration of physical toil combined with long, idealized descriptions of the countryside. It is an exaggeratedly bucolic scene conjured up by an aristocratic and wealthy poetess. The resulting chocolate-boxy preciousness is seen in such descriptions as this, of a shepherd:

> He shall turn little rams to little tegs,
> And dock their tails, but on a different day;
> Then, well content, sit down to watch them play,
> Companioned by his pipe and towzled pup;
> Watch them, appraising strong and frisky legs
> And grin when little ewe butts little tup.[21]

In contrast with such stuff, Campbell's satire is sharp and pleasingly
earthy:

> Seek some old farm (the image of your mind)
> Where in some farmer's ledger you may find
> Fodder . . .
> Which, thrice-digested, into cud refined,
> May clatter down in cantos from behind . . .
> Your soulful face will scare away the rooks,
> While wondering yokels all around you sit,
> Relieved of every labour by your wit,
> Which, while it fetches, carries, ploughs, or digs,
> Or trickles into hogwash for the pigs,
> At the same time will leave your talents free . . .
>
>   (CP, I, 229)

The verse of John Squire (himself a noted parodist) was even more
vulnerable to Campbell's darts than that of Vita. Prude, socialist,
vegetarian, dog-lover, and poetaster, Squire represented everything
that attracted Campbell's derision. Squire's two best-known poems,
'The Rugger Match' and 'To a Bull-dog', fairly invited mockery.
Campbell's ridicule of 'The Rugger Match' was no doubt intensified
by his knowledge that Squire himself, despite his enthusiasm for
'rugger', was too short-sighted ever to play it.[22] In 'To a Bull-dog',
Squire addresses his pet on the subject of a recently killed friend,
Major William Smith. His maudlin sentimentality renders the poem
ludicrous:

> We shan't see Willy any more, Mamie,
> He won't be coming any more:
> He came back once and again and again,
> But he won't get leave any more.

Campbell, who disliked dogs and hated sentimentality, reacts with
what Squire's biographer Howarth terms 'viciousness':

> . . . Jack Squire through his own tear-drops sploshes
> In his great, flat, trochaical goloshes . . .
> Now as he would exalt to deathless Fame
> His vanished Lycidas, 'Willie' by name,
> And to the dead man's pet his grief expresses,
> Outslobbering the bulldog he caresses . . .
> The patient monster as he listens drops
> A sympathetic trickle from his chops,
> And both together mix the mutual moan,
> Squire for the dead, and Fido for a bone.

> Partners in grief, in watery tourney vie
> The rheumy jowl and the poetic eye,
> While with his tail for baton, keeping time,
> The poet wags his mangy stump of rhyme.
>
> (CP, I, 211)

One of Campbell's techniques consists in making the animals representative of their masters, who share the manners and morals of their pets. The Nicolsons' sexual 'freedom' was such that, as Lady Sackville wrote of Vita and Harold, 'she is not in the least jealous of him, and willingly allows him to relieve himself with anyone'.[23] Campbell saw this as bestiality:

> The garden lawn provides a sort of Lido
> For basking 'Billykins' and sprawling 'Fido,'
> The garden path – a sort of Rotten Row
> Where oft a merry pick-a-back they go;
> While 'Snap' and 'Spot' their playful whiskers twitch
> The lustful 'Towser' quits his lawful bitch,
> The bashful 'Mamie,' famed in Georgian lay,
> Who straight is covered by the faithful 'Tray,'
> And so the amorous springtime glides away.
>
> (CP, I, 211)

The Nicolsons were indeed fond of dogs – they had at this time a particularly foul-smelling spaniel – while Campbell had disliked the animals since being attacked by one as a child,[24] but his urbanity and wit transform what might have been a banal comment on 'cynolatry' into a particularly biting criticism of his former hosts.

The same wit is at work when Campbell attacks the Georgians' 'Cult of Youth'. This was a point which Campbell almost certainly came upon in Lewis's novel *The Apes of God*, where it is derided at exhausting length. Campbell took it up partly because one of the cult's chief exponents was Edward Shanks, who happened to be Squire's assistant editor on the *London Mercury*. At the time of his association with the Nicolsons Campbell was only twenty-five, and his jibes at the ageing 'Peter Pans' are therefore the more pointed:

> 'Young poets' as they call them in 'The Nation'
> Or 'writers of the younger generation' –
> Spry youths, some under ninety, I could swear,
> For two had teeth and one a tuft of hair
> And all a die-hard look of grim despair . . .
>
> (CP, I, 214)

Apart from the other characteristics of the loose grouping of writers he attacked, however, Campbell attacked the very fact that they formed a coterie. Their views and their values, he felt, were standardized, and they tried to force their opinions on others.[25] (This is the point of *The Georgiad*'s opening lines, with their attack on Graves and Riding; Campbell believed they were trying to impose their critical standards on all writers. In 1927 he had attacked them in an article written for the *Calendar*, but the magazine died before Campbell's piece could appear. Late in 1927 he published a very critical review of Graves's work in the *Athenaeum*; another similar attack, which he planned to publish in 1928 in Lewis's magazine the *Enemy*, was never finished.) He had always felt himself to be a proud and rugged individualist. With his innate anarchism, he reacted strongly against the 'levelling' influence of Bloomsbury, where, he wrote,

> . . . modesty's the measure of renown:
> And so, as one, when wolves are on his course,
> To save his life will sacrifice his horse,
> He who would rise must rather walk than ride
> And fling to tugging curs his hamstrung pride.
> Then farewell, Pegasus . . .
>
> (CP, I, 215)

He rejected what he saw as the clique standards of the Nicolsons and their friends, who were

> . . . drilled, like Fascists, to enforce on all
> The standards of the middling and the small . . .
>
> (CP, I, 240)

All these criticisms of 'Georgia', however – its members' affectation, bad verse and mutual back-slapping, their worship of dogs and youth, and their group values – were really side-issues, buttresses of the central quarrel which provoked *The Georgiad*. It was his wife's unfaithfulness to him that excited Campbell's rage in the first place, and ultimately it is on Bloomsbury's sexual mores that he focuses most clearly.

The final form of *The Georgiad* was influenced by the publication in 1930 of Wyndham Lewis's satirical novel *The Apes of God*. It was an attack on everything Campbell himself wished to attack: '. . . the dog-loving lady-artist, the champion practical-joker, the would-be caveman of Bloomsbury, the Psycho-analytical bore, the nancy-boy and the would-be child, who pathetically strives to maintain his youth instead of trying to grow up.'[26] Campbell had reviewed two of Lewis's earlier novels for the *New Statesman*, and the journal asked him to review *The Apes of God* when it appeared. He responded with enthusiasm, but his laudatory review was turned down by Ellis Roberts, the acting editor. Angered by what he saw as a literary clique ganging up to suppress the work of its critics, Campbell wrote an abusive letter to Roberts, and then printed his review in Lewis's 'Enemy Pamphlet No. 1'. The matter ended when Roberts abandoned his standpoint on *The Apes of God*, apparently under the influence of his editor, Sharp, who wrote apologizing to Campbell and calling Roberts 'a bloody fool'.[27] Roberts, humbled, published his own review of *The Apes of God*, praising it as 'a brilliant novel'.[28]

This was Campbell's first open rift with the English literary Establishment, and it left him triumphant. He saw the publication of Lewis's book as preparing the ground for his own attack, which he finished hastily and which was published by Boriswood after months of delay. He seems to have been pleased by the minor sensation it caused. In a letter to Lewis late in 1931, he listed the reviews of the poem which had already appeared, and added,

MacCarthy Nicolson and Co are paralysed . . . Since the Georgiad (I hear) the Nicolson menage has become very Strindbergian. Each accusing the other for it and smashing the furniture about; but they are rotten to the core and I don't care about any personal harm I have done them – I take their internal disturbances as a justification of the Georgiad.[29]

The poem as it finally appeared in the autumn of 1931 is, despite its title, Popeian only in that it is a satire in heroic couplets. It is, as Campbell himself wrote, 'about 1200 lines of coarse, swinging doggerel: but it has some pretty lively moments. I don't think anything so scurrilous has appeared in England for about 150 years. Nearly everyone is mentioned by name.'[30] The literary coteries reacted with laughter; *The Georgiad* sold well. The reaction of the reviewers was strangely muted, but by February 1934 Campbell could write, 'The number of squibs excited by The Georgiad amounts now to about fifty . . . I only want six or seven more to rival the bibliography of the "Dunciad"'.[31] From the victims themselves came no reaction other than (according to Campbell) seven anonymous letters.[32] One reviewer commented on this silence: 'It is shameful, but comprehensible, that a satire of this power and scope should have been hushed up by the reviewers whom it scarifies.'[33] Another journal remarked that the absence of reviews of *The Georgiad* was a conspiracy of silence 'signalising the clique-spirit in English literary criticism'.[34]

Among both reviewers and public, however, there was considerable puzzlement as to what had provoked this onslaught. After all,
Campbell's relations with the people he was now attacking were
known to have been warm. He had contributed poems and reviews to
the *New Statesman* and the *London Mercury;* his work had been included
in Moult's *The Best Poems of 1930*; and, most significantly, it was
known that he and his family had enjoyed the Nicolsons' hospitality.
Many members of the literary world viewed *The Georgiad* as (at best)
evidence of Campbell's gross ingratitude towards his hosts. As Harold
Nicolson was to put it,

The current legend is that out of charity we lent him the gardener's cottage at
our home at Long Barn, Sevenoaks Weald. That we there introduced him to
several of our literary friends who came down to dine or sleep or to stay from
Saturday to Monday. That some of these friends, notably Raymond
Mortimer and Edward Sackville-West (my wife's cousin) did not pay
sufficient attention to the Campbells and in fact talked about people whom
they did not know or books in French or German which they had not read.
That Roy Campbell was incensed by this behaviour and acquired angered
feelings of inferiority. That he therefore quitted the house and thereafter
revenged himself on all of us in 'The Georgiad'.[35]

And though Harold Nicolson (in a private letter) was quick to point
out that this was a distortion of the truth, Campbell had to live with
this 'current legend' for the rest of his life, his pride preventing him
from rebutting it. The poem he had begun writing as a simple act of
revenge had become an investigation of his own divided nature, and
an indictment of a whole society sliding towards what he called 'the
great Anonymous'[36] – a society from which he drew further and
further away. For all its light-heartedness *The Georgiad* is an
acknowledgement by Campbell that the gulf between himself and his
fellows was steadily widening.

VIII

Provence

1929–1933

WHILE Campbell was composing *The Georgiad* during 1929, Mary's dominance over him, and his dependence on her, continued to grow. From this time on he worried less about money, simply handing over to her whatever he had, and receiving in return a weekly allowance – an arrangement that also gave her some slight control over his drinking. She was always the first to read what he had written, and often suggested what he should write about. She acted as his secretary in his dealings with publishers. It was she who dealt with tradespeople, she who arranged holidays for the children in England, she who decided when the family should move house, and she who found the new house. She took care of the practical details of life and left Campbell free to write. It was an arrangement which, once they had settled into it, satisfied something in each of them. A photograph of this period says it all: Campbell, seated, looks with mute appeal at Mary who, standing hand on hip, stares unsmiling down at him. Their relationship henceforward was one which recognized and accommodated the feminine elements in Campbell's personality, and the masculine in Mary's. It was an accommodation which considerably strengthened their relationship, and allowed it to weather the storms that lay ahead.

It may have been about this time that Campbell wrote his fine sonnet 'The Sleeper', in which he pictures himself watching over his sleeping wife:

> She lies so still, her only motion
> The waves of hair that round her sweep
> Revolving to their hushed explosion
> Of fragrance on the shores of sleep.
> (CP, I, 48)

She sleeps unaware of him, self-involved as a foetus, uncaring, unconscious of his spirit brooding over her. Yet what Campbell seeks to stress in this poem is not his isolation, but his unity with her, and the image he uses is an extraordinary one. Mary's physical appearance, he says, is an embodiment of his own spirit;* her beauty watches through his eyes:

> Is it my spirit or her flesh
> That takes this breathless, silver swoon?
> Sleep has no darkness to enmesh
> That lonely rival of the moon,
> Her beauty, vigilant and white,
> That wakeful through the long blue night,
> Watches, with [my] own sleepless eyes,
> The darkness silver into day . . .
>
> (CP, I, 48)

'The Sleeper' ends on a note of quiet triumph won through suffering, and the same quiet note is struck in that strange poem, 'Silence', in which Mary is seen as the 'sister' of Campbell's 'Psyche'. Their marriage was beginning to work once more, but on a quite new basis. By July 1929 Mary was able to write to Vita that she and Roy were 'reconciled again'. Vita, relieved, soon began to terminate the correspondence, and by August 1929 Mary's tone was becoming one of querulous despair: 'Why do you write less and less often? I fear it is indifference, Vita, or forgetfulness. I get so unhappy, so miserable – Vita it's unkind of you . . . without you I can do nothing.' Daily letters became weekly ones; the correspondence faltered into silence, killed by Vita's lack of interest.

The immediate crisis over, Campbell settled down to an idyllic life in Martigues. He had had a steady income of £20 a month since the death of his father in 1926, and the Campbells found they could live very comfortably on this sum in France. They soon moved from the house in the Rue St Mitre to a small, airy farmhouse, Tour de Vallier, about two miles out of the town. It was set in fragrant pinewoods on a low hill near the Étang de Berre, the lake of Martigues; from the terrace there were glimpses of the lake, and superb views of St Victoire and the hills around Marseilles, with the snowy Ventours gleaming like a bank of clouds on the horizon.

Campbell, who never lost his gift for striking up friendships with the common people of whatever country he lived in, was soon on good terms with the fishermen of Martigues; he would frequently spend

---

* He seems never to have put into verse the corollary to this idea (also found in 'Pomegranates' and 'Reflections'): that his own body was a physical counterpart of Mary's spirit.

nights at sea with them seining in the Mediterranean or spearing mullet by the flare of an acetylene torch on the Étang. One of the fishermen he met in this way was a tall, blond, strikingly handsome youth named Marius Polge, whom everyone called 'Grandpère'. He and Campbell became fast friends. Together they bought a boat, a ten-foot *bette* named 'La Clemence',[1] and their partnership became closer when Mary's sister Helen, visiting the Campbells, quickly became Polge's mistress, and subsequently his wife.[2] 'We are starting a regular family-business here', Campbell wrote to an acquaintance.[3] He soon acquired a second boat, which he called 'Teresa and Anna' after his daughters. In this on summer evenings the Campbell family and their friends would go out on the lake, and there row and bathe while the dusk gathered and the moon rose. Campbell and Grandpère would dive for mussels and bring them up in handfuls and Campbell, who prided himself on his cooking, would prepare them for dinner.

Perhaps in reaction to the sedentary life he had so hated in Kent, he gave himself over to vigorous pursuits: boxing, fishing, rowing, and swimming. Under Grandpère's influence, he also took up water-jousting, a violent sport popular along that stretch of the Mediterranean coast. The jouster, balanced on a small platform mounted on the back of a boat, wears a protective wooden shield on his chest, and uses a heavy lance to knock his opponent, similarly armed and mounted on an approaching boat, into the water as they pass. Campbell describes such encounters in his autobiography, *Light on a Dark Horse*:

The first pair [of jousters] having been drawn, the boats advanced from about a hundred and fifty yards away, accelerating to a speed of twenty knots as they passed, almost grazing each other's gunwales, with the kettle-drums rolling louder and louder as they approached. They sometimes capsize in each other's 'wash.' The antagonists stand on raised platforms, two feet by two and a half feet square and ten feet above the water, and projecting from the stern. . . . One should gauge the weight, height, and force with which one's antagonist will strike, so as to be at such an angle when the lances meet the shields that the force of the collision will shoot one straight back to one's previous position. As when standing on horseback at a gallop, the body leans quite a long way forward at an angle one could never keep while standing still.[4]

Campbell, with his massive build and great strength, proved very good at this dangerous and exacting sport. He was soon accepted as a permanent member of 'La Joyeuse Lance Martegale', one of the best jousting teams on the coast, and he proudly sported the green beret by which a team member could be recognized. Jousting not only gave him the opportunity to display the individual prowess and courage that meant so much to him, and which he constantly celebrated in his verse, it also gave him that sense of camaraderie and security he longed for.

The constant exercise, the companionship of men among whom he was an equal, his comparative affluence, and the beauty of the countryside so reminiscent of South Africa, combined to make this a very happy time for him. Years later he was to look back with longing on this period of his life:

> That sacrament of friendship, a good Provençal meal . . . is best honoured in the open air, and best of all, in the evening, with the limitless sweep of the Crau, the Camargue and the sea, under a crimson and violet sky with the stars coming out and the crickets relieving the cicadas . . . .
>
> If you, my reader, at any future date find yourself sitting there with your arm round some young beautiful living torso, and as you drink your wine looking down over Camargue and the Crau from the old ruins of Fos . . . say a Grace for me and my beloved and my friends, for we also knew what you know,
>> 'Yet, though knowing naught,
>> Transcended knowledge with our thought.'[5]

The peace and happiness he found in Provence were increased for Campbell by the turbulence he had come through in South Africa and Kent – beginning with *Voorslag* and climaxing in the shock of Mary's infidelity. In consequence, the poetry he produced during 1929 and 1930 is among the most serene he ever wrote; but in every poem the serenity is heightened by the suggestion that it has been won only at great cost. 'Autumn', which Campbell wrote late in 1929,[6] expresses in the image of a tree bare against the sky the way in which Campbell felt himself to have been purified by his experiences:

> I love to see, when leaves depart,
> The clear anatomy arrive,
> Winter, the paragon of art,
> That kills all forms of life and feeling
> Save what is pure and will survive.

The storms of approaching winter, the poem suggests, are productive as well as destructive: they bring down the olive's fruit for men to collect:

> Strained by the gale the olives whiten[7]
> Like hoary wrestlers bent with toil

> And, with the vines, their branches lighten
> To brim our vats where summer lingers
> In the red froth and sun-gold oil.

And Campbell closes the poem with two phoenix images of creation through destruction – the fire, on which the 'rotted stems' sprout new and more beautiful leaves; and the wine, in which crushed and trampled grapes achieve their full glory:

> Soon on our hearth's reviving pyre
> Their rotted stems will crumble up:
> And like a ruby, panting fire,
> The grape will redden on your fingers
> Through the lit crystal of the cup.
>
> (CP, I, 52)

As winter was 'the paragon of art', he believed, so he had become a better and a clearer poet as a result of his experiences. It was not in his marriage alone that he saw improvement.

He was not mistaken. There is in his poetry of this period greater clarity and purity of line. The barbaric splendour of epithet of *The Flaming Terrapin* has gone; the lyrics he wrote in 1929 and 1930 have an almost classical simplicity. 'Autumn' is a good example. The violent energy, the headlong, dizzying rush of words, so characteristic of the early Campbell, would be quite out of place here. The movement now is considered and deliberate, and one has the impression that each word was chosen carefully, and carefully weighed. Campbell's early self-confidence has gone; the poems convey a distinct sense that during this period he had been stopped in his tracks. A re-evaluation of his life, a searching for some new direction, would certainly come; but for the time being he was simply grateful to have got through the crisis so well.

His relief and gratitude are seen clearly in another classically simple poem, 'Mass at Dawn', one of his most beautiful lyrics. In it, he drew upon his own experiences at sea to give vibrant life to an age-old symbol of rest after labour, the weary fisherman regaining the harbour:

> I dropped my sail and dried my dripping seines
> Where the white quay is chequered by cool planes
> In whose great branches, always out of sight,
> The nightingales are singing day and night.
> Though all was grey beneath the moon's grey beam,
> My boat in her new paint shone like a bride,
> And silver in my baskets shone the bream:

My arms were tired and I was heavy-eyed,
But when with food and drink, at morning-light,
The children met me at the water-side,
Never was wine so red or bread so white.

(CP, I, 47)

The extraordinary richness of this poem derives not simply from the fact that it springs from Campbell's personal knowledge (he must often have sailed in so after a night's fishing, to be met by his daughters on the sunny quay), nor even from the fact that it reflects his feelings at having survived a deeply wounding personal crisis. The range of suggestiveness of the poem is the result of the particular images he has assembled: the sea, the fisherman, the bride-like boat, the dawn, the children, and the sacrificial food. They are images with profound religious connotations, and though those connotations are here half-submerged, they stir associations in the mind in such a way as to give this poem great significance. The fisherman, tired and heavy-eyed, has reached a turning-point, as Campbell felt his life to be at a turning-point. He is exchanging the moon for the sun, solitude for company, the sea for the land, night for day, labour for rest, and though the religious symbolism is older than Christianity, the 'Mass' of the title sums up the way all the images hint at a renewal, a triumph-through-suffering, which the fisherman shares with nature.

Campbell was not a Christian at this time. But neither was he the agnostic scoffer he had been at Oxford and in South Africa during the Twenties. Unsure of the very ground of his existence, he was turning increasingly towards religion; not the rigid Presbyterianism of his upbringing, nor the dutiful Anglicanism of his wife's childhood, but the Roman Catholicism he saw in the lives of the people around him. 'Mass at Dawn' perhaps marks the beginnings of his slow and erratic movement towards conversion, a process that was to take at least four years. As a result of his upbringing, he had always associated religion with 'wowsers' (as he liked to call killjoys), and it was a long time before devotion replaced mockery in his references to religion.*

* For an example of his earlier antagonism to Catholicism, one may quote the last verse of 'Solo and Chorus from "The Conquistador"', written in 1926:

> Then fly, my wolf-pack, on before,
> Swift in your pilgrimage of hope,
> And I shall follow on your spoor
> To kiss the bunions of the Pope:
> A thousand priests, behind our thunder,
> Shall follow with the crow and kite,
> To cure the wounds of those we plunder
> With words of mercy, hope and light!
> (CP, I, 187)

Another poem reflecting his experience as a fisherman, and his search for religious belief, is 'St Peter of the Three Canals'. When he published it in *Adamastor* Campbell classed it among his 'Early Poems' because he began it in 1920, when he visited Martigues briefly for the first time. But it was the last *Adamastor* poem he finished, in 1930, after coming upon the early fragmentary verses scribbled on the fly-leaf of one of his books.[8] In this delicately ironic poem he begins his approach to the Church by a curiously oblique route: an investigation of the pagan elements in the Catholicism of southern Europe.

The 'St Peter' of the title is a statue of the saint, represented as Neptune, standing in a niche in a church tower high above the three rubbish-filled canals of Martigues.* He is, says Campbell,

> An old green idol, thunder-scarred,
> On whom the spray has crusted hard,
> A shell-backed saint, whom time maroons
> High stranded on the Rock of Ages . . .
> > (CP, I, 182)

Campbell clearly finds Peter as an idol more approachable than Peter as a saint. His tone is one of gentle mockery both of the 'Peter-Neptune' and of the simple fisherfolk's superstitions concerning him.

For Campbell, the saint-as-idol is attractive because it has none of the Sunday-glum connotations of his father's Presbyterianism; on the contrary, he imagines this pagan Peter in a context of sunny lust,

> Where Dagon weds with Mother Carey,
> Jehovah woos a Mermaid Mary,
> And Thetis sins with Davey Jones.

But Campbell is not simply mocking. His light tone is very reminiscent of the delicate banter of some of T. S. Eliot's slighter poems. Lines such as Campbell's

> Deep in his bosom nest the doves
> In token of seraphic loves,
> To keep his garments – white as snow.

are reminiscent of Eliot's 'The Hippopotamus' in their general tone and in the direct echo of the final phrase. And as the poem progresses,

---

* This statue is today nowhere to be found in Martigues. But a huge bas-relief on one of the churches overlooking the canals represents the faithless Peter sinking into the sea.

its tone changes. The extended comparison of the Church to a ship is
lightly done, but when the speaker addresses St Peter directly, his
sincerity is unmistakable. The tone is humble but direct, one
fisherman appealing to another:

> Remember in your high promotion
> How once, poor flotsam of the Ocean,
> You followed such a trade as mine.
> The winter nights, have you forgotten,
> When hauling on a seine as rotten
> You cracked your knuckles on the line?
>
> Have you forgot the cramp that clinches
> Your shoulder, turning at the winches –
> And not a mullet in the mesh?
> Have you forgotten Galilee –
> The night you floundered in the sea
> Because your faith was in your flesh?

Campbell has talked his god down to himself; the 'Amphibious saint'
is one he can both understand and believe in. And the final appeal,

> Be with me, then . . .
> Increase the horse-power of my engine,
> Hallow my petrol ere I go!
>   (CP, I, 185)

an appeal which might have been mocking earlier in the poem, has by
the last stanza acquired a gravity that forbids us to smile. The
movement through 'St Peter' – from irony towards faith – is prophetic
of Campbell's spiritual progress over the next few years, and his
method of approaching Christianity through paganism ultimately led
him to faith. 'Mass at Dawn' and 'St Peter' look forward to his volume
Mithraic Emblems, as *Mithraic Emblems* looks forward to the fully
Christian poems.

As 'St Peter' shows, Campbell was sympathizing more and more
closely with the simple people of the Rhône mouth, whom he saw as
being close to nature and to God in a way he envied. Even Mary came
to feel this about them. After a brief visit to London in 1929, she
wrote to William Plomer,

The day after I arrived there was a great feast at our house. Five jouters,
fishermen, invited themselves to a bouillebasse [*sic*] which they brought

caught and cooked themselves. They made a large fire in the open air and all helped with this sacred rite! One felt they were the remote descendants of the men the gods [?loved]. I don't love them; as soon as I had eaten & drunk with them I hid myself in my room – but I must say I have more respect for them than many rooms full of the London Paris New York intelligentsia. I believe there is a quality in this air & soil & sea to be found nowhere else in the world.[9]

Campbell believed in the primitive virtues of Provence too; the horsemen and fishermen of southern Europe, he wrote, constituted an aristocracy that stood alone against the levelling influences of technology and trade. He took his stand with the cowboy and the fisherman, as the possessors of the virtues he cherished:

If we are the last of one great era, and the shopkeeper is to take eventual control, at least it will have to be admitted that we did not struggle for 'existence'; we struggled for life against death, we had physical joys, we had chivalry, kindness, generosity . . .[10]

The idyllic primitive life of his African childhood had given him an intense admiration for such virtues, the virtues of an older, more individualistic time. Provence, that 'little bit of Africa in Europe',[11] seemed to instil them as he fancied Natal and Rhodesia had done.

In 'Horses on the Camargue' (CP, I, 47), which harks back strongly to the animal poetry he had written in Africa, Campbell expresses his love for the area and for the values it instils, symbolized for him by the small white horses of the Camargue, that area of swampland (even now only partially drained) stretching westward along the coast from the mouth of the Rhône. Herds of cattle and white horses still roam there. Campbell's intense awareness of the power and passion of such animals is evident in earlier poems,[12] and the combination of horses and sea which the Camargue provided was a particularly evocative one for him. His earliest memory, he was to write in *Light on a Dark Horse*, was of seeing the sea through the legs of a horse:

A horse had its head over the wire fence, and as we rounded the hedge and surprised it, it reared up and turned away: and I, looking down the grassy slope through its legs, saw a huge living expanse of glittering azure, like a peacock's tail, electrified with winds and solar fire.[13]

It is clear that the Camargue horses had great personal significance for him. His treatment of them is in several ways reminiscent of 'The Zebras'. Where the animals in that poem were seen as dispelling the night, these bring life to a dead landscape; they are not only a vivifying force, they are symbols of freedom and security. The narrator, solitary and depressed, was clearly under the spell of the 'grey wastes of dread' before he saw the galloping herd, and it is equally clear (though Campbell does not say so) that the horses break the spell for him. 'Horses on the Camargue', though it was written at least a year after Campbell's complete reconciliation with his wife, shows the continuing effect on him of Mary's affair with Vita. Even by 1930 that three-year-old wound had not fully healed. Just as Campbell had fled the humiliating security of Sevenoaks to Martigues, he pictures the horses as 'silver runaways', and tells the tale (to which he alluded in 'Mazeppa') of the wild horse who 'hurls his rider' and makes his way home oblivious alike to distance and danger.

Campbell certainly believed that the Rhône had helped him to forget his torment in England; it was, he said in a later poem, a sort of Lethe that

> . . . from the Wound its anguish drains –
> as you may hear from one who drank,
> down on his knees, beside the bank,
> and lost the memory of pain.
> ('Death of the Bull', CP, I, 123)

The situation of the narrator in 'Horses on the Camargue' focuses Campbell's essential loneliness very sharply. He is the loner drifting about in the waste places of life, observing from afar the joy and companionship he can never share. The effect on the observer would be quite different if there had been only one white horse. He is stirred by their 'harmony of hooves', by the fact that they are so clearly at one with each other and with the landscape in which they move. The horses in fact become yet another way of expressing that triumph-through-suffering which had become Campbell's constant theme. He believed that as the horses gained 'power and beauty and delight' from being at one with their surroundings, so his verse could gain impact from the same source; the wildness of Provence was the right environment for a poet. The very wind was inspiring. Praising Provençal literature, he later wrote,

The same fiery spirit that inspires the works of these poets and breathes in all the prancing wild horses and fighting cattle of the Crau and the Camargue, roars in the charges of the mistral through the crags of Provence. It thunders down from the high forested peaks of the Alps, the Ventour and the Alpilles in the rock-rolling spates of the Isère, the Durance and in the headlong Rhône. That spirit lives in the bulls when they meet to celebrate their 'Ramadans' by moonlight and the air is hoarse with their bellowings. . . . Meanwhile plunging through the reeds and tamarisks, the great bull-deity of Provence answers their voices with his own, heaving forever onward through the pines and the waves.

Provence! Your memory is as rousing to those 'who have the passion' of poetry, as the mistral is to the waves.[14]

'Horses on the Camargue' provides a good example of the way Campbell drew inspiration from his own experience, but it is also an example of how his wide reading complemented that experience. He drew upon Provençal and (extraordinarily) Red Indian poetry in writing the poem. It owes something to the description of Camargue horses in the fourth canto of the Provençal poet Mistral's long work, *Mirèio*;[15] and it also draws upon the verse of Michawayo, the son of Sitting Bull, whose work Campbell read in a French prose translation by a Martigues friend of his, Jean Toussaint Samat.[16] Campbell admired the Red Indian's verse for its 'high powers of conscious imagination, [and] intelligence'.[17] Perhaps paradoxically, the varied origins of 'Horses on the Camargue' show the power of Campbell's poetic vision, which indelibly stamps every line as his own. His 'liftings' (as he called them with the modesty that characterizes his references to his work) were not so much theft as alchemy.

The deep loneliness revealed in such poems as 'Horses on the Camargue' affected Campbell all his life, and several acute observers recognized in his very conviviality a symptom of his isolation. William Plomer thought him cut off from humanity, 'in spite of all his bonhomie in bars';[18] and Wyndham Lewis wrote of him, 'he is like a man who rushes out into the street when the lonely fit is on him and invites the first dozen people he meets to come up and have a drink'.[19] During this period in Provence he kept in contact with a small and diminishing circle of artistic acquaintances. He saw a good deal of Augustus John, who had a big house in Martigues, and of Aldous Huxley, then living in Sanary, who would sometimes spend the weekend with the Campbells.[20]

The Campbells had met and befriended Sybille Bedford, then an unknown young woman living with her mother and step-father, Lisa and Nori Marchesani, in Sanary. It was while the Campbells were staying with the Marchesani, in the spring of 1930, that Campbell introduced her to Huxley, at the time the Huxleys were moving into

their newly built Sanary house. Sybille Bedford later described the
meeting:

We stepped across some planks and approached a hole in the façade. Inside
sitting on the floor beside a large revolving book-case, sorting books, was
Aldous.

He was dressed in khaki shorts, sandals without socks and a light shirt; he
looked up and one saw the large round spectacles. Roy spoke, 'Aldous – this
is Roy'. 'Roy,' Aldous said in a high silvery tone. He got to his feet, uncoiling
length. 'Dear Roy – how are you?'[21]

It is typical of Campbell's sensitivity that he remembered to identify
himself by voice to his nearly blind friend.

After this reunion the Campbells visited Huxley frequently. On
one occasion they arrived in Sanary on the yacht of some acquaintances, the Ofairs, who were sailing about the Mediterranean. Huxley
met them on Sanary beach, and they spent the afternoon swimming
together, Huxley splashing about in a small blue rubber boat, peering
short-sightedly around him. Afterwards he helped Mary Campbell
dress, feeling for the complicated buttons of her blouse with his long
fingers.[22]

Apart from such semi-residents as John and Huxley, the Campbells
saw few of their artistic friends regularly. The journey from London
was a long one in 1929. They received occasional visits from Enslin
du Plessis, Anna von Schubert (who having originally been attracted
by Roy, was now very attached to Mary), the Irish writer Liam
O'Flaherty, the painter Tristram Hillier, and – very rarely –
Wyndham Lewis. In June 1929, the American poet Hart Crane
turned up in a taxi and stayed for a week, at Campbell's invitation. He
proved something of an embarrassment, however; Campbell had to
restrain him from jumping off the bridge in a fit of alcoholic
depression, and a little later had to rescue him again, this time from an
angry sailor to whom he had made homosexual advances.[23] 'He is a
good poet . . . but he went off his rocker completely', Campbell wrote
to Enslin du Plessis:

We had to get him to go away but we parted good friends. . . . We found him
sitting at 12 at night in the middle of the road with his typewriter on one
side of him and his portmanteau on the other crying like a baby. Then he
tried to jump off the bridge. I think it was dope. I managed to get him back to
his own people.[24]

A comparison between this letter and another (to Wyndham Lewis)
describing the same visit, affords a good example of Campbell's

growing habit of representing himself as both tough and ruthless. It is clear from the letter to Du Plessis and from Campbell's conversations years later with David Wright that he went to considerable trouble to save Crane from himself. But in recounting the affair to Lewis, Campbell represents himself as pitiless and relentlessly logical, the persecutor rather than the protector. Crane, he says, had criticized the reasoning of Lewis's magazine the *Enemy*:

He started banging the table and shouting so I made him shut up. Then I threw a bucket of water on him to make him perfectly sober. I kept him till 2 am and retraced everything he had said. He then wept, and said he was coming over to Europe with a brigade of Americans to shoot every European. Then I thought it was about time to show him what he would get if he did. His chief quarrel against Europe it seems was that the sailors and fishermen were not pederasts. I chucked him out of the house when he became so truculent. He was so worked up, he was crying like a great fat baby and said he couldn't walk through the forest at night. I said he'd have to or the wolves and wild boars would bite him and he believed it. I put his typewriter into one of his hands and the valise in the other and gave him a kick behind to get him moving . . . . The garde champêtre found him sitting in the middle of the main road with his typewriter and valise, howling and howling . . . . [He] is a disgrace both intellectually and morally, a howling, ugly-looking, lachrymose devil, like nothing that I have ever seen before.[25]

The way in which Campbell presents the visit (and his own conduct) to Lewis is startlingly different from the more objective account he gave Du Plessis. The point is worth pursuing, because it became habitual with Campbell in later years to misrepresent his actions in this way. The pitying affection evident in his references to Crane in the letter to Du Plessis is replaced in the Lewis letter by hatred and contempt; it is no longer he who finds Crane crying in the road, but the *garde champêtre*, and Campbell implies that Crane was sobbing because of Campbell's treatment of him. The account is coloured throughout by Campbell's suppressed or overt violence, and he represents his actions as having been in defence of Lewis. In just the same way he was after the war to represent his imaginary violence against Louis MacNeice or Geoffrey Grigson as being in defence of Edith Sitwell. The fact is that Campbell needed to believe that he was fighting for a cause, and he searched for enemies with diligence. He recognized this quality in himself; *Don Quixote* was one of his favourite books.

In fact he seldom fought physically with anyone, and when he did generally came off worst. For instance, in 1932 he had a drunken fight with his brother-in-law, Grandpère. His daughter Teresa wrote of it,

One afternoon we children and the maid were returning from the lavoire [where the Campbells did their washing] when I saw a whole lot of people assembled in front of the house and a big man with a straw hat on lying on top of my father trying to strangle him . . . . It was Grandpère fighting my father. . . . My sister, seeing my father was being beaten, rushed at Grandpère from behind, caught hold of his leg and bit it. Grandpère got such a surprise that he let go of my father and the fight ended.[26]

This situation, from which Campbell was rescued by his six-year-old daughter Anna, says much about the poet's vulnerability, which his assumed aggressiveness was a largely successful attempt to hide. He was painfully sensitive to any adverse criticism and would brood for days over a bad review or a thoughtless letter from a friend, and these bottled-up feelings too often burst out into violently abusive replies. He would seek to hurt as he had been hurt, and his very sensitivity gained him a reputation for brutality.

His relationship with William Plomer shows how he alienated people through his extreme reactions to them. When Plomer arrived in England from Japan, early in 1928, Campbell wrote him letters of introduction to people he thought might be useful,[27] and repeatedly invited him to stay in Provence – invitations Plomer never took up, though he replied very amiably. In May 1929, on a visit to London, Mary Campbell met Plomer and spent an enjoyable time with him;[28] it is impossible to know whether she told him of her marital difficulties, and their causes, but from this time onwards her letters to 'Dearest William' became more frequent. Campbell, on the other hand, found corresponding with Plomer more and more of an effort:

You cannot imagine the nervous strain it causes me when I write to you and even more so when I get letters from you. It is a relic of the Neurasthenia I had in Africa and somehow I associate you with it. I know that after we meet again it will disappear. But please forgive it while it lasts.[29]

Mary, on her occasional trips to London, saw Plomer roughly every six months; but on the one occasion when Campbell and Plomer met in London, early in 1930, they found they had drifted apart. Plomer was irritated when Campbell gave the manuscript of *Adamastor* to Enslin du Plessis, having forgotten that he had promised it to Plomer. Plomer had also become a personal friend of Harold Nicolson and Virginia Woolf, and of several other people whom Campbell was about to attack in *The Georgiad*, and he was disappointed to find

Campbell more interested in travelling to Dublin with Liam
O'Flaherty to watch the Springboks play rugby than in meeting
Plomer's new friends. (Campbell and O'Flaherty seem to have been
drunk most of the time in Ireland, and it was only through the
personal intervention of Senator Oliver Gogarty* that they avoided
arrest and imprisonment, after a series of extraordinary escapades.)[30]
Though Campbell wrote apologizing to Plomer for his behaviour
('London completely got on my nerves, not to speak of my liver'),[31]
the rift continued to widen. When Campbell wrote jocularly to
Plomer, on holiday in Greece late in 1930, 'There is something
mysterious and sinister about your trip to Greece. I suspect you are
taking a class of young English girls or boys around . . .', Plomer,
who was very sensitive about his homosexuality, reacted angrily.[32]
He deplored the publication of *The Georgiad*, in October 1931, but the
relationship dragged on, steadily deteriorating, until August 1933. In
that year Mary paid another of her irregular visits to London, taking
the two children to spend a holiday with their grandmother in
England. On this visit, as she had done on earlier ones, she dined with
Plomer, and afterwards, in the taxi, she embraced and kissed him.
Plomer, an austere man and a confirmed homosexual, seems to have
been shaken and alarmed; he disengaged himself hastily. Later he told
this story to Laurens van der Post, who told another South African,
Uys Krige – and Krige told Campbell. Campbell was bitterly hurt at
this fresh evidence of Mary's continuing connection with the 'Bloomsberries', whom Plomer had now definitely joined – in Campbell's
mind at least. The result was a furious letter from Campbell to
Plomer, accusing him of representing Mary as being in love with
himself (Plomer), and continuing, 'I am not temperamentally equipped to fox out your motives but they smell Freudian enough: and
knowing your general hatred of women and marriage in particular
coupled with your nancydom it points to a very different sort of
triangular predicament. . . .'[33] And just as he had hit back at Vita
through *The Georgiad*, he struck at Plomer now with a poem entitled
'Creeping Jesus', which he published in his volume *Mithraic Emblems*
three years later:

> Pale crafty eyes beneath his ginger crop,
> A fox's snout with spectacles on top –
> Eye to the keyhole, kneeling on the stair,
> We often found this latter saint at prayer,

* Oliver Gogarty was a poet, a friend of Yeats, and the original of 'Buck Mulligan' in James
Joyce's *Ulysses*.

Mary and Roy Campbell, 1929

Tour de Vallier, 1930: a party of the Campbells and their friends on the terrace

Altea. From the left: Campbell's mother, Campbell and Mary, with Tess and Anna on donkey, Uys Krige's friend Emelia in the foreground. May 1935.

'For your own sake,' he'd tell you with a sigh
(He always did his kindness on the sly).
He paid mere friendship with his good advice
And swarmed with counsels as a cur with lice:
For his friends' actions, with unerring snout,
He'd always fox his own low motives out . . .   (CP, I, 270)

In his rage Campbell seems to have forgotten the original reason for
his outburst. He alludes to it only in one line, accusing Plomer of
having 'slandered women he could not supplant'. In this way a
friendship which had for years been extremely close ended in a
permanent rupture, and one which both men later regretted. 'It is well
known how difficult it is to forgive those whom one has wronged',
wrote Plomer of this quarrel, years later. 'I think W. P. [i.e. himself]
and R. C. wronged one another and neither made enough effort to
make amends.'[34]

Through such breaks in relations as this (and Plomer was by no
means the only friend Campbell lost in this way)[35] Campbell reinforced his reputation for violent and intemperate behaviour. It was a
reputation that gained credence from his much-advertised physical
pursuits, for to jousting he added, in 1929, bullfighting. The
bullfight fascinated Campbell; it seemed to him to combine art with
the physical prowess and courage he so much admired. He had had
considerable success at the Provençal game of cocarde-snatching, in
which amateurs attempt to pluck a piece of ribbon from between the
horns of a bull, but his great ambition was to become a professional
matador. He wrote to his generous friend C. J. Sibbett,

If I take off another cocade [*sic*] I will be given a trial at the mise a mort with
the sword which has always been my ambition. For a cocade one gets 500
francs for a mise a mort 1000 frs after that you can become an entrant for
being a matador. If I could get that job I would sell my boats at once . . . I
would give anything to become absolutely good at it.[36]

And a little later he was writing melodramatically to Sibbett, 'In strict
training – not even allowed the perfectly legitimate joys of marriage,
and living in barracks. Have written Mary to reply to your letter if I
don't come through . . . "Morituri te salutamus"', and signing himself
'Toreador de la Joyeuse Lance'.[37] However, his ambitions were
dashed when on two successive occasions at Istres in August 1929 he
was caught by a bull, which trod on his foot and then tossed him. He
was soon writing shamefacedly to Wyndham Lewis, 'I have given up
any thought of bullfighting in an expert way – the last affair was a

fiasco and I felt a fool for having written about it in such a confident way. It will take far too long for me to learn anything but cocarde-snatching.'[38] But bullfighting did not lose its attractions for him, as 'Estocade', the earliest of his poems on this subject, shows. The fascination of the fight seemed to grow with the realization that he would never perform an estocade himself. Like Hemingway, he thought bullfighting the noblest of sports. Each fight was the climax of the bull's life, and one of the high points of the torero's. It was the very antithesis of the dull, safe, pedestrian life he rejected, and increasingly in his verse after 1930 the bullfight is used as the symbol of the simple, personal virtues of skill and courage which he lauded. Thus he subtitled *The Georgiad* 'A Charlottade', (after the mock-fight in which a clown dressed as Charlie Chaplin does battle with a cow) to show his amused contempt for those he satirized in that poem. And from 1930 onward, he began to wear a toreador's cloak and hat on his visits to London.[39] (It is worth remarking, as another instance of the contradictions in Campbell's personality, that from about the age of twenty he had been an ardent conservationist who refused to kill any animal. More than that, he could scarcely endure to see an animal killed, and would, for instance, hide in his room when it was necessary to drown a litter of kittens.)[40]

Campbell had by the end of 1929 banished, by a concentration on vigorous physical activity, his 'revulsion from the life of letters'.[41] He began to get together another volume of verse, in which he was to include all the shorter poems as yet unpublished. *The Wayzgoose*, published in 1928, had done his reputation little good, and six years had passed since the publication of *The Flaming Terrapin*; he was in danger of being forgotten. *Adamastor* changed all that.

Whatever poems of mine I remembered I wrote down; and others we found in old magazines . . . . But I lost more than half of what I had written. When we got the rest together we sent it to T. S. Eliot, and this was my book *Adamastor* . . .[42]

Jonathan Cape, who had published *The Flaming Terrapin* and *The Wayzgoose*, refused *Adamastor* – a refusal he was to regret. The critics welcomed *Adamastor* with almost as much enthusiasm as they had *The Flaming Terrapin* in 1924. Desmond MacCarthy, in a long review, professed himself 'embarrassed' to assist at the birth of a book destined to be famous.[43] Arnold Bennett, calling Campbell 'a master of words', wrote of him, 'Mr. Campbell is quite outrageously a poet. He has

plenary inspiration. Emotions, crude and primeval, surge out of him
in terrific waves. . . . He rides on words as on horses, loving them as
violently as he whips them. His is indeed the grand manner.'[44] Harold
Nicolson, to Campbell's intense amusement, praised him in the *Daily
Express*; so did Vita Sackville-West in the *Fortnightly Review* of June
1930. Once again, as on the appearance of *The Flaming Terrapin*, a
few critics expressed disquiet at Campbell's 'bombast and noise', and
from such important critics as Middleton Murry there was silence. On
the other hand, T. S. Eliot liked *Adamastor* enough to give it the
coveted Faber imprint, and he wrote a very appreciative letter to
Campbell, who replied, 'Few things have given me more pleasure and
confidence than your last letter. A word of encouragement from you is
worth far more to me as a poet than any other sort of notice I could
get. I shall do my best to live up to it and I am very grateful indeed.'[45]
The critics who did review *Adamastor* provided a remarkable chorus of
praise. By May 1930 Campbell was able to write jubilantly to Du
Plessis, 'I understand from Faber that the 3rd edition of Adamastor is
just coming out – not bad in one month!'[46]

From *Adamastor* Campbell earned more money than he had ever
had in a lump sum before. Characteristically, he spent it as quickly as
possible: on a fur coat and other gifts for Mary, bicycles and toys for
his daughters, great dinners at the plush Restaurant du Canal for all
his friends – and a sardine net for himself.[47] He seemed, as he had
seemed after the publication of *The Flaming Terrapin*, to be on the crest
of a wave that would sweep him to wealth and literary fame. The
financial success of an expensively produced book of his verse, *Poems*,
privately printed by Nancy Cunard in Paris, further increased his
confidence and expectations.[48] *Poems* appeared shortly before *Adamastor*, and Nancy Cunard had met Campbell in Marseilles to discuss the
volume, bringing with her her negro lover of the time. Campbell, who
hated pretension of any kind, later wrote of her,

When superannuated English society-tarts take up negro lovers, it is
generally a sort of perversion like the exaggerated feeling for dogs and cats. I
knew one who went negro in order, as she said, to 'study conditions amongst
the negroes'. Having selected the negro with the largest 'condition' she could
find, she brought him to Europe.[49]

This was the period when Lewis paid his visits to the Campbells,
the first of them to plan *Satire and Fiction*, the pamphlet in which he hit
back at those who attempted to impose a literary boycott on *The Apes
of God*. This first visit, in mid-July 1930, was the one which Lewis

records so vividly in his novel *Snooty Baronet*,[50] in which Campbell appears as 'Rob McPhail'. Lewis's love of secret-agent tricks was growing during this period, with his sense of being persecuted (a sense that communicated itself to Campbell), and his black cape and black hat, his sudden arrivals and equally sudden disappearances lent him an aura of mystery which fascinated the Campbell children. He bought Campbell's daughter Anna a long balloon one day as they had lunch outside Pascal's restaurant in Martigues, and when she accidentally dropped it into her soup and burst it, he gave her a horrible look which she never forgot.[51] Even the balloon appears in *Snooty Baronet*. Lewis and Campbell would hold muttered conversations which went on long into the night, and from which everyone else was excluded. Campbell admired him enormously. For his part, Lewis found in Campbell a sympathy and a similarity of views which surprised him. He wrote in *Snooty Baronet*, 'the likeness of our respective ways of feeling (on a number of points) is exceedingly marked. I am astonished at the likeness. It is on account of this I value him so much I think. I feel towards him as I should towards a brother.'[52]

Campbell set store by these contacts with Lewis. For one thing, they provided him with something he badly needed: a cause to fight for. Lewis, in turn, welcomed Campbell's support. In 1932 he wrote to Campbell,

At a point in my career when many people were combining to defeat me (namely upon the publication of the *Apes of God*) you came forward and with the most disinterested nobleness placed yourself at my side, and defended my book in public in a manner that I believe no other work has ever been defended.[53]

Early in 1931 Lewis asked Campbell whether he would consider writing a monograph about him, to be published by Chatto; Campbell, who had just finished writing *The Georgiad*, agreed. In writing this short book* Campbell soaked himself in Lewis's work for several months. 'I am convinced that Lewis is a writer of the stature of Swift, and certainly a very great thinker indeed', he wrote, going on in the same letter to compare Lewis with Nietzsche, Cervantes, and Rabelais.[54]

His support for Lewis's *The Apes of God* had involved no small sacrifice; he lost many of his own friends when *Satire and Fiction* appeared. Augustus John's frequent visits terminated abruptly, and

---

* It was, for reasons that remain unclear, withdrawn before publication, and the MS has been lost.

Aldous Huxley no longer came for weekends.[55] Campbell regarded
the sacrifice as well worthwhile. To be involved in battle, and with an
ally like Lewis, was exhilarating to him. The letters convey something
of his excitement: 'It was great that the Apes and the Georgiad were
published simultaneously – I can almost hear the thud from here!',[56]
he exulted to Lewis in November 1931. He was later to realize how
much harm *The Georgiad* had done to his reputation, but for the
moment he felt he had exacted full compensation from Vita. And in
one sense his victory was complete: Mary, reconciled with him, was
no longer corresponding with or seeing her former lover. Campbell
seems to have felt all the triumph of a Greek warrior returning from
the destruction of Troy, his Helen at his side. 'Song', probably
written at this time, is an exploration of the battle implicit in his love-
making:

> You ask what far-off singing
> Has mingled with our rest.
> It is my love that, winging
> The deep wave of your breast,
> With white sail homeward turning,
> Sings at the golden oar
> Of a white city burning
> On the battle-tented shore.
>
> (CP, I, 97)

Campbell felt that all was right with the world in 1932. He was
drinking less, and feeling healthier as a result; the Joyeuse Lance, the
jousting team of which he was a member, had won the championship
for the second successive year; his work was going well; his marriage
was working tolerably well; and he was making money. He moved
into a larger house, Figuerolles, set still further away from the town
than Tour de Vallier. Figuerolles was an old pink farmhouse over-
shadowed by a great cedar. In addition to the maid they had always
had to do the housework, the Campbells now employed a tutor for
their children – the young Afrikaans poet, Uys Krige, who was later
instrumental in precipitating Campbell's break with Plomer. Krige,
then earning a precarious living as a professional rugby player in
Marseilles, sought Campbell out in October 1932. He found Campbell still asleep at midday – sleeping, as he habitually did, in his
clothes on the floor. Krige was touched by the warmth of the
reception he got from this famous poet who had not been expecting
his arrival, and to whom he was a stranger. His description conveys

something of the impact Campbell made on those who met him for the first time, a sense of elemental force that seemed to wash around him in waves:

A tall figure came stumbling down the dark rickety staircase. He wore a rough pair of sailor's trousers and a dark blue jersey. It was obvious that he had slept in his clothes. The next moment he was standing on the doorstep, blinking his large greenish-blue eyes in the sudden sharp sunlight and shaking, vigorously, my hand.

Something big and generous seemed to flow out of the man in that firm clasp, that forthright look and Roy's whole intensely alive, eager bearing . . . .

But it was when he opened his mouth that I got a shock. He had been on the binge with some Martigues fishermen, he said, he had a hell of a thirst, would I mind walking fifty yards to the well with him? There had been a Krige with him at Oxford, Jack Krige of Johannesburg, the best student of his year, a first-rate fellow, must be one of my cousins . . . .

The large dented bucket rattled to the bottom of the well, shattering our two calm images on its still, greenish surface into a thousand splinters of dancing light. Back wheezed the bucket. Grabbing it in his two hands, Roy emptied it over his head in a single abrupt gesture. Straightening up, he shook his head ponderously, a couple of times, his face set in a surly expression throughout, as if along with the glittering drops that were splashing off his pate, he wanted also to scatter the last grey cobwebs from his brain.

'That's better!' he boomed at me. 'Much better. Come on, man, let's get going! It's getting late!'[57]

And he whirled Krige back into the village for yet another binge with the fishermen. When the two of them recovered, the next morning, he invited Krige to come and stay with them, and Krige did – for eight months. Campbell ungrudgingly provided him with board and lodging and small sums of money from time to time. As a partial return Krige tried to teach Teresa and Anna their letters, though he was never able to discipline them. They found him amusing rather than informative. One day he made them laugh, for instance, by asking in genuine puzzlement, 'Do cows have horns?'[58] He and Mary became very friendly. She took up painting again at this time, and Krige sometimes posed nude for her.

Only his magnificent constitution allowed Campbell to live as he did, drinking much, eating and sleeping little. He lived at a pace that made Laurens van der Post's pronouncement on him seem accurate: 'Born on fire, it was as if his whole being had already irrevocably accepted that he could only live by burning himself out.'[59] But though Campbell seemed physically able to keep going for the moment, he was outrunning his resources in other ways. In the flush of *Adamastor's* success he had enlarged both his house and his household as if indifferent to the financial crisis the world was going through. He treated the money he made from *Poems*, *Adamastor*, and *The Georgiad* as if it were part of a steady income rather than a windfall that would not recur. But the economic facts gradually made themselves felt. In the autumn of 1931 Britain abandoned the gold standard, and the value of the pound fell immediately against other major currencies, including the French franc. Campbell's income was considerably reduced in value, at a time when his expenditure was increasing. It was some time before the poet realized that the pound's devaluation was likely to be permanent. He began living on credit, and piling up considerable debts. To increase his income he began writing prose. In 1932 he published a volume called *Taurine Provence*, which his publisher described as a study of the 'Philosophy Technique and Religion of the Bullfighter'. Its genesis had been an article on bullfighting which Campbell had written in 1929, at T. S. Eliot's urging.[60] Campbell himself called *Taurine Provence* 'a bloody pot-boiler', and told Lewis, 'I had to get drunk to write it, and it is written like a Baedeker and copied out of a few French newspapers'.[61] Campbell was overmodest about *Taurine Provence*, which contains many fine passages. A companion volume, *Marine Provence*, was written early in 1933, during a stay in the ruined Gascon castle of a friend, the painter Tristram Hillier;[62] but though Campbell was paid for it, the book was never published.*

* The publisher, Desmond Harmsworth, ran into financial difficulties. The MS of *Marine Provence*, like that of *Wyndham Lewis*, has been lost.

IX

Flowering Reeds

1933

CAMPBELL began 1933, the year Hitler came to power, with a sense of deep foreboding. In January the poet wrote presciently to C. J. Sibbett, 'This year nineteen thirty-three promises to be the dirtiest since the war – the Europeans are becoming barbarians again, I fear, and rapidly too.'[1] He had much to be depressed about. It was gradually coming home to him that his mounting debts were not just going to go away, and his prose books earned very little. In any case he hated writing prose, because it kept him from poetry. He began making plans to move to Spain, where he knew he could live more cheaply than in Provence. His financial problems depressed him deeply; it seemed to him that material security had been snatched away from him again just when it had seemed within reach. He felt the world was conspiring against him. At intervals his anxieties would boil over in furious rages which he usually vented on his daughters' dog or their cats, cursing them and throwing at them any object that came to hand.[2] The strain of supporting his family, despite the amount of responsibility which he had surrendered to Mary, was beginning to tell. His self-doubts, allayed for a time by the idyllic conditions of life in Martigues, rose again stronger than before. He was, after all, older now, nearly thirty-two; his waist was beginning to thicken; his head was quite bald. He was still being saluted as 'a poet of promise', but when would that promise be realized?

Early in 1933 he began to gather the poems he had written since the publication of *Adamastor* into a volume he called *Flowering Reeds*, not because he wanted to publish them but because he needed the money. He was no more able to support his wife now than he had been when he first married her, and he felt that he had not much longer to make his mark on the world. Time, and his shortage of it, began to obsess him.

By his high tower of creviced rock
The time is always twelve o'clock –
High tower, high time to save our souls!
(CP, I, 183)

he had written in 'St Peter of the Three Canals': and the sound of 'Time's winged chariot' is heard again and again in *Flowering Reeds*.

Most of the poems in this volume were written between 1930 and 1933, though two of them were published in magazines as early as 1929. Another, 'Choosing a Mast', has a tranquillity and purity of tone which links it more to the 'classic' poems of *Adamastor* than to the troubled lyrics of *Flowering Reeds*. In his celebration of the strength, beauty, and fragrance of the pine he selects as a mast for his boat, Campbell shows again that deep influence of the landscape of Provence which was so evident in *Adamastor*, and which is seen again and again in his letters:

Today the mistral decapitated one of my favourite pines and cracking it in half with the sound of a rifle-shot, threw its upper extremity, 30 feet in length, into our olive-orchard about forty yards away. These pines, that grow all over Provence, are magnificent trees, they seem made to resist the wind – they are as pliant as bamboos though they carry a weight of foliage that would lay any bamboo flat in a mistral. They move in the wind like huge waves there is something liquid and fluid in their motion and in their eternal roaring and thundering, which never ceases day or night. . . The mistral blows away all cobwebs of the mind. It is cold, yet sunny: and at night there is nothing I like better than to hear it plunging in the pines outside while one sits in front of a log-fire . . .[3]

This love of the tree's resistance and strength is apparent in the poem too. He chose the pine, Campbell says,

> . . . for her stormy watches on the height,
> For only out of solitude and strife
> Are born the sons of valour and delight . . .
> (CP, I, 104)

– a restatement of the need for pain that looks back to many of the *Adamastor* poems (from 'Mazeppa' to 'The Palm') and forward to the Christian poetry he was to write later. The final mood of the poem, though, is peaceful. The last part of the letter quoted finds expression in the lines

> It was the pines that sang us to our rest,
> Loud in the wind and fragrant in the fire . . .

And the poem ends with Campbell at one with nature and with himself, enjoying the gale as the 'Horses on the Camargue' do in that earlier composition, and finally shooting home to harbour as he did in 'Mass at Dawn'.

But 'Choosing a Mast' is an exceptional poem in *Flowering Reeds*. Much more typical of the prevailing mood of this volume is 'The Gum Trees', which had been written in 1929, just too late for inclusion in *Adamastor*, and published separately by Faber. It is a keynote poem in *Flowering Reeds*, for it sets the tone of self-criticism and doubt that permeates the volume. The eucalyptuses form one of the long avenues that flank the arrow-straight roads of Provence. To the poet in the opening stanzas, they seem to be racing along on either side of the road as he stands between them, and the susurration of their leaves becomes the rush of motion. Once more, in the avenue, Campbell finds an image to express his divided nature.

The connection for him lies not simply in the fact that the trees rush as precipitately to the horizon as he through life; it lies in the fact that an avenue consists of two lines of trees, mirroring one another, linked together by contiguity, yet eternally divided. And as his split nature was a fruitful source of verse, was in a sense the channel through which many of his finest thoughts were transmitted, so the trees line and define the road along which the life of Provence passes.

Campbell tried, in his verse and in his life, to unite the warring elements in his nature, and he appears to take comfort from the fact that the avenue, as it progresses into the distance, seems to achieve the longed-for unity:

> Far on the sky, with crests aflame,
> The tapering avenues unite. . .
> (CP, I, 111)

His obsession with the passage of time, though it is subtly handled in this poem, is always present. The trees are first presented to us in the evening; they are seen 'with crests aflame', and they run 'along the red-lit rim of space', and we watch them through the night, as they 'flicker to the moon's white fire' until the coming of day. But whereas Campbell felt the passage of time as a constant threat, the trees seem to triumph over it. The illusion of speed which their beauty gives rise to

> Is like a silver current hurled
> Majestic through the noiseless reeds
> Of some less transitory world;
> (CP, I, 111)

They are free of the earthly dimensions that shackle the poet.
Whereas his progress is inexorably towards the grave,

> Their march is one victorious race
> Of immobility with time . . .

But just as Campbell felt success was snatched away from him each
time it seemed within reach, so his sense of the trees' movement,
unity, and eternity is revealed for an illusion with that rising of the
sun for which they seemed to strive. They stand as rooted as they
were the day before, as divided by the road as they were the day
before, and as tormented by the elements; and at last he explicitly
draws the parallel between the trees and himself:

> They, too, have dreamed they sought a goal
> When merely from themselves they fled!
>   (CP, I, 112)

He had begun to realize – at least in the context of this poem – that not
only was his a divided nature, but that his enemies were extensions of
himself. The mob, the bourgeoisie, tradesmen, supporters of apartheid or Christianity, the herd, homosexuals, intellectuals, all the
groups he attacked most fiercely, all are groups of which he was a part
or longed to be a part. This is true of the groups he was to attack in
future years, too: Communists, 'Saxons', Protestants, Jews, and many
others.* He was 'fleeing from himself' in attacking them; if trouble did
not come to him, he went looking for it, because an external struggle
stilled his internal strife. Even the poverty from which he suffered so
much at this time was at least partly the result of his own extravagance. All his life he was a spendthrift – money existed to be got rid
of. In his early days in Oxford he would spend £30 in a weekend,
mostly on drinks for his friends; a legacy of £100 from a cousin was
spent on a black cape, a guitar, some books and similar 'frivolities' in a
few days. In 1930 he and Mary squandered £180 in a week in
London.[4] The adversities which so oppressed him rose again and
again from his own subconsciousness ('caves of sleep') to confront him:

> The dusty winds begin to sweep,
> The distance stretched before them lies,
> Antaeus-like from caves of sleep
> Their old antagonists arise.
>   (CP, I, 112)

---

* In view of the loudly expressed anti-Semitism of Campbell's later years it is worth
mentioning that Mary believed herself to be partly Jewish.

He had reason to write of the repetitive nature of his problems. Ever since the shock of learning about Mary's affair with Vita, he had feared that she would sooner or later be unfaithful to him again, though he affirmed in prose and verse that his marriage had been strengthened by the strain, as if willing it to be so. In his letters to Mary during her periodic visits to London one discerns his fear that this time, perhaps, she would not come back to him. If she failed to write to him he would panic and fire off telegrams begging her to rejoin him immediately. There is pathos in this correspondence, full of frankly expressed physical passion (in a simple code, using b for a, c for b and so on, which Campbell used on postcards, with a touching faith in the privacy thus achieved) and equally full of fear about what she might be doing while she was away from him: 'Come back at once *when it's time* we are all wearying for you. But have a thoroughly good time first but *please not more* than you said',[5] he writes urgently in 1932. But when Mary did take another lover it was not in London but in Campbell's own house; and once more it was a woman. Late in 1932 two English girls came to stay with the Campbells: Lisa and her sister Jeanne, a beautiful, dark-eyed girl, who was unhappily married. Jeanne and Mary had been friendly for some years; late in 1932 they became lovers. It may be that Mary did not try to hide the affair from Campbell this time; perhaps past pain had made him wary. However it was, he seems to have realized quite quickly what was going on. To him it must have seemed like a recurring nightmare; all his half-healed wounds gaped anew. Again he was being 'cuckolded by a woman'. But he had learned something from his previous experience: whatever pain she caused him, he could not live without Mary. This time he did not pack a bag and run away as he had run from Long Barn. Instead, perhaps out of spite, perhaps in an effort to woo Mary through jealousy, he took a lover of his own: Lisa, the sister of Jeanne. Years later Mary was to describe her as 'fat and yielding'.[6] Like Jeanne she was unhappily married. The extent of Campbell's attachment to her can be judged from a postscript to one of his most passionate letters to Mary:

I wrote a semi-love letter to Lisa: 'May Venus shower a 1000 blessings on her valiant little soldier' that was the worst I said but I also said I was glad and better that she had gone away (and I only sent her my *spare* love *left over from Mary*. I love only Mary hotly and fiercely).[7]

It seems clear that Campbell was consoling himself with this casual relationship in order to win back Mary, and it appears that his ploy was successful. Mary later described both her and Campbell's affairs at this time as 'very light-hearted and frivolous',[8] and it is true that this affair was much less intense than that with Vita, and much briefer. But it is quite evident from his poetry that Campbell's sense of the wearisome, recurrent nature of his problems was increased by this revivification of the ghost of Vita, which he believed he had so thoroughly laid in *The Georgiad*.

He knew now that Mary could never be wholly his as she had been for a time after their marriage. 'I wish you belonged [to me] altogether',[9] he wrote wistfully to her. The poems reflect his tormenting sense that she belonged to the world as much as to himself. 'A Sleeping Woman' presents the same situation as 'The Sleeper'; the poet, sleepless and isolated, broods over his unconscious wife. As in the earlier sonnet, the situation suggests powerfully both his love for her and her indifference to it; it is as though he can fully enjoy her beauty only when she is unaware of his attentions. It is too as if Campbell's vaunted dominance over Mary[10] exists only while she is asleep. The difference in emphasis between 'A Sleeping Woman' and the earlier poem lies in Campbell's description of the sleeper. In the earlier poem she was simply withdrawn from him and from existence, lying still 'on the shores of sleep'. In 'A Sleeping Woman', however, she is not so much withdrawn from life as absorbed into it; she reflects it, and it partakes of her:

> From skies the colour of her skin,
> So touched with golden down, so fair,
> Where glittering cypress seems to spin
> The black refulgence of her hair,
> Clear as a glass the day replies
> To every feature . . .
>
>   (CP, I, 110)

Campbell is shut off from Mary's existence, not because of her self-containment (as in the earlier poem) but because she seems united with the whole world. Jeanne had followed Vita; who would follow Jeanne?

It is in that superb sonnet, 'The Road to Arles', that he most vividly expresses the despair he felt at this time. Again the symbolic avenue appears,* this time 'shorn of any veil', and the wintry twigs become the horns of a helpless Actaeon, hunted down by the pitiless moon-goddess he made the mistake of loving. The image powerfully

---

* Even today the fine avenue of plane-trees lines the old road between Martigues and Arles.

suggests Campbell's vulnerability and the degree of suffering to which his love for Mary, 'the cold huntress', exposed him:

> Bare trees, the target of her silver spite,
> Down the long avenue in staggy flight
> Are hunted by the hungers of the gale:
> Along the cold grey torrent of the sky
> Where branch the fatal trophies of his brows,
> Actaeon, antlered in the wintry boughs,
> Rears to the stars his mastiff-throttled cry.
>
>   (CP, I, 99)

The Greek myth gains enormous force from Campbell's evident personal feeling, compressed into the rigid sonnet-form; the fatal trophies are the horns not only of Actaeon, but of the cuckold. C. S. Lewis's thoughtlessly cruel words lie behind this throttled, thrilling cry of pain. There is great pathos in the fact that even at this point of renewed betrayal he could not bring himself to blame Mary explicitly. Instead he blames his own pride for making him resent her behaviour, for making him vulnerable; it is his own pride that has laid his life waste:

> Pride has avenging arrows for the eyes
> That strip her beauty silver of disguise,
> And she has dogs before whose pace to flee –
> In front a waste, behind a bended bow,
> And a long race across the stony Crau
> Torn in each gust, and slain in every tree.
>
>   (CP, I, 99)

Mary's affair with Jeanne was short-lived, to Campbell's relief, and Lisa, having served her purpose, went too; the most Bohemian of households could not have sustained such a *ménage à quatre* for long. And Mary's dominance over Campbell seemed to gain in strength, just as it had after the affair with Vita. His fear of losing his wife tied him more closely to her. This perhaps explains the inclusion in *Flowering Reeds* of the fine translation of Rimbaud's 'Les Chercheuses de Poux', a translation which Campbell had made some years before, and which had influenced his earlier poems 'The Sisters' and 'The Zulu Girl'. In the translated Rimbaud poem a child tormented by lice is approached by two mysterious sisters, their fingers tipped 'with silver-pointed nails'. In lines heavy with implicitly sexual imagery, at once attractive and repellent, they search his hair for lice:

Into his heavy hair where falls the dew,
Prowl their long fingers terrible in charm.

He hears their breathing whistle in long sighs
Flowering with ghostly pollen; and the hiss
Of spittle on the lips withdrawn, where dies
From time to time the fancy of a kiss.

(CP, I, 107)

The child, acted upon by the women, sinks into a trance of melancholic delight. Dominated, outnumbered, and mastered by the fearsome women, he is a passive sexual object in the same way the horses in Campbell's poem 'The Sisters' are passive sexual objects. It is evident from its influence on Campbell that Rimbaud's poem struck a deeply responsive chord in him, expressing something that perhaps he could not bear to approach in his own writing.

The growing menace in Germany had now become the backdrop against which the sadness of his own life played itself out. He found the conferences of statesmen vainly trying to relieve the pressure building up in Europe a sad sight. He wrote to Sibbett in June,

I find the atmosphere of the London Conference as depressing as that of Geneva especially as we are nearing the dog-days now. The old fellows might just as well have stayed at home and saved hotel expenses. Roosevelt seems to be the only man with any ideas and he is tied up with his party.[11]

The disorder in the world at large seemed to be reflected in all aspects of his own life.

This pervasive depression lies behind 'Overtime'[12] in which he describes seeing anatomical pictures in a medical textbook: flayed lurid figures displaying muscles and blood vessels, glands and nerves. Campbell reflects lightly and wittily on these pitiful figures, but the humour evaporates when he relates the pictures to himself, his bitterness is unmistakable, his longing for death genuine:

The lucky many of the dead –
Their suit of darkness fits them tight,
Buttoned with stars from foot to head
They wear the uniform of Night;
But some for extra shift are due
Who, slaves for any fool to blame,
With a flayed soul the ages through
Must push the shovel of their fame.

(CP, I, 113)

In closing *Flowering Reeds* with this witty but deeply sad poem Campbell seems to be regretting having made himself a motley to the view, setting before the eyes of coming generations his inmost sorrows and their cause.

His own generation, however, paid very little attention of any kind. *Flowering Reeds* was reviewed, and generously reviewed, by William Plomer in the *New Statesman*,[13] and the *Adelphi*[14] and the *Times Literary Supplement*[15] noticed the volume briefly; but there was none of the widespread interest which its appearance warranted, and which the author of *Adamastor* might have expected. Campbell was in no doubt as to the reason for the surprising silence of the reviewers. It was, he believed, a literary boycott like that which had greeted Lewis's *The Apes of God*; its cause was his defence of that book, and his publication of *The Georgiad*.

This silence on the part of the critics had two effects. It increased Campbell's sense of isolation and persecution, and it meant that his hopes of increasing his income came to nothing. He was by now deeply in debt, and as a result becoming unpopular with the tradesmen of Martigues. The idea of a move to Spain became increasingly attractive to him. He began writing prose again, this time an autobiography, which he hated. He was encouraged to press on with it by a new acquaintance, John Greenwood, whose recently established publishing house, Boriswood, had published *The Georgiad*, and who was anxious to print more of his work.

The visits of two friends he had made in South Africa during the *Voorslag* period, Anna von Schubert and Cecil Sibbett, coincided in August 1933 and provided an interval of calm. Anna von Schubert stayed a month, and both the Campbells enjoyed her company immensely. They took her to a bullfight, which horrified her so much that she stayed in bed all the next day,[16] and they were sorry to see her go. But such pleasant interludes did not alter their financial plight. Sibbett had suggested that life in Spain might be cheaper for them, and Campbell had long been thinking of going there. His interest in Spanish literature was growing; as early as 1932 he showed Krige an American anthology of South American poems, and spoke with great enthusiasm of Chocano, Lugones, and other Latin American poets.[17]

The move to Spain was eventually precipitated by a ridiculous incident. Late in 1933 the Campbells' pet goats broke through a neighbour's fence, and in the course of a night destroyed a number of valuable young peach-trees. The neighbour demanded compensation.

When he failed to get it, he sued the Campbells for a considerable sum, and won.[18] Campbell had no way of paying. To avoid the ignominy of a prison term, he began making hasty plans to decamp across the Spanish border. The begging letters he wrote to Greenwood and to Sibbett attest to his desperation in the face of this new crisis:

Do you think you could be able to help me as before? I write this in an agony of terror for my little family. Such an act would double my everlasting gratitude to you and I should see that it was rewarded in posterity . . . Could you manage to lend me £50? Never have I been so desperate as at this minute. If only I could shift out and get to Spain – I could keep the ground under my feet . . . I despair of going on living.[19]

Faced with such appeals, his friends paid up, and late in November 1933 Campbell and Mary travelled by train to Barcelona, followed a few days later by their children, Uys Krige, the French maid Thérèse, a large black dog named Sarah, and a small mountain of luggage. Because of the need to leave quickly and quietly, they abandoned all their more bulky possessions – books, paintings, and furniture – crossing the border as if they were refugees fleeing a war. They found rooms in a tenement in the Barrio Chino, the prostitutes' quarter of Barcelona. The violent Anarchist strikes that followed the elections of 1933 were in progress in the city, and the streets echoed with exploding bombs; a revolution seemed imminent.[20] Sallying out into Las Ramblas, the broad, shady boulevard that runs down to the harbour, on their first evening in the city, the Campbells were alarmed to find machine-gunners at both ends and the pavement cafés eerily silent. They had eight pesetas left; they knew no Spanish. In Provence Campbell had once again found security and a home, only to lose it; once more he had to endure exile and destitution, his work ignored, his marriage fragile. What further blows could life deal him? 'God knows what we are going to do,' he wrote.[21]

X

Spain

1934–1935

THE Campbells' most immediate need, once they had settled into their rented rooms, was for money. Their landlady, finding them penniless, seized their luggage as security on the rent.[1] Campbell knew only one way of earning money. He had written 20,000 words of his autobiography before leaving France, and now he raced to finish it, writing the last chapters standing up against a bureau so as not to fall asleep. He wrote the African chapters last, finishing with one on Rhodesia. He padded the book with any story he could remember, adapting the anecdotes of friends into autobiography, and giving himself a leading role. Few of his stories are entirely imaginary; fewer still are entirely accurate. For example, his stories about boating on the lagoon in Durban, being chased by a python or being nearly drowned by the tidal bore, are true enough – but they happened to his elder brother George, not to himself.[2] A tale about kidnapping dogs in Cannes was taken from a book of reminiscences by the editor of the *Sporting Times*, J. B. Booth. Another yarn, of sailing a drunken doctor out to Bardsey Island in a storm, was the genuine feat of the barman in the Ship Inn in Aberdaron, the Welsh village in which the Campbells had lived immediately after their marriage.[3] In most of these tales, Campbell figures as the sort of assured, devil-may-care man of action he would so much have liked to have been, the sort of man he felt his father and brothers would have admired. Of his poetic achievements he said virtually nothing. This became the pattern of his myth-making; he seldom boasted of things he could do.

There is another element worth noticing in the book: Campbell's love of expressing opinions calculated to shock and enrage the type of intellectual he had encountered at Long Barn: '"Shocking the bourgeois" is the silliest thing that we do. I have always preferred to shock the shocker of the bourgeois, who is naturally and always a tame little figure, an inverted bourgeois himself . . .'[4] He succeeded all too well in his object. The bourgeois-shockers (and almost everyone else) believed him when he claimed to be in favour of slavery or Mussolini, and against everything modern, from machinery to Charlie Chaplin.

The £100 he received from Boriswood for this book, which he aptly named *Broken Record*, together with gifts from his friends in South Africa, relieved him of financial anxiety for the moment. Whatever lay ahead, he was at least out of France and out of debt. One catches his relief in a letter to Sibbett:

Since I last wrote the revolution has calmed down: and everything is normal. For weather we might be in the Cape and for tranquillity, thanks to you, in the fortunate islands . . . For the first time in a year I am free from all worries and working at poetry: and I owe all this to you. I am glad unspeakably glad to have finished with all this filthy prose which I can't write anyway . . . I just stretch my arms and yawn with relief.[5]

He loved Barcelona, with its combination of magnificent public buildings and intimate, cool-fountained courtyards, its peculiarly Spanish fusion of Europe and the Middle East. The Campbells' rooms were in a decaying building in the Calle San Pablo, at number 28. Running off Las Ramblas, with its fashionable crowds sipping coffee or promenading under the great planes, the Calle San Pablo dives into a warren of mean streets, itself becoming narrower and darker as it goes, until it is little more than a gloomy alley, loud with the song of caged birds and the laughter of the prostitutes who cluster towards evening in the wine shops. With his experience of the Old Quarter of Marseilles Campbell felt at home almost from the start, and quickly began making friends with a group of disreputable characters, among them an Italian named Collini, who claimed to be a spy for his government, and who would talk revolutionary politics for hours on end. On Sundays the Campbells would go to one of the city's fine parks, where Catalan dances were held on the grass; often they would all join the rings of dancers. They began learning Spanish with the help of the Nicaraguan poet Rubén Darío, whom Campbell had met in a bar in the Barrio. They picked up the language with ease, though Campbell never learned to speak it faultlessly. He admired Darío's poetry, and made free adaptations of at least two poems – 'After Rubén' and 'Toril'.

The Aldous Huxleys, on a tour of Spain with Sybille Bedford, spent a day in Barcelona and took the Campbells out to dinner in the Plaza de Cataluña, one of the great squares of the city. Huxley, who was shortly to leave Europe for America, spoke pessimistically of the political situation of the Old World: of rearmament, of Hitler, of the Anarchist bomb which had just been thrown in a nearby street, injuring several people and overturning a tram.[6] Campbell, who had little interest in politics, listened without comment. At this stage he still regarded Spanish politics with amused tolerance, and as something of no concern to himself. 'For the Catalans as with the Irish, politics is a national industry,' he wrote.[7]

Despite his uncertain situation and his depressing surroundings in this strange new country, he was writing well. He was revising a set of poems he had written in France, a sequence he called 'Mithraic Emblems', the strangest and most obscure poems Campbell wrote.

It was in Provence that he had grown interested in the dead and mysterious worship of Mithras, a religion which struggled for dominance with Christianity in the early centuries of the Christian era. Mithraic relics were scattered all over Provence, as the Marquis of Baroncelli-Javon (an antiquary, author, and friend of Campbell's) pointed out to the poet. The church in the Camargue village of Saintes Maries de la Mer, which Campbell visited on his first trip to Provence in 1920, may have been a Mithraic shrine before being taken over by Christianity. In his reading of Gibbon's *Decline and Fall* Campbell came across references to Mithraism and, his interest once aroused, he almost certainly read Franz Cumont's definitive book on the religion.[8] (In *Snooty Baronet* Wyndham Lewis implies that he drew Campbell's attention to Mithraism, but it seems much more likely that it was Campbell who first interested Lewis in the subject.)

There was much about Mithraism to attract Campbell. His South African upbringing, and his unhappy experiences in England, had given him a near-mystical belief in the value of what he called 'real sunlight';[9] here was a religion that worshipped the sun. His preoccupation with the passage of time, apparent throughout the poems of *Flowering Reeds*, was satisfied by Chronos, the Supreme Deity of Mithraism. Campbell's love of individualism, courage, and personal achievement drew him to a religion which, as Cumont puts it, 'was particularly adapted to fostering individual effort and to developing human energy . . . for them [Mithraists], the good dwelt in action. They rated strength higher than gentleness, and preferred courage to lenity'.[10] It was the religion of the soldier rather than the slave.

Above all, however, Mithraism attracted Campbell because of its central myth, which he had seen represented on several great bas-reliefs in the British Museum.[11] According to this myth, the super-human Mithras (God of Light) had captured a wild bull, symbolic of the forces of life, and taken it to his cave. But the animal succeeded in escaping, and the Sun sent a raven to order Mithras to slay the bull. This he did, much against his will, stabbing the animal with his hunting knife. Then a miracle happened. From the blood of the victim sprang a vine, from its spine wheat; from its body all the useful plants on earth. The Evil Spirit, in an attempt to nullify the miracle, sent the ant, the scorpion, and the snake to consume the body-fluids of the stricken beast, but his malice was in vain. Mithras had, through his reluctant sacrifice, enriched the world.[12] It is clear that the bull-slaying was a creative, beneficial act, linking Mithraism with the other ancient religions in which the annual renewal of vegetation plays a central part.[13]

Campbell had always believed that (in his words) 'The administration of death to a beautiful animal is a sacred sort of rite';[14] and here was a religion whose central rite was the hunt. He believed that Mithras loved the bull and killed it with great reluctance[15] – an idea supported by Cumont.[16] And in this Mithraic sacrifice, the slayer suffering with the slain, Campbell found yet another image for his divided, self-tormenting nature, which vented its suffering in poetry as the bull's death enriched the world. In addition, he saw in the bullslaying the symbolic meaning and justification of the bullfighting he so loved. He affected to believe that bullfighting was the living remnant of Mithraism: 'tauromachy is both the most Ancient and the most *living* of all Aryan religions; and it numbers more passionate believers and more devoted priests (devoted even in the face of death) than any other religion, to this day. How many parsons would do as much for their creed, as a torero does for his?'[17] Not only was bullfighting a religion; it was a religion very closely resembling Christianity. Cumont points out that the sectaries of Mithras practised baptism and a form of confirmation, held Sunday sacred, celebrated the birth of the Sun on 25 December, and believed in Hell, Heaven, a Flood, the immortality of the soul, and in a Resurrection and Last Judgement.[18] Campbell believed that Mithraism was as prophetic of Christ as the writings of Isaiah.[19] It is clear that Mithraism provided him with an approach to the Christianity from which he still shrank, but which drew him steadily. In this sense 'Mithraic Emblems' is, on a much larger scale, that approach to Christ through paganism which first appears in 'St Peter of the Three Canals'. And Mithraism did something more for Campbell; it provided his poetry with the sort of framework of personal mythology which Yeats had sought and found in the occult.

The sonnet sequence which Campbell entitled 'Mithraic Emblems'* is built round the seven 'Sword-sonnets'. He wrote these first, publishing six of them in 1933, in the *New Statesman*, before he left France. The Third, Second, and First Swords, in that order, appeared on 8 April 1933 (p. 445); the Fourth Sword on 29 July 1933 (p. 134), and the Sixth on 26 August 1933 (p. 237). The poems vary only in minor ways from the form in which they were to be published in 1936.[20]

Campbell seems to have found the idea of the seven swords in Guillaume Apollinaire's sequence 'Les Sept Épées', in the long poem 'La Chanson du Mal-Aimé',[21] in which the seven swords are the griefs that wounded Apollinaire's heart in the course of an unhappy love affair. More immediately, Campbell came across the image of swords gashing a heart in churches throughout southern France and Spain: little painted statues of the Virgin, her heart transfixed by the swords of human sin.[22] Campbell had already alluded to such figures in the final stanzas of 'Canaan', in *Flowering Reeds*:

> . . . the young Madonna's heart
> With rosy portals gashed apart
> Bleeds for the things I say.
>   (CP, I, 97)

The sword image gains further significance for Campbell from the climax of the Spanish bullfight, in which during the 'estocade' the matador thrusts the bull through the heart. And yet another layer of symbolism is added by those Mithraic sculptures which depict the sun god with a seven-rayed halo, one ray of which shines out towards Mithras at the moment he slaughters the animal he loves.[23] In a drawing Campbell made to illustrate *Mithraic Emblems*, but which he never published, these strands of symbolism are drawn together. Mithras is depicted plunging a sword into the kneeling bull, while the scorpion stings its genitals and the dog and serpent attack it; the raven flies overhead. And behind Mithras rises an oddly shaped sun, from which seven rays emerge, so that they look like blades transfixing Mithras's heart.

The 'swords', then, are symbolic of suffering, the suffering of the bull, of Mithras, of the Virgin, and of Campbell, but it is suffering that brings enrichment, creativity, forgiveness, and illumination.

---

* Mithraic Emblems is the title both of a sequence of poems and of the volume in which it first appeared. In this discussion of them, *Mithraic Emblems* is the volume, and 'Mithraic Emblems' the poem sequence.

With this background in mind, we would expect to find in 'Mithraic Emblems' an examination of the stages by which Campbell was approaching a conversion to Christianity. Further evidence that he saw 'Mithraic Emblems' as a symbol of spiritual progress can be found in his later plan to write a similar series of poems, this time entirely Christian, to be called 'The Stations of the Cross'.[24]

The Mithraic sequence opens with 'The Altar', in which Campbell's obsession with the passage of time emerges anew. Campbell compares his squandered years with the 'flower-fed bulls' of the Mithraic sacrifice which, having been consumed by a funereal pyre, ascended in smoke to be made immortal in the heavens. His years, slain, leave behind them verse ('the lily's ghost and bleeding wine') and so triumph over their own passing.

In the second sonnet, 'The Solar Enemy', Campbell addresses the Sun which in its passage kills his years one by one. It is, he says, the 'enemy of my inward night', for as he moves closer to the grave he comes to understand himself and the goal of his life more clearly. The illumination is within him; as in the drawing he did to illustrate the poems, the Sun and his heart are one and the same. The sun which the dying beast sees is

> my own lit heart, its rays of fire,
> the seven swords that run it through.
> (CP, I, 116)

The third sonnet, 'Illumination', elaborates this view of the growth of self-knowledge. Campbell's gaze is directed upon 'the white abrupt sierras of my days' by the star which shines within him, so that his flesh glows like 'a rose against the dawn'. He sees his own skeleton as 'a frond of snow', and every nerve is visible,

> fine as the thistled hair of fays
> and myriad as the coloured rays
> an eyelash fibres from the sun.
> (CP, I, 117)

The fourth sonnet, 'The Seven Swords', makes it plain that the Swords are 'swords of vision', seven in number because of the seven colours into which sunlight can be refracted. The number seven was sacred to Mithraism for several reasons. Apart from the seven-flame halo worn by Sol, the religion recognized seven stages of initiation, symbolized by ladders constructed of seven different metals. When the swords combine (as the seven colours combine to form pure white when painted on a whirling disc)[25] the result is a clear vision of the ultimate destination of the soul – immortality such as the Mithraic bull achieved through death. Under the guise of Mithraism Campbell is approaching the mysteries of Christian salvation. The seven combined hues show us 'that sole star' (the Sun, God) which perceives in us kindred sparks of its own life, like the egg of the Phoenix, an age-old symbol of immortality, within a hardened shell.

The fifth sonnet is the first of the Seven Sword poems. There can be no doubt that Campbell deliberately made them both complex and obscure. He was, after all, dealing with moments of personal crisis and pain which he would not willingly open to the public gaze. In a later poem, 'Orpheus', which could be described as a review of his life, he refers to the seven swords as a code, a

> . . . morse of green and crimson fires
> whose messages must not be told –

and goes on,

> decoding the forbidden words
> I sang them to my starving herds,
> the stock of Seven Deadly Sires
> whom only harmony can hold.
>
> (CP, II, 127)

These seven poems detail moments of suffering or illumination – and moments of sin. For the seven swords in the Virgin's heart represent the seven deadly sins of mankind, and Campbell came to believe that his sufferings were the result of his sins. Pain implied guilt. Each of these poems marks what Campbell saw as a stage in his spiritual advance.

From Apollinaire and from the rainbow Campbell had got the idea of giving each sword one of the seven colours. It seems too that he originally contemplated linking each with a metal or other substance, and with an emotion or state of mind. If that was his plan, he did not bring it to fruition. The colours of the swords are, in order, clear (crystal), blue, green, red/orange, silver, golden, and clear again. They seem to be made of crystal, air, ice, flame, silver, lightning, and flame again; and the states of mind they represent are ecstasy, peace, sorrow, anger, grief, joy, and lust. The basis of the plan is there, but Campbell did not carry it through in detail.

The first Sword poem hints obliquely at the chief sorrow that affected his life, his unhappy relationship with Mary:

> The first's of lunar crystal hewn,
> a woman's beauty, through whose snows

the volted ecstasy outglows
a dolphin dying in the noon;
and fights for love, as that for life . . .
(CP, I, 118)

In *Light on a Dark Horse* Campbell noted, 'I have seen that famous fish which sailors correctly call the "dolphin". . . dying on the deck of the *Inkonka* and the gorgeous colours swirling, in humming-bird tornasols, through its greenish-silver body . . .',[26] and in comparing Mary to the captured fish, Campbell shows again his awareness of the degree to which she felt herself trapped by his love. This first Sword poem was almost certainly written early in 1933, when Mary's affair with Jeanne had just ended. And as, after winning Mary back from Vita, Campbell had celebrated his triumph in the 'Song' in *Flowering Reeds*, so the last lines of 'The First Sword' sound the same note of triumph in the same Homeric terms:

this sword was tempered in my blood
when all its tides were at the flood
and heroes fought upon the strand.
(CP, I, 118)

If the first of these seven sonnets is a celebration of Campbell's achievement of a partial reconciliation with his wife, the second reveals him gradually coming to terms with himself. It has something of the mood of 'Mass at Dawn', and draws inspiration in the same way from the peace Campbell found in working as a fisherman on the Étang de Berre:

a low blue flame, the halcyon's flight
passing at sunset swift and free
along the miles of tunny-floats . . .
when evening strews the rosy fleece
and the low conches sound from far,
a lonely bird whose sword of air
is hilted with the evening star
has slain upon the shrine of peace
the daily slaving forms I wear.
(CP, I, 118)

Campbell put the experience that lies behind this sonnet into prose, in *Light on a Dark Horse*:

Far out on the milk-white dead calm waters of the Mediterranean, in late spring . . . when the tunny-floats lay out in mile-long straight lines behind the drifting boats; when wine had been drunk, the lanterns lit, and the last conch had sounded its mournful signal across the bay; when it seemed blasphemy even to speak or whisper a single word, and sacrilege to move, except from one elbow to another – the only perceptible movement in the whole gulf would be the low flight of the sacred halcyons, always taken singly along the line of the tunny-floats, moving about a foot above them . . . Bird after bird would silently cross the bay in this manner till long after nightfall, and it seemed that this low, level movement was the only possible expression of that supernatural radiance and peace.[27]

Like 'Horses on the Camargue' or 'St Peter of the Three Canals', 'The Second Sword' records the period in Provence when Campbell began to draw closer to the simple belief of the Provençal fishermen, by living in daily contact with nature as they did.

'The Third Sword' was originally printed as the first sword, and it is a picture of what Campbell felt to be his original isolation from God. Campbell draws for imagery on the arctic landscapes of the Yukon poet R. W. Service, who had so influenced his boyhood verse. The third sword is a green aurora borealis flickering about the arctic horizon, preventing Campbell from reaching 'the grail', as the miners of Service's lugubrious ballads so often freeze before finding the lode.

This sombre mood is lifted by 'The Fourth Sword', with its picture of the crimson-and-gold tiger-fly probing the depths of a grape for sweetness. In the same way, Campbell suggests, God will seek out the best in him despite his 'soured and black despairs'. The 'toreadoring sylph' will rouse him in rage if not in love, as the bullfighter provokes the bull to act out the climax of what Campbell thought was a Mithraic ritual. The connection between fly and bullfighter is made through the brilliant red-and-gold 'suits of light' which matadors wear in the Spanish course of bulls.

'The Fifth Sword' (which in the volume *Mithraic Emblems* is subtitled 'In memory of my father') expresses Campbell's grief and lifelong guilt at the unsettled quarrels he had had with his adored father just before the latter's death. In terms heavily influenced by Apollinaire[28] he laments the memory which,

> . . . a lifetime to consume,
> in vigilance is still the same,
> a sword of silver in the gloom
> it guards a grief that is my shame . . .
> (CP, I, 120)

The significance of this grief and shame here is that in moving closer to God Campbell felt he was also closing the rift between his strictly religious father and himself; he was moving closer to the traditional family values his father had symbolized, and against which he had rebelled.

'The Sixth Sword', as it was reprinted in *Collected Poems* in 1949, is a straightforward salute to Franco's Spain ('her, by all the world betrayed'), to the 'last Crusade' against the Spanish Communists, and to Franco's red-and-gold flag. But in 1933, when the poem was originally written, Campbell cared nothing for the coming conflict. As he first wrote it, the poem ended

> forged only of those living rays
> of whom its lustre is the praise
> the sixth salutes with lifted blade
> the passing oriflammes of days
> to whose white prancing cavalcade
> the red blood drums the Marseillaise.[29]

Far from being a declaration of religious and political affinity with the Franco regime, it was originally a restatement of Campbell's concern with passing time, and like 'The Altar', with which the sonnet sequence began, it is triumphant. Campbell was coming to terms not only with himself and his God, but with advancing age.

The Sword sonnets end, however, on a note of irresolution. In 'The Seventh Sword' Campbell comes back to the problem he dealt with in 'The First Sword': his troubled relationship with Mary. The seventh sword is a phallic symbol:

> The seventh arms a god's desire
> who lusts, in Psyche, to possess
> his white, reluctant pythoness . . .
>   (CP, I, 121)

Mary is seen once again as the personification of Campbell's psyche, as she was in poem after poem in *Flowering Reeds*; and once again she evades the union he seeks with her. She is, Campbell says, arctic ice fleeing his fire, and though he pictures her reflecting the light he sheds (as 'arctic crystals' each reflect the 'living sun') the image merely reinforces our awareness of the distance between them. The final sexual image is equally strained:

> so to the shining sword he probes,
> her breasts are lighted, and their globes
> each to a vase of crystal wrought.

In the last of these important Sword poems Campbell has combined his longing to draw closer to Mary and his search for God, and the images he uses are such as to make us doubt the success of either quest. One further point reinforces this uncertainty – 'The Seventh Sword' has only thirteen lines. This is not an oversight; Campbell was a careful workman, and 'Mithraic Emblems' was hammered out over several years. It seems clear that in leaving 'The Seventh Sword' incomplete he is hinting at the impossibility of his fully achieving union with the objects of his desire, the 'grail/whose glory I shall never see'.

The Seven Swords are stages in Campbell's quest for unity: unity of being, union with Mary, and union with God. They represent a turning away from his youthful revolt against religion, against the conventional morality of his family, and against his fellow men. His desire to turn to God, to bind his wife to himself, to share the companionship of his fellows, to be reconciled to the traditions of his family – none of these needs was entirely new to Campbell, but each is given new expression in the seven Sword poems. The stages of development they represent foreshadow dramatic changes in him. Within a few years of writing them the one-time revolutionary would be an arch-conservative; the hermit a town-dweller; the atheist a Christian; the Bohemian a devoted family man; the anarchist a lover of military discipline. His conversion was not as wholesale as he liked to think it, but in a sense the seven Sword poems mark the pivot on which his life turned, though the change was neither immediate nor complete.

The remaining sonnets, the two 'Raven' poems and 'The Raven's Nest', elaborate Campbell's application of the details of the Mithraic sacrifice to his own life. He connects it with the Phoenix (which like the Raven was associated with the Sun and with immortality) and uses it to restate his obsession with the passage of time. In a powerful image, he pictures time as the slow piling-up of the bird's nest, composed of the memories of once-vivid life – an image which conveys his new belief that the end of life would be, for him as for the Phoenix, a beginning:

> . . . steeper yet he stacks the pyre
> to tempt the forked, cremating fire
> to strike, to kindle, and consume:
> till answering beacons shall attest
> that fire is in the Raven's nest
> and resurrection in the tomb.   (CP, I, 122)

It is clear from his letters that the first fourteen sonnets were all Campbell had completed of 'Mithraic Emblems' before he left France at the end of 1933. He had certainly completed only fourteen sonnets by January 1934;[30] and of the remaining nine several were not added until 1936. 'Death of the Bull', for instance, was not written before the end of June 1936,[31] though it is deeply imbued with the landscape of Provence, as deeply as any of the poems which Campbell actually wrote there. 'Mithraic Emblems' falls into two distinct parts. The first fourteen sonnets deal with Campbell's slow and hesitant conversion, and his coming to terms with himself and his wife; the remaining nine, written after his conversion, are much less complex and obscure. The last of them, 'To the Sun', is openly Christian, the Sun/Son quibble becoming explicit. (For this reason Campbell separated it from the rest in *Mithraic Emblems*.) These nine reveal steadily increasing religious commitment, and in Spain, as the Civil War drew near, religious commitment had dangerous political consequences.

Campbell was very slow to commit himself politically to the right wing in Spain. This is the more surprising when one observes that he had been moving away from the left-wing views of his youth ever since he had left England for France in 1928. His reaction against 'Bloomsbury' had included a rejection of the generally left-wing values he had encountered at Long Barn. In *The Georgiad* he had linked socialist views with the levelling mediocrity of literary cliques:

> They hatch Utopias from their dusty brains
> Which are but Hells, where endless boredom reigns –
> Middle-class Hells, built on a cheap, clean plan,
> Edens of abnegation, dread to scan,
> Founded upon a universal ban:
> For banned from thence is all that fires or thrills . . .
>
> (CP, I, 223)

Increasingly he associated socialism with the death of individuality, of the personal achievements he valued so highly. And as he saw in the ordinary people of Provence (jousters, cattlemen, and bullfighters) the personification of the individual valour he advocated, so he pictured all his enemies as a vague composite figure, Charlie Chaplin, Bernard Shaw, and a crooked businessman rolled into one:

> There is a kind of man who wears woollen under-pants, carries horrible little black umbrellas, is afraid of Germs and objects to almost everything in life, especially to anything that surpasses him in valour or skill. This type is

the ancient Nordic Barbarian or Druid breaking free from the chivalry of the Celt, the civilization of the Roman, and the culture of the Greek. . . .[32]

he wrote confusedly in *Taurine Provence*. He was hardly more coherent or logical when trying to express the nature of the 'Nacion Gardian' (the imaginary Nation of Horsemen) which he so admired:

The Nacion Gardian can never die; shoved into the last corner of Europe it has fought one of the most powerful 'progressive' governments [that of France]; it has thundered down democratic and liberal ideas . . . it is founded on very deep intellectual traditions dating back to Cervantes, Velasquez, Greco, St. Theresa, and St. John of the Cross. If, as I do not believe, the modern equestrian can be chased out and destroyed by mechanical people and Shavians . . . at least it will have to be admitted that we did not struggle for 'existence'; we struggled for life against death . . . [33]

The fact seems to be that Campbell had no theoretical political views, he had only personal likes and dislikes. He was in no sense a deep political thinker. His attempts to weld his likes and dislikes into a coherent system invariably failed. He was not unaware of this. In *Broken Record* he wrote significantly, 'Like other poets of the past, I am more interested in my friends, neighbours and enemies, than in the newspapers or vast distant groups. My reactions come out of personal contacts, and not group urges.'[34]

Wyndham Lewis tried hard to convert the poet to his own brand of right-wing thought. Early in 1930, for example, he sent Campbell the series of articles he was later to print as his book *Hitler*, in which he lauds the Nazi leader as 'a man of peace', and praises the way the Nazis were 'cleaning up the moral filth' of Germany.[35] Campbell, in striking contrast to his usual fervent praise of Lewis's work, told his friend that he found the articles 'very interesting', and the result of all Lewis's efforts was a mildly approving reference to the dictator in *Broken Record*.[36] Lewis was eventually to conclude, with some exasperation, that 'of politics he [Campbell] has none, unless they are such as go with a great antipathy for the English "gentleman" in all his clubmanesque varieties; a great attachment to the back-Veldt of his native South Africa; and a constant desire to identify himself with the roughest and simplest of his fellow-creatures in pub, farm, and bull-ring.'[37]

What Lewis terms his 'great attachment to the back-Veldt' emerges most strikingly in a poem Campbell had begun in August 1933,[38] shortly before deciding to leave France for Spain, though the final draft was not completed before July 1936.[39] The poem is 'Junction of

Rails'. It shows perhaps more clearly than any other how much, and how hopelessly, Campbell longed for a pastoral world of nobles and peasants, and how much he hated, or pretended to hate, trade and technology in all its forms – trains and telegraphs, cities, radios, capitalists, ships and even macadamized roads. He longed naively for a simpler world, with a Romantic longing that is reminiscent of D. H. Lawrence's constant dreams of a 'colony of escape'. 'Junction of Rails' is spoken by the very spirit of steel, which serves man obediently and waits for his downfall. The poem begins with a vision of a distant city, wittily conceived of as a prosperous capitalist:

> Cities of cinemas and lighted bars,
> Smokers of tall bituminous cigars,
> Whose evenings are a smile of golden teeth –
> Upon your cenotaphs I lay this wreath
> And so commend you to the moon and stars.
>
> (CP, I, 149)

And in contrasting the electric lights of the city with 'the moon and stars' Campbell in the first stanza sums up in a single deft touch his attitude to all that the city stands for. It is as dirty as the smoke it produces; it is as showily and artificially attractive as a gold tooth; and above all it is impermanent. One remembers Campbell's evocation, in a much earlier poem, of

> The timeless, surly patience of the serf
> That moves the nearest to the naked earth
> And ploughs down palaces, and thrones, and towers.[40]

It is because the city, by its very nature, is removed from 'the naked earth' that Campbell predicts and desires its destruction. The more rapid the advance of technology, he suggests, the more certain its defeat.

> Though they have taught the lightning how to lie
> And made their wisdom to misread the sky
> I hold their pulses: through my ringing loom
> Their trains with flying shuttles weave a doom
> I am too sure a prophet to defy.
>
> (CP, I, 150)

The 'doom' the steel speaks of is a universal cataclysm that will crush the fruits of technology at once – a great war of the sort Campbell by 1933 foresaw very clearly. After the holocaust, he liked to believe, there would be left the green world he dreamed of, a simpler world of cowboys and ploughboys and poets. Characteristically, he sees this cleansing destruction in religious terms, likening it to the destruction of the Cities of the Plain, and the poem ends with a paean almost mystical in its fervour:

> A sword is singing and a scythe is reaping
> In those great pylons prostrate in the dust,
> Death has a sword of valour in his keeping
> To arm our souls towards the future leaping:
> And holy holy holy is the rust
> Wherein the blue Excaliburs are sleeping!
>
> (CP, I, 152)

In a curious passage in *Broken Record*, Campbell expresses this mystical faith in the ultimate triumph of those whose lifestyle is in harmony with nature:

> While the solar, yellow and blue spirits of gold and steel revolt against their misuse in the modern world . . . as if they wanted to come back to their native use, as the swords, tools and ornaments of men; the iron of trident forged in Cailar* will never rust, nor the studs tarnish on the bridles of the *gardiens*; and they will live to make anachronisms of the 'Flying Scotsman', the 'Berengaria', and all our oversized, unwieldy hustling mechanical burdens . . .[41]

How far Campbell had come from the days when, at Oxford, he had read and quoted Marinetti with approval, and from the description in *The Flaming Terrapin* of

> . . . a fierce train, maned like a ramping lion
> With smoke and fire . . .
>
> (CP, I, 84)

Increasingly during the Thirties he came to see scientific progress as a regression, and in many ways his views look forward to those of the conservationist movement of our own time, its roots deep in Romanticism.

Shortly after sending off an early draft of 'Junction of Rails' to his publisher Greenwood, who included it in the *Mithraic Emblems* volume, Campbell received a copy of Wyndham Lewis's *One Way Song*, in November 1933. In this long poem Lewis expresses views very similar to those Campbell had put forward in 'Junction of Rails'. Lewis derides at length the modern obsession with machinery, making his characters talk like steam-engines ('Say it with locomo-

---

* The 'trident' is the long, three-pronged cattle-goad of the Provençal cowboy or *gardien*.

tives!'), but the focus of his attack, like Campbell's, is on what Lewis saw as the growing tendency to ignore the lessons of history, and to imagine that all problems could be solved by 'progress'. Campbell was surprised at the similarity of Lewis's views to his own; at the way Lewis refers to the train as 'half a horse' which has 'eclipsed' the real animal and 'shrivelled stooks and stubble'; at the way Lewis described progress as

> All temporal hustle, tantamount to a stunt
> To affect to run – all the wild gestures of speed –
> Stock-still in fact, we stamp out Change's seed . . .[42]

and at the way Lewis believed that technology would destroy itself:

> Important as are power stations, the clock
> Is more so. *Este Memor!* Sedate tick-tock!
> It's my belief that Master-Clock does hold
> The death-warrant of the four-faced time-manifold.[43]

With his usual modesty about his work, Campbell wrote at once to Lewis to acknowledge his 'debt':

The whole of One way is a great treat – it made me laugh like hell. My 'Junction of Rails' is not properly satirical but the similarity is striking and I must have been thinking in precisely the same direction as you since we last met, my mental pendulum of course having been given a swing by you. Idea after idea are similar yet I've seen nothing out of England since Snooty and a book of poems by Spender, but I cottoned on at once . . . To return to the Flying Scot, it is astounding how many ideas I have got the same as you – I call it an 'iron rocinante of the rail':* I use the words Tick-tock in the same way etc.[44]

Lewis, on seeing Campbell's poem, called it 'an amazing instance of Telepathy'.[45] But Campbell was too ready to pay, and Lewis to receive, homage. The romantic and conservative values Campbell expresses in 'Junction of Rails' were deep-rooted in his character from the first; despite the similarity of occasional phrases in the two poems, there are differences which are still more striking. For Lewis condemns those who (like Campbell) seem to want to return to the past, as strongly as he condemns those who try to ignore it:

> Try and walk backwards: you will quickly see
> How you were meant only *one-way* to be! . . .
> Endeavour to re-occupy the Past:
> Your stubborn front will force you to stand fast!

* A phrase he deleted before publishing the poem.

(No traffic-caption of *Sens Interdit*
Is necessary for this clearly one-way street.)[46]

Campbell's debt to Lewis was not as great as either of them imagined.
Campbell echoed the views he expressed in 'Junction of Rails' in
several later poems, also published in *Mithraic Emblems*. In 'Rust' he
presents a horrifying picture of the war which was going to consume
the world. In imagery that invites comparison with the work of Owen
or Sassoon, he describes a war where

> . . . dropped asphyxiating dung
> Shall fall exploding blood and mire;
> Whose cropping teeth of rattled fire
> Shall make one cud of old and young;
> (CP, I, 148)

and from which will spring, when the carnage is done,

> . . . the dainty flower
> That, herding on that blasted heath,
> A cowboy chews between his teeth.
> (CP, I, 148)

The same simplistic longing for a return to the primitive, independent
world of the cowboy is found in 'Vaquero to his Wife', and in 'To the
Survivors'. Campbell, of course, had no assurance that he himself
would survive the coming cataclysm. He sees the ultimate triumph of
his ideals in terms of the 'new heaven and new earth' of the book of
Revelation; he certainly did not foresee the form the coming conflict
would take.

The most unpolitical of men could not have failed to notice the violent
unrest that was sweeping through Spain in wave after wave. After the
elections of November 1933 the country sank steadily towards chaos
and war. Strike followed strike; political murders became common;
the Communists plotted and the Anarchists planted bombs, the right
wing talked darkly of the need for a military takeover to prevent
anarchy.[47] Even the Campbells, with their limited Spanish, could
clearly understand the signs of coming trouble. When the bombing
eased off in Barcelona, and the government machine-guns disappeared
from the street corners, the atmosphere of unrest persisted; they were
often turned back by the Guardia Civil when they set out for their
evening stroll on the Ramblas.[48]

Though Campbell was writing well in Barcelona, they soon grew tired of their cold and crowded rooms in the Calle San Pablo. In any case the brothel-quarter of a Spanish city hardly seemed the place to bring up their two daughters, now aged eleven and seven. They decided to find a village where they could resume their country existence and eke out their allowance (£20 still coming each month from South Africa) by growing some of their own food. They used most of their remaining money to buy tickets to Valencia; they said goodbye to Uys Krige who had decided to stay on in Barcelona; and in March 1934 they piled all their luggage, their dog and themselves into a third-class compartment, and went looking for a new home. It proved to be a nightmarish journey. Occasionally, at likely-looking villages, they would leave the train and go exploring. If the village seemed a pleasant one, they would try to find a house to rent. They had no success. The villages were as much alive with politics as Barcelona had been; each little dusty square was loud with the drilling of its young men – Falange or Anarchist, Carlist or Communist. The local people were suspicious of these foreigners with their shabby luggage and stumbling Spanish. As they went from village to unfriendly village, turned away everywhere, spending their nights in bug-ridden inns, the Campbells grew more and more desperate. Campbell as usual imagined himself to be ill or about to go mad, and took to drink again;[49] their money dwindled faster than ever.

They arrived in Valencia tired, cold, and virtually penniless. In the Calle de la Padilla, near the Arena, they found a room even more squalid than the ones they had left in Barcelona, and in an area as sordid. The city was paralysed by a general strike. Campbell, in moments of sobriety, got a temporary job as an unskilled worker in the bullring.[50] It was in Valencia that their miseries culminated in a furious quarrel which went on for days and ended in Mary's decision, not for the first time, to leave Campbell. Their two frightened daughters never forgot this quarrel. Tess, the elder, decided that when the break finally came she would go with her mother.[51] But this new low point in their married lives passed, as others had done, and when Campbell won 1,000 pesetas, then worth about £17, on the National Lottery, it seemed a good omen.[52] They set off again, always moving south, and at last their luck changed. They stopped in Alicante, then still innocent of tourists, and it was near Alicante that Mary 'found' the village of Altea, in May 1934. Superbly set between the mountains and the sea, Altea attracted the Campbells at once. They stayed for a week at the local inn, the Fonda Ronda, until they

were able to rent a small peasant house, and after a few months move
to a bigger one, set on a few acres of land among scrubby olive trees
about a mile out of the village, with orange groves all around.[53] They
bought a donkey to cart their supplies from the village up a rutted
track, and even to fetch water from a nearby spring, in great
containers slung in panniers. Their life was, in material details, not
unlike that of the threadbare peasants around them.[54] Campbell wrote
with relief to Wyndham Lewis, 'I seem to have got into heaven – with
no debts, nothing annoying or troublesome. But I had a fierce time of
it for some months. . .'[55]

It was in Altea that their conversion to Catholicism, so long
portended in Campbell's verse, took place. Characteristically, it was
Mary who made the decision. Like Campbell, she had had a strictly
Christian upbringing; like him, she had broken away from belief in
her teens. Now the uncertainties and miseries of her life with
Campbell revived her need for faith. For some time she had been
reading the letters of St. Teresa of Avila (after whom Tess had been
named), and the quarrel in Valencia had the effect of bringing to a
head a process that had been going on in her as it had in Campbell.
Not long after their arrival in Altea she announced abruptly, 'I'm
going to become a Catholic.' And Campbell without hesitation
replied, 'Well, kid, if you're going to I will too.'[56] They presented
themselves to the village priest, Father Gregorio, announced their
intention, and asked for instruction in their new faith. The simple
man was delighted by the idea of a whole family of 'English' being
won over to the Church.

Campbell poured some of the fervour of his belief, and also the long
struggle that lay behind it, into one of his finest poems, 'The Fight',
written at this time. In it, he symbolized his movement towards belief
(indeed, his whole life up to this point) as an aerial dogfight:[57]

> Two aeroplanes were fighting in the blue
> Above our town; and if I held my breath,
> It was because my youth was in the Red
> While in the White an unknown pilot flew –
> And that the White had risen overhead.
>
> (CP, I, 155)

Campbell undoubtedly saw his youth as 'red' not only because it had
been sinful, but because of his earlier strong left-wing views; while the
'white' symbolizes Mithras's united seven colours, and the purity of
Christ. Campbell describes the battle in vividly realistic terms:

From time to time the crackle of a gun
Far into flawless ether faintly railed,
And now, mosquito-thin, into the Sun,
And now like mating dragonflies they sailed . . .

The Red craft is shot down, flaming, and out of that flame, phoenix-like, rises the White. Campbell points the significance of the poem in terms that are explicitly and triumphantly Christian:

The towers and trees were lifted hymns of praise,
The city was a prayer, the land a nun:
The noonday azure, strumming all its rays
Sang that a famous battle had been won,
As signing his white Cross, the very Sun,
The Solar Christ and captain of my days
Zoomed to the zenith; and his will was done.

(CP, I, 156)

After plumbing the depths of misery in Valencia the Campbells had found a home and a faith in Altea. Life there came close to satisfying Campbell's ideals of a primitive, pastoral world free alike of modern conveniences and modern tensions. His letters paint a picture of almost complete withdrawal from the world:

We have a lovely house. Huge square and roomy with olive trees and locust trees all round. There are no roads here except the one main road to Alicante from Valencia . . . We have lost all our books clothes and furniture in France . . . I have become almost ascetic as I always do when I get going with poetry and I hardly eat or sleep at all . . .[58]

Until today I haven't seen a peseta since April 24th: and I had to give the postman a fowl for my last stamp to you. I live entirely on my farm and what it produces . . . I am even growing my own Tobacco. Beyond my rent I have no other expenses and believe I have at last found the way to deal with the crisis – i.e. by living without any cash at all.[59]

He began making friends with the other foreigners in the neighbourhood: with Bill Sykes, a large and amiable American, and with two Norwegians, Helge Krog and Erling Winsness. Krog, whom the Campbells had met in a local tavern when he admired their dog Sarah, was a playwright, and Campbell at his request rephrased the English translations Krog's wife had made of his plays, and got them published as his (Campbell's) own translations. He wrote of these men,

Helge was a Communist and Erling was a Nazi, but they were both staunchly united in their hate of Christ and Christianity . . . These men were like children; they would argue violently and then totter up, helping each other from side to side, lovingly to bed. Oh! If only people could take their politics as lightly and boozily as Norwegians!⁶⁰

His own political commitment, meanwhile, was growing steadily. The influences of friends and enemies, and of his own background, caused him to incline towards the Right; but the decisive factor was his conversion to Catholicism. Belief in God, in Spain at this time, was itself a political act. The Church was inextricably linked with the great quarrels which were now coming to a head: the struggle between the Separatist movements and the central authority, and the struggle between the bourgeoisie and a large section of the working class. The Church was committed to the maintenance of the old order, and in consequence the Left's hatred of established religion reached in Spain an intensity such as the world has seldom seen. Campbell, holding to his new faith with all the passion of a recent convert, could not and did not stand aloof. The battle lines were being drawn, and he was no longer in doubt as to what side he was on.

In Altea late in 1934, however, the issues still seemed more academic than real. The Campbells read no papers and owned no radio. The mail was unreliable at best, and when the little river came down in flood they were cut off from the outside world for days at a time. Campbell could occupy his time with writing, or drinking with Krog; in the evenings he and Mary would play their guitars together, singing sea-shanties or Scots and Spanish songs. They took long walks into the mountains. As Campbell wrote to a friend, 'We often go for 20 mile walks inland to delightful mountain villages. Festivals are in full swing, and everybody seems happy . . . I hope to stop here for many years. It is a good base for wandering through Spain. Mary and I are going to take a mule-trip through the country. Horses for the present are beyond my purse . . .'⁶¹

Freedom from worry enabled him to work extremely fast at this time. On 1 September 1934, for instance, he completed the drafts of six poems in a single night.⁶² He balanced these intense spells of writing with days of healthy physical activity. Often the family would load their donkey with pots, and make a day-long pilgrimage, in company with their maid's family, through the vineyards to the spring of Santa Ana, whose water was renowned for its taste and purity. They would roast a picnic lunch of *boboches* (skewered meat) over a fire, returning to their house at sunset. It was about a glass *botico* of the water of Santa Ana that Campbell wrote his poem 'A Jug of Water',[63] which opens with a unique description of the interplay of light in water, 'this frosty chrysalis of flame':

> The silver life and swordplay of the noon
> Caught in mid-slash; the wildfire of the scar
> Whose suds of thunder in a crystal jar
> Compose a silent image of the moon.
>
> Shut rainbow; hushed appeasement of the spray . . .
>   (CP, I, 132)

And Campbell goes on, with a metaphysical ingenuity reminiscent of Vaughan or Crashaw, to explore the implications of water's beauty and indestructability:

> Pool in the grime by city lanterns scarred,
> Stainless it still from every contact came
> As the light incense, orphan of the flame,
> Survives the baser fuel it has charred.
>   (CP, I, 134)

Water, changeless through many changes, reflecting the light whether it be that of street-lamp or star, is for Campbell an image of Faith – faith to remain constant through 'the world's great autumn' which he thought imminent. And the lesson he drew from the water is

> That love is God, that dying is renewal,
> That we are flames, and the black world is fuel
> To hearts that burn and battle for delight.
>   (CP, I, 135)

It seems clear that Campbell expected the approaching conflict to culminate in an all-destroying Armageddon, and that the triumph he hoped and longed for was the triumph of the Resurrection.

The same hope for resurrection closes another poem for which Campbell found inspiration in Altea. The village itself had no bullring, but there was one in nearby Alicante, and it was almost certainly in the Alicante arena, in May 1934, that Campbell saw a young bullfighter, Florentino Ballesteros, killed. Campbell was a man easily moved to tears, and one who therefore took pains to hide his emotional vulnerability, but there is no disguising the pity and terror that speak through the vivid opening of 'The Dead Torero':

> Such work can be the mischief of an hour.
> This drunken-looking doll without a face
> Was lovely Florentino. This was grace
> And virtue smiling on the face of Power.

Shattered, that slim Toledo-tempered spine!
Hollow, the chrysalis, his gentle hand,
From which those wide imperial moths were fanned
Each in its hushed miraculous design!

                                                                    (CP, I, 143)

Campbell's new faith made him a much happier and more stable person. He drank rather less at this time, and made several valiant attempts to stop drinking completely; his relationship with Mary as a result seems to have been less strained. He began resuming contact with his literary friends. He wrote to Wyndham Lewis that he was breeding 'pigs and donkeys which I hope to sell to the British public as poets'.[64] Lewis ignored this sally and, after letting more than a year elapse, replied,

Much blood has flowed beneath the arches of my ribs since I last wrote you. *All* my juvenile inattentiveness to the dictates of sex hygiene came home to roost. To cap everything else I have for six months been engaged in a battle royal with a lump of scar-tissue – the upshot of a wound inflicted upon me by a dangerous surgeon . . .

I should like to hear your voice again – both in the flesh & in the fields of letters. As for me I have written a large political book, about the ideas behind current events – 'Red', 'Black', 'Brown' & of course Blue. Cassells have had a 150 thousand-word novel of mine in their blasted office for 3 months now; as Boots is their master* they want Boots to be my master. Impasse! It is about the revolt in the Asturias.[65]

This 150,000-word novel was *The Revenge for Love*, whose central character, Victor Stamp, a large, sincere, naive Australian artist, bears resemblances to Campbell.

Tristram Hillier visited them once again in June 1934, and took them touring for a week, along the coast.[66] Uys Krige, who had been living for some months in Valencia, came to stay with his mistress Emelia, a pretty, crippled Catalan girl, early in 1935. He left her for seven months with the Campbells while he went off to find work in Belgium and Holland, promising to return and marry her. And Campbell's mother, then touring the world as she had done several times since the death of her husband, arrived and stayed in Altea for several weeks, in May 1935. Accustomed to luxury, she was taken aback by the Campbells' spartan life-style: by the bare whitewashed peasant house, the outside toilet, the water that had to be fetched in

---

* Cassells were afraid that Boots Lending Library would demand the censoring of *The Revenge for Love*.

pots, the threadbare clothing, the donkey that was led through the house each night to his stall at the back. She had never imagined that Roy would let his family live like this. She bought them a new stove, and introduced them to some of the American gadgets she had discovered on her travels; she bought them all new shoes and new clothes. And she decreed that Tess and Anna should be sent to school, for their education had been extremely haphazard, although Mary had taught them English and History, and Campbell had given them lessons in Geography and Astronomy. Tess, now nearly thirteen, should be sent to school in England, and the Campbells should move to a town where Anna could attend a Spanish school. Mrs Campbell would pay for all this.[67]

Early in June 1935, then, the Campbells left for Madrid with Campbell's mother. They were to look for a new house, and Campbell wanted to consult a doctor about the backache he had, one of his perennial ailments, while Tess was to go on with the energetic old lady to a school in England. On the way to Madrid, and again on the way back, having parted from an excited Tess, they made a detour to Toledo, staying for a day each time in the Hotel Lino.[68] They liked the city at first sight. Perched on its rise above the gorge of the Tagus, its grey houses gathered tight under the walls of a great fortress, the Alcazar, it seemed to preserve still the spirit of the noble, Christian Spain of the Emperor Charles V, whose arms, massively carved in stone, still adorned the city's Visagra gate, facing Madrid. And in fact Toledo had changed remarkably little since the days when it had been Charles's capital. It was a severe, introverted city of narrow streets up which donkeys carried panniers, a city of little hidden plazas that had been Moorish market-places, of medieval battlements and fifteenth-century palaces. Above all, it was a city of churches, monasteries, and convents, extraordinarily numerous for a place of such small popula-tion.* The contrast between the grave beauty of Toledo and Madrid's feverish glare struck the Campbells forcibly. They rented a small house just opposite the cathedral, 18 Calle Cardinal Cisneros, and then went back to Altea to pack up.

They had all this time been receiving instruction in Catholic doctrine from the priest in Altea, and two days before leaving the village for good they were received into the Church, re-baptized and remarried, most of the population of the village turning out for the ceremony and for the party which followed it. Father Gregorio

---

* 28,000, by the last census before the Civil War.

declared roundly that it was the best day of his life; the peasants wept and embraced the converts. Campbell chose as his patron saint Ignatius Loyola, founder of the most militant of monastic orders; Mary, no less significantly, chose Mary Magdalene. The next day Campbell wrote to Enslin du Plessis, 'At last I am in the land of my dreams!'[69] The same letter contained the first hint any of his friends had had about his religious conversion; and linked with it was evidence of his growing political awareness:

I don't know much about communism, but I have seen that many valiant and generous men take up that form of imitation-christianity. But they are not happy.

Yesterday I had the good fortune to be baptised and married in the Catholic Church. I wish you the same luck.[70]

Thus religion and politics, Campbell's life in Toledo and his life in the Church, were from the start linked in his mind. The city in which he was about to take up residence, cramped, stony, and backward, was for him the City of God.

XI

Toledo

1935–1936

IT was very shortly after their arrival in Toledo that the Campbells, drinking at a café one night, met a young Englishman playing a violin in the main square for coppers. He told them that he was tramping through Spain; they invited him home for dinner. His name was Laurie Lee. In *As I Walked Out One Midsummer Morning* Lee records the meeting:

There were four of them: a woman in dazzling white, a tall man wearing a broad black hat, a jaunty young girl with a rose in her hair, followed by a pretty lacy child.
    They were clearly not Spanish, yet they had a Spanish air. I thought they might possibly have been Portuguese. The man sat at the table with a distinguished stoop . . . . He had a long scorched face and the eyes of a burnt-out eagle. He offered me a strong but shaky hand. 'Roy Campbell,' he said. 'South African poet. Er – reasonably well known in your country.'
    His voice was musically hoarse, yet broken and interrupted as though ·being transmitted on faulty wires, and it seemed to quaver between bursts of sudden belligerence and the most humble of hesitations.[1]

Campbell proceeded to tell Lee that he hated England, that all his friends were English, and was Lee broke and could he do with any help? Lee was fascinated by Campbell, and intoxicated by his poetry. He stayed with the Campbells for a week, scribbling in his notebooks during the day, drinking with Campbell at night. Campbell told him that he drank four and a half litres of wine a day. Mary Campbell tried, without success, to convert Lee to Catholicism.

Shortly after Lee left to continue his travels (depositing with the Campbells several notebooks which he later came back to collect) the poet moved with his family to a much larger and grander house, number 13, Airosas. Once the summer villa of a cardinal, it was built into the moorish ramparts near the great Visagra gate. With its lofty rooms, its great stone staircase, and its deep cool garden, it was easily the biggest and best house Campbell ever rented.* 'Prosperity such as I have been experiencing for about the first time in my existence since I first ran away from Oxford, has a very good effect on my work . . .', he wrote to Greenwood his publisher.[2] The house even had its own large fountain, which froze in winter and stank in summer. One evening Campbell, drunker than usual, stumbled against this fountain and fell into it. When he sat up, gasping and bubbling, he found his landlord standing staring open-mouthed at the sight. To save face, Campbell had immediately to pretend he had jumped into the fountain to refresh himself. He ducked his head repeatedly into the foul water, with every appearance of enjoyment, and then climbed out and staggered up the steps of his house, dripping green slime as he went, leaving the astonished man to reflect on the eccentricity of writers.[3]

It was at this time that Campbell wrote most of the last nine poems of the 'Mithraic Emblems' sequence. His back again gave him trouble at this period, and he spent some days late in 1935 in the hospital in Toledo being treated for it. From this experience sprang the poems 'The Mocking Bird' and 'Christ in the Hospital'.[4] He also engaged in a little horse-trading, not so much for money (though henceforth he often described himself as a professional horse-dealer) as in the hope of acquiring really good horses for his family to ride. On several occasions Campbell lost a good deal of money at his horse-dealing hobby – as when he bought a mule for a large sum, and then found that it was stone-deaf and therefore almost useless. He had always identified himself with the simplest of his fellows, and in Spain his style of life brought him frequently into contact with them. 'Thank You Very Much',[5] inspired by one of many trips he made to the nearby village of Casas Buenas, shows the deep love he had for Spain and the Spanish people. The poet arrives on his mule, tired and elated by his ride, and catches his first sight of the village,

> The church with storks upon the steeple –
> And scarcely could my cross be signed,
> When round me came those Christian people,
> So hospitable, clean, and kind.
> Beans and alfalfa in the manger
> (Alfalfa? – there was never such!)
> And rice and rabbit for the stranger –
> Thank you very much!
>
> (_Mithraic Emblems_, 166–7)

* It is now an expensive, sixty-room hotel.

It is clear that Campbell believed he had found in Castile the simple bucolic world he had longed for. It was a world which time seemed to have passed by, a world of peasants and horsemen, in which a train or a motor car would have seemed an anachronism. Even in Toledo, of course, there were motor cars, radios, and cinemas; but Campbell resolutely turned his eyes from them. His Utopian landscape forms the background to several other poems, such as 'Posada',[6] and 'After the Horse-fair', which ends with the poet's compassionate prayer uniting him with all his fellow-men:

> He prayed for lonesome carbineers
> And wakeful lovers, rash of years . . .
>
> For thieves: the gate-man late and lonely
> With his green flag; for tramps that sprawl:
> And lastly for a frozen guy
> That towed six mules along the sky
> And felt among them all the only,
> Or most a mule of all!
>
> (CP, I, 138)

The whole passage, with its humorous reference to himself as the 'frozen guy', shows that Campbell regarded the unity of all men in Christ as more than a phrase.

It was this very contact with gypsies and beggars and tramps, however, that made him aware of the approach of the now-imminent Civil War. Toledo, until early in 1936, had largely escaped the political killings and bombings which were becoming daily occurrences in cities like Madrid or Barcelona. But the situation changed dramatically after the elections in February, in which the various left-wing parties, united in the Popular Front, came to power. The elation of the Left, and the frustration of the Right, at this development, caused a great tide of violence to wash across the country.* The Church was an obvious target for the attacks of the Socialists and Anarchists; churches were desecrated and burnt all over Spain. Even in Toledo, which had inclined to the Right in the February elections, there was strong anticlerical feeling, and it culminated in a series of violent riots in March 1936, in which churches were burnt and priests and monks attacked in the streets. During these bloody days the Campbells (who had struck up a close relationship with the

---

* Though the Popular Front established itself as the leading party, it did not secure an overall majority of votes. Campbell claimed that he had been forced at gunpoint to vote for the Left in February, using a dead man's card. I have not been able to verify this story.

Carmelite friars of Toledo, some of whom became their personal friends and confessors) sheltered several monks, in lay clothes, in their house. This was, to say the least, a very dangerous thing to do, but the Campbells felt passionately that they could do nothing else. As Campbell wrote later, 'Better a broken head than a broken spirit every time!'[7] For him, the March riots were a violent shock; his idealized view of Toledo as the holy city set in a timeless pastoral world peopled by Christian peasants was smashed almost overnight. The serpent had come to power in Eden.

His relations with the common people whom he had thought his friends deteriorated rapidly. Even before the elections a local bar-keeper had shown him a formidable collection of automatic pistols, and told him that he would be shot when the time came, 'if you are still here . . . and haven't been bumped off by anyone else'.[8] A gypsy whom he had employed out of charity unexpectedly sued him for unpaid wages. The Campbells were in danger not only because they flaunted their Christianity and were known to have sheltered the hated monks, but because their big house and their two servants showed that they were rich. On 16 March 1936 Campbell was stopped by two Assault Guards (a force generally left-wing in sympathies) while he was out riding. They questioned him and, not liking his answers, beat him severely and paraded him back into town to be thrown into prison.[9] He gave a histrionic description of the scene in 'To My Jockey':[10]

> I never felt such glory
> As handcuffs on my wrists,
> My body stunned and gory
> And toothmarks on my fists,
> The triumph through the square
> (My horse behind me led),
> A pistol at my cutlets,
> Three rifles at my head.
> And four of those black bastards
> To hold a single man:
> And four to take him to the gaol –
> Proclaiming thus my clan.
>   (*Mithraic Emblems*, 99)

Campbell was questioned by the Chief of Police and released because he was a foreigner; he later invented two quite distinct stories of an heroic escape. He was very lucky not to have been shot as so many Spaniards were under similar circumstances, and as his companion that day, a gypsy named 'Mosquito' Bargas, who did occasional odd jobs for him, had been shot by the roadside just minutes before Campbell's arrest. The poet's letters convey something of the chaos of those lawless days. He sent off to Greenwood the manuscripts of the remaining 'Emblem' poems, together with 'The Family Vault' (written in December 1933),[11] 'The Crystal', 'The Argonauts', and the witty 'Fable for my Children'.[12] And he wrote dramatically,

I am rushing this off to you, as I have twice been put against the wall. The handwriting is very bad; I am sorry, but I have been so hit with rifle butts that my hands don't work . . . . I am sending this now in case I get bumped off. But I advise you to wait until I write again. If not the rest of my work will be at the house of the gypsy Rodrigo (the young one) near the Puerta del Sol, Toledo.

. . . For some reason I collect more blows than Don Quixote. God knows why! for I am amicable to everybody. But I have been run in twice, for *nothing*! Because they say that I look like a gipsy. But I have given *all* my clothes to the poor and have passed this winter in the coldest quarter of Europe (except Berlin) without any socks or under-clothes. Really bolshies make me laugh. 'Liberty'? It is *death*![13]

His narrow escape merely increased Campbell's religious enthusiasm. His obsession with the passage of time, and the approach of death, had been swept away by his conversion. Far from bewailing the approach of physical decay, he seems to have looked forward to death now that he faced it every day:

> Our tired old men lament increasing age
> Because they have no Christian Faith

he wrote in *Mithraic Emblems* (p. 101), adding defiantly,

> I do not fear to die, nor beg to live –
> This world is full of graves!

It was at this time, partly in recognition of the aid they had given the Carmelite friars during the riots, that the Campbells were confirmed in a secret ceremony, before dawn, by Cardinal Góma, the white-haired old Archbishop of Toledo and Primate of Spain. No longer need Campbell seek a cause to defend, or a group to ally himself with; the cause had sought him out, the group was well-defined, and his enemies were numerous and powerful. It was becoming dangerous to worship openly; the armed youths of both sides swaggered about the streets with increasing freedom; portraits of Marx and Lenin appeared on the walls at every street corner. From the villages tales of horror came ever more frequently: here a priest would be shot, there a rich man butchered in front of his family. The forces of the law were either helpless or partisan. Mary, going with missal and mantilla to Mass each morning, would be confronted by grinning *pistoleros* drawing their fingers threateningly across their throats.[14] Campbell grew more and more alarmed as the heat of the Castilian summer grew and the country slid towards anarchy. For once, he was more in contact with reality than Mary was. 'Kid, there's going to be a shemozzle here,' he told her fearfully. 'Let's get out.' But Mary flatly refused to leave, and it was Mary who made the decisions; they stayed.[15]

In the blazing days of early July, the narrow streets of the city trapped the heat and radiated it long after dark. Nobody could sleep. The loudspeakers in the streets relayed the braying voices of Radio Madrid, increasing tension in the promenading crowds by exhorting everyone to remain calm. The 'hit' tune of the moment, 'The Music Goes Round and Round and it Comes Out Here' echoed from a thousand radios. The Campbells' garden seemed full of hoopoes that year; the poet regarded them as birds of ill-omen, and during these quivering white days their melancholy crying filled the air with dread.

The outbreak of hostilities, when it came, was almost a relief. The Army, under General Franco, revolted against the Popular Front government on 18 July, and garrisons all over Spain and Morocco rose to seize, or attempt to seize, the town and cities. In Toledo, apart from some firing at night, and some sniping at the Civil Guards in the main square, there was comparative calm. But on the evening of 20 July the Civil Guards from outlying villages began gathering in the city, bringing their families and possessions with them.[16] The next morning Campbell and Tess (who had returned to Spain in May) were busy watering their horses and mules when they heard the sudden rattle of rifle fire. Pouring down the Madrid road, which sweeps across the low dusty hills from the north before entering Toledo by the Visagra gate, was a column of government militiamen from Madrid, four armoured cars at their head. They were already exchanging heavy fire with the men of Toledo's garrison, who had only that morning openly declared themselves in revolt. In the crisp morning air of Castile every detail of the engagement stood out clearly. Campbell spent no time in watching it; with his daughter and the animals he fled back to his house, his only concern to get out of Toledo as quickly as possible. This was by no means easy. Apart from the practical difficulties involved in organizing anything at such a time, Campbell had no ready money. With the arrival of the column from Madrid, sniping had broken out inside the city; it was dangerous to move outdoors. That afternoon and evening there were bombing raids by government aircraft on the Alcazar. On the streets, nothing moved.

When darkness fell the Carmelite monks called on Campbell: would he help them again? They wanted refuge this time not for themselves but for their priceless archives, among them the personal papers of St John of the Cross. Campbell agreed, and during the hours of darkness a heavy trunk of ancient documents was safely conveyed from the Carmelite library and deposited in the Campbells' hallway. There was another air raid early the next morning, and when it ended a battery of government guns began firing on the Alcazar from the hills north of the town. These guns were at first very inaccurate; one shell fell near Campbell's house, though without doing great damage. To proclaim his neutrality, Campbell displayed a Union Jack in his corral, but took it down hastily when he found that it drew the fire of both sides.

That afternoon the defenders of the city began to fall back towards the Alcazar itself, fighting a fierce rearguard action against the advancing Madrid militiamen. Some of the most desperate fighting took place very near the Campbells' house, for the Visagra gate and the Carmelite monastery were easily defensible positions.[17] Campbell's sonnet 'Hot Rifles'[18] conveys something of the experiences of this day, and a moment of the fighting is captured in another sonnet, 'Christ in Uniform':

> Close at my side a girl and boy
> Fell firing, in the doorway here,
> Collapsing with a strangled cheer
> As on the very couch of joy,
> And onward through a wall of fire
> A thousand others rolled the surge . . .
>
> (CP, I, 154)

The very title of this poem shows how closely Campbell identified the defenders of the Old Spain with the defenders of Christianity. For him, already, this was a holy war of Christians against the Anti-Christ.

By 22 July, the third day of the fighting, the Toledo garrison under Colonel Moscardó, with the Civil Guards and some of the richer citizens of the town, had withdrawn into the Alcazar and was being besieged by the militiamen, who began searching the city for possible supporters of the rebels. Churchmen were among the first to die; the seventeen Carmelite monks were shot in a group and left lying where they fell. Campbell, sallying cautiously out that evening, found them covered with a tarpaulin. From his house he could see the smoke of their burning library, so close that falling roof-timbers could be clearly heard; the building and the priceless collection it housed burned for days. From their back door the Campbells could see a great iron cross on the monastery roof, silhouetted against the flames. It became a symbol of resistance to them, and they would go out every morning to see if it had fallen. It never did.[19] Campbell's sonnet, 'Toledo, July 1936' shows the extent to which the fate of the Carmelite friars symbolized Toledo's agony for the poet:

> Toledo, when I saw you die
> And heard the roof of Carmel crash,
> A spread-winged phoenix from its ash
> The Cross remained against the sky!

Now, more than ever, the city of his adoption was sacred to him:

> . . . high above the roaring shells
> I heard the silence of your bells
> Who've left these broken stones behind
> Above the years to make your home,
> And burn, with Athens and with Rome,
> A sacred city of the mind.
>
> (CP, I, 153)

The same day as that on which their confessors were killed, the Campbells' house was searched, probably because of its size and prominence. The Campbells had had time to remove the crucifixes and religious pictures from their walls, but the trunk of precious Carmelite manuscripts still stood in the hall when the sweating, boiler-suited militiamen pounded on the door. The possession even of a missal could mean death at the hands of an anticlerical labourer drunk with the power possession of a rifle gave him. The search of the house was thorough, but though the militiamen leaned their rifles on the Carmelite trunk, they never thought of opening it. There was an ugly moment, however, when one of the few literate militiamen took up Campbell's copy of Dante's *Divine Comedy* and puzzled out the title. 'Italian!' he announced to his comrades: 'Fascist!' The situation would have been amusing had it not been terrifying. But Campbell, with admirable presence of mind, showed them some of his Russian novels, and so convinced them that he was neutral. With a few coarse jokes, at which Campbell laughed heartily, they left at last. The

Campbells believed that their lives had been saved miraculously.[20]

They were by now reduced to living on cucumbers picked at night in their garden, and sheltering from the daily shelling and bombing in a gloomy passage of their house.[21] They were beginning to despair of ever escaping from the city (for a thorough and ruthless purge of the *bourgeoisie* was now in progress)* when fate again took a hand. With his usual generosity, Campbell had for some months been instructing an idiot poetaster, Angel Monico, in the art of writing verse. This young man now turned up at the Campbells' house carrying a dead child and a paper bag. The child had been killed by a shell; in the paper bag were 3,000 pesetas tied in bundles. Monico, a Communist, had been the sole witness to the murder of a priest by a militiaman, who had divided with him the money the priest was carrying.[22] Angel now asked the Campbells to use the money, 'in case you're in need'.[23] They who had for days been preparing themselves for death, thought the money a godsend and Angel well named. During the next few days they planned their escape, eventually managing to bribe some militiamen into giving them a lift out of the city in the back of a lorry used for conveying corpses. As it crossed the Alcantara bridge the truck, despite the skull and cross-bones painted on its side, came under fire from the Alcazar, one tower of which had been set alight by shell-fire, so that it blazed like a farewell beacon against the evening sky.[24] The Campbells arrived at Algodor, a village ten miles away, shaken but unharmed. There they spent the night dozing uneasily on sacks on the station platform. The next day, by wearisome stages, they made their way by train to Madrid, and then to Valencia; in every village they saw burnt or burning churches. The whole of Spain seemed aflame with hate.

In Valencia the British Consul put them aboard a refugee ship, the HMS *Maine*, bound for Marseilles. The ship was crowded with Britons fleeing Spain, among them Robert Graves, Laura Riding, and Alan Hodge. The dramatic circumstances of this meeting on 9 August 1936 smoothed away all memories of Campbell's attacks on Graves and Riding during the late Twenties and early Thirties. Campbell apologized to them and the apology was accepted. The Campbells were soon on very good terms with them, and they travelled together via Paris to London. When they reached England

---

* According to McNeill-Moss, '. . . practically all the well-to-do were shot. The rough rule appears to have been this: that anyone who had employed a servant in his house or more than two workers in his business, merited death. There were exceptions: not many.' (McNeill-Moss, pp. 150–1.) The Campbells employed two housemaids.

Laura Riding approached Campbell quietly: 'Roy, you look starving,' she said. 'Would £500 be any good to you?'[25] Campbell's pride would not let him accept, but he never forgot the generosity of this spontaneous offer. The whole incident sheds light on the many literary quarrels he was to have after the war: he generally disliked, and was disliked by, people he had never met, and the antipathy seldom survived close acquaintance.

The Campbells had fled Spain with little more than the clothes they were wearing. Even Campbell's manuscripts had had to be abandoned. He had entrusted his dog to friends, and left the stable-door open so that his two horses could take their chances. The money from *Angel* would not go far. The Campbells were lucky, then, to be offered a temporary home in Binsted, near Arundel, by the wealthy publisher Wishart, who had married one of Mary's six sisters, Lorna. The Wisharts, who were going off on holiday, offered the Campbells the run of their luxurious home on its large estate.[26] The lush beauty of Sussex in late summer was overwhelming to the Campbells; after the danger, privation, and exhaustion they had suffered, Wishart's farm seemed a vision of heaven. The orchards were heavy with soft Victoria plums and apples; there was thick cream, and butter, and eggs, and fresh vegetables from the kitchen garden, while indoors the linen sheets and hot baths, the silver and mahogany, were to them a taste of luxury such as they had never enjoyed before, and never were to enjoy again.

Meanwhile the siege of the Alcazar was big news. Campbell had been swooped on by reporters when he landed in England, and his story appeared under such headlines as 'British Bullfighter Trapped by Rival Armies'.[27] Throughout August and September the Campbells bought several papers each day to follow the course of the siege. Their distance from the conflict paradoxically increased their involvement in it; the abundant food of Marsh Farm brought vividly to their minds the starvation in the Alcazar. Each piece of good or bad news from Toledo elated or depressed them. The besiegers sprayed petrol on the building and tried to set it alight; they tunnelled under it and blew it up with huge charges. The Campbells fought each day of the siege vicariously. And they began to nurse an antipathy towards those who did not share their sympathy for the defenders.

In these circumstances they drew closer to Wyndham Lewis, who thoroughly shared their enthusiasm for the Nationalists, and who ended his letters to Campbell at this time with 'Long live the New Spain!'[28] They saw a good deal of him during August and September.

He came down to Arundel, planning to paint a six-foot group portrait of the Campbells with the Alcazar looming romantically in the background, but he seems never to have completed it.

The Alcazar's defenders under Moscardó were still holding out when, on 27 September, the siege was lifted by advancing Nationalist forces. Years later Campbell wrote that his joy at the news of the relief of the fortress was 'as fresh today as when we first heard it in September 1936'.[29] For the Campbells, as for supporters of the Nationalists generally, the siege of the Alcazar became the symbol of the struggle of 'Christian Spain' against the 'Marxist hordes'. For Campbell, it was the rock on which faith was founded, the rock which that faith had made immortal in spite of physical destruction. His sonnet on 'The Alcazar Mined' begins,

> This Rock of Faith, the thunder-blasted –
> Eternity will hear it rise
> With those who (Hell itself out-lasted)
> Will lift it with them to the skies!
>
> (CP, I, 154)

He added the final poems to *Mithraic Emblems* when it was already in the hands of the printer, at the end of August, and the volume, published by Boriswood, appeared in October 1936. Faber & Faber, who had wanted to publish it, were very disappointed. Geoffrey Faber had written to Campbell, 'It beats me to understand why after the success of *Adamastor* you should have decided to take your poems elsewhere instead of enabling the publishers of *Adamastor* to go on building up your reputation and position as a poet.'[30]

In fact *Mithraic Emblems* did little for Campbell's poetic reputation. It was largely ignored by the critics; apart from a review in *The Tablet*[31] (a Catholic paper) it went almost unnoticed. Nearly three months passed before the *New Statesman*[32] and *The Sunday Times*[33] paid attention to this, his biggest volume of verse. They were the only important papers to do so. It was the third of his books to be so treated. The reasons for this neglect are not easy to make out. Campbell's political views are not explicitly expressed in these poems: Desmond MacCarthy, reviewing them, was unable to say on which side Campbell's sympathies lay.[34] Many critics were undoubtedly repelled by the vigour with which he expressed his dislike of 'Charlies', 'Pommies' and 'Red-necks' in the inferior 'Horizon' section of the volume. G. W. Stonier, for instance, in the *New Statesman*, noted acidly,

Not only do Commando and the Charlies, Christ-Mithras, the garlanded bull, Toledo, become as monotonous as a Southend carnival, but a number of verse-formulae are relentlessly repeated. . . . I do not know of any previous volume of Mr. Campbell's in which you could find these ineptitudes. For the first time I have found myself reading through to find the good ones. They are here, if one looks . . . *Mithraic Emblems* might have been cut down to a third of its present size (150 pages). It would still not be on a level with *Adamastor* or *Flowering Reeds*, but it would be real Campbell and not fake cowboy.[35]

In fact the 'ineptitudes' Stonier found in *Mithraic Emblems* had made their appearance before, in such volumes as *The Wayzgoose*, and a dislike of these aspects of Campbell's work does not convincingly explain the almost complete silence that greeted *Mithraic Emblems*. Campbell himself believed that he was the victim of a continuing literary boycott, and he may well have been right. This was the period when the great newspaper barons could and did conspire to stifle all favourable mention of one public figure while 'puffing' another, and in the literary world the animosity of one of Campbell's powerful detractors would be sufficient to deter those who might have expressed their admiration of him. Thus Stephen Spender, who secretly admired Campbell's poetry while decrying his politics, never dared to write a favourable review of it; and he admitted after Campbell's death, ' . . . the main reason why I never wrote about Campbell during the 1930's was Auden's very critical view of him as a poet'.[36]

Campbell had had high hopes for *Mithraic Emblems*; for months his publisher had been assuring him that it would finally establish his reputation in the forefront of English poetry. The volume's almost total failure was a cruel disappointment to him. In addition his relations with his brother-in-law Wishart, an outspoken left-winger, had deteriorated rapidly. Wishart supported the Left in Spain, and Campbell, who knew that people like Wishart were among the first to be shot in the Spanish Republic, thought him perverse. Mary's brother Douglas Garman, at this time a member of the Communist Party, often visited Marsh Farm with Peggy Guggenheim, whose lover he was.[37] Campbell was soon writing defiantly to Lewis,

We are still in our 'Alcazar' in Bolshevik Binsted. I only wish you were here. Our hosts are trying to turf me out (my three brothers-in-law). I refuse to go – I am abolishing property and practically demonstrating their theories with uplifted fist – they send their ultimatums now by the chauffeur who laughs at them because they dare not come near here![38]

But he did not sincerely enjoy such quarrels, and he decided to try to return to Spain. English writers, he found, supported the Republican side in Spain almost unanimously, and he felt ever more strongly that England was not his country. On his trips to London he visited only the low-life characters he had known during his Oxford days, avoiding other artists; as always, he was more at ease among the poor. He wrote to Wyndham Lewis,

I have seen enough of my old 'pals' to realize that they are a humiliated race and will coolie for anything that menaces them, instead of fighting it. All I like is those rattled [*sic*] old whores who are susceptible to Christianity. But I never had any sexual business with them. Only they used to give me food, and I would be a shit if I forgot them in their old age.[39]

He was increasingly alienated from the political views of other intellectuals. He could not see that Germany was the enemy to be feared; he was convinced that the coming war would be fought against Communism, and that the English in siding with the Spanish Republicans were siding with their own future enemies. On the other hand, he was as far from English Fascists as he was from the Left. Wyndham Lewis arranged a meeting between Campbell and Oswald Mosley, late in 1936. It was not a success. Mosley began questioning Campbell about the use of mortars in street-warfare. 'Why do you ask that?' said Campbell. 'Because we may have to use them here before long,' said Mosley.[40] The idea appalled Campbell. He returned to Arundel pale with emotion, and told Mary, 'He's on our side, but for all the wrong reasons.'[41] From this lunch one can date the beginning of the estrangement between Campbell and Lewis. They continued to exchange occasional letters until the early Fifties, but the warmth of their relationship was never revived. With this last link severed, Campbell began to find the political atmosphere in England insupportable. 'Everybody is cynical and fatalistic now – it is terrible to see,' he wrote to a South African poet.[42]

The Campbells were joined at this time by a Spanish girl, Josephine Bosch, the daughter of a Spanish millionaire brewer. She had been at a finishing school in England when the Civil War broke out, and, finding herself stranded and penniless, she advertised for employment. She acted as a governess to Tess and Anna, much as Uys Krige had acted as tutor. She had no idea whether her parents, trapped in Barcelona, were alive or dead, and for six months she cried every morning.[43] Each night she and the Campbells would say the rosary together and pray for Spain. They longed increasingly to be near the conflict in which their involvement was so deep. The unexpected gift of £150 from an old acquaintance, Izaac Rousseau, who had shared his sitting-room with Campbell in Oxford seventeen years before, gave Campbell the opportunity he sought of taking his family south again. On 29 January 1937, a day of whirling sleet, they sailed for Lisbon on a German boat.

XII

Wanderings

1937–1942

THE wintry passage to Portugal was a rough one, and Campbell was one of the few passengers not to be seasick. Having survived a terrible storm in the Bay of Biscay, the *Nyasa* sailed into Lisbon harbour past the tangled masts of sunken or beached boats. The Campbells asked for a cheap hotel and were directed to the Pension Luz in the Avenida de Liberdad.[1] After their uneasiness in England, waking to find themselves in Lisbon was a delight. The sunshine, the noisy, dark-skinned women with baskets of fish on their heads, and the saunter-ing, careless pace of life soothed Campbell's nerves and reminded him of Spain. But they had all had enough of cities; they studied maps and looked for a village in which to settle. They asked the pension owner for advice. 'All you English go up the coast, to Estoril,' he said.[2] That was enough for Campbell; he turned his eyes south.

After three days in the Pension Luz, they took the train to Setúbal, and during the five days they spent there, they heard of the little fishing village of Cezimbra. It proved to be just what they were looking for, somewhere quiet, beautiful, and cheap. They took a room in the Pension Chic, which though it was most unchic was clean, and so cheap that they gave up any immediate thought of renting a house; they simply lived in the pension for five months. They expected the war in Spain to end at any time, and they were waiting for an opportunity to move back to their Toledo house, on which they had paid a year's advance rent. Although Toledo was in Nationalist hands, the front was only three miles away, and the city was still being shelled intermittently.

It was while the Campbells were staying at the Pension Chic that a family of English-speaking Portuguese, the Caupers, arrived to see them one day, saying they had heard of an English family living in the village. Cauper, a member of the wealthy Braganza family, was a director of the Shell Oil Company in Portugal. He and his wife, intelligent and highly cultivated, were very kind to the Campbells.

They invited them frequently to stay at their beautiful old summer residence in the next village, and helped them a good deal during these early months in Portugal.³ Their children were about the same age as Anna, and the Campbell daughters picked up Portuguese quickly. The friendship begun in this way between the two families was to prove close and lasting.

As the weeks passed and Franco's initial rapid advances were halted, it became clear that the war was going to be a long one. Campbell's money from South Africa had begun arriving again, and with it, late in May 1937, they rented a house with a fine view over the village, the port, and the sea. During this time Josephine Bosch, the Spanish girl, who lacking the money to travel had stayed on in England, joined them and lived with them until the end of the Civil War.

Campbell had been planning, since he left England, to return to Toledo to check on the safety of the Carmelite archives, still in the trunk in the Campbells' house. Before he left England he had persuaded a recent acquaintance, Tom Burns, who worked on *The Tablet*, to sign him on as a special correspondent, and to provide him with an official letter of accreditation. Soon after the Campbells had moved to a second, larger house in Cezimbra, Campbell set off alone by train for the Spanish border. He travelled north to Coimbra, and then across the border to Salamanca, which he reached on 24 June. Salamanca was at this time the home of the Nationalist Head of State, and the embassies, the Falangists, and the Press Service were sited there. Armed with his letter from *The Tablet*, Campbell saw Señor Merry del Val, chief of the Nationalist Press Service, and was given safe conduct to the Madrid front, together with letters to authorities in other cities, including General Queipo de Llano, the bombastic Governor of Seville.⁴

He loved being back in Spain. The discipline of the Nationalist regime impressed him as a great improvement on the chaos that had gripped Spain before the outbreak of Civil War. His daily letters to Mary were full of enthusiasm: 'If it were not for the wounded soldiers, everything is so beautifully run here, that you would not know there was a war on – except for the expression of the soldiers – such a fine mixture of determination & confidence. You can feel Victory tingling in the air!'⁵ In Portugal he had begun a poem in memory of the murdered Toledo Carmelites. The atmosphere of Nationalist Spain inspired him, and while he waited in Salamanca for a military car to take him round the fronts, he finished the poem, perhaps the most humbly moving of all his Christian writings. It is a poem that leaves no room for doubting the sincerity of his conversion, filled as it is with pity, and envy of his martyred friends:

> . . . well might Hell feel sick and sorry
> To see the brown monks lying dead . . .
> (CP, II, 31)

It was in Salamanca that (according to his own account)[6] he offered to fight for Spain in the ranks of the *requetés*. It was typical of him to want to enlist as a monarchist soldier rather than as a member of Franco's regular army. But Merry del Val was firm: what the Right in Spain needed was good propaganda, not soldiers, he said. 'Pens, not swords.' And Campbell, filled with enthusiasm, promised to do his best. With his journalist's pass, he travelled by car to Toledo on 28 June 1937. From there he wrote to Mary:

I have just got here by Special Car from Salamanca, via Avila Talavera etc, through snowy mountain passes and castled towns with hundreds of storks nesting in the battlements. Nationalist Spain is far more peaceful than before the war; except for the smashed houses you see nothing but Millet scenes, smiling peasants at work etc . . .
Dozens of people recognized me in the street: the estanco-keepers etc. I have never done such a lot of handshaking in my life. Coming into Toledo by the Avila road we saw it a long way off. You remember how it was when we left it with one tower of the Alcazar in flames. The town is still completely dominated by the Alcazar: it looks grander if anything. . . . Really it is wonderful to tread on this Holy ground again. Tomorrow I will go to Mass at the Carmelites; and then get down to work and show up the English Press.[7]

He spent three days in Toledo, and on 30 June drove to Talavera, where he spent the night, and where he somehow twisted his hip badly in a fall, an injury that was to have serious consequences. From Talavera his special car travelled southwards down the front, and by 1 July, as his daily letters make clear, he was in Seville, from where he travelled by train back to Lisbon. It is worth tracing this journey into Spain in detail, because all the evidence suggests that it was the only one he made to the front. For the rest of his life Campbell was to claim that he fought for Franco. So he did, with his pen. But his actual experience of the battlefield was confined to this tour by car on the single day of 1 July 1937.

On his return to Lisbon from Seville, his train had passed along the beautiful Algarve coast of Portugal, and he had been greatly impressed by the scenery. Early in September, therefore, the Campbells moved south once again, this time to the village of Estombar, where again they found a cheap pension. It was in Estombar that Campbell settled seriously to work, writing a 5,000-line poem which he originally called *A Legionary Speaks*, but later renamed *Flowering Rifle*, and sub-titled 'A Poem from the Battlefield of Spain'. Openly propagandist in intent, it glorified the Nationalist forces generally and Franco in particular. The greater part of it was composed in a mere two weeks, in March 1938. Faber having refused it, it was published by Longman's on 6 February 1939. With the appearance of this poem Campbell's relations with his fellow-writers in English (already strained by *The Georgiad*) were finally broken. *Flowering Rifle* convinced all who read it that Campbell was a thorough-going Fascist; it was a slur from which he was never fully to free himself. It is largely upon this poem that the charges alleging Campbell's Fascism rest, and they are charges that cannot be ignored.

It should be said at the outset that, as propaganda, *Flowering Rifle* fails completely; in the English-speaking world at least, it almost certainly did more harm than good to the Francoist cause.[8] One reason for this ineffectiveness is that Campbell makes little attempt to seem unbiased; the preface of the volume concludes with the words VIVA FRANCO! ARRIBA ESPANA! and almost every line of the poem proclaims his prejudice equally loudly. Even neutral readers were put off by this stridency, and left-wing critics were enraged by it. Secondly, the poem is very badly written. In later years Campbell was to claim defiantly that he thought it his best work, but shortly before its publication he wrote rather ruefully to a friend, 'I should have kept it by for revision for a year at least but preferred to strike while the iron's hot. . . .'[9] It seems clear that he scribbled it as quickly as possible and then published it without attempting corrections (though he was to revise the version that was printed in the second volume of his *Collected Poems*). The mechanical rhythm and inevitable rhymes of the iambic couplets give large sections of the poem an almost stupefying monotony, and the effect is increased by the vagueness of Campbell's imagery, his use of slang and tremendously long sentences, and his habit of repeating arguments, images, and jibes again and again. Not infrequently, one finds him repeating an entire passage which he had used twenty or thirty pages earlier. Thus the quotation of Lenin's phrase 'Our mightiest weapon is the Lie' recurs at least four times; comparisons between the generous, open-handed salute of the Right and the clenched fist of the Left occur in at least three extended passages; attacks on 'Charlies', 'Wowsers' or 'red-necks' occur throughout the poem, as do the claims that even Nature refused to serve the Communists, boasts that Campbell prophesied the outcome of the war before its start, and assertions such as that Russian tank-crews had to be bolted into their vehicles to stop them from deserting. It is clear that *Flowering Rifle*, like Campbell's other long poems, was written in sections which were later slotted into the finished work wherever they seemed to fit. The poem is easily the most undisciplined he ever wrote, linked as it is by nothing except the violence of his invective against the Left. There is no 'plot', and no attempt to impose a structure on the work.

Flowering Rifle provides some extraordinary examples of the shallowness and naivety of Campbell's political judgement, and the way he tried to build up a system of political opinions out of his personal likes and dislikes. It is clear, for instance, that one major reason for his support of Franco was his observation that food was more plentiful on the Nationalist side of the lines:[10]

> The loaves and fishes of an 'outworn creed'
> Suffice the starving multitude to feed . . .

In the left-wing Republic, on the other hand,

> Shiploads from Britain, loaded trains from France
> Served but the march of hunger to advance,
> As Bread to famine, water turned to thirst,
> The miracles of Jesus were reversed:
> In vain the Gaucho toiled for their relief
> On Pampas thundering with tons of beef –
> Round up the plains, or trawl the teeming sea
> Where the Red Curse is, there will Hunger be![11]

There is very little to sustain the reader's interest. Only towards the end of *Flowering Rifle* does the dense fog of rhetoric lift briefly, when Campbell gives us what may be an eyewitness account of Franco's cavalry going into action against troops of the Republic:

> Under our horses smokes the pounded thyme
> As we go forward; streaming into battle
> Down on the road the crowded lorries rattle
> Wherein the gay blue-shirted boys are singing,
> As to a football match the rowdies bringing –
> But of this match the wide earth is the ball
> And by its end shall Europe stand or fall . . . .

Past dead men lying nonchalantly round,
As if in brief siestas on the ground,
The horses, trotting, lift the town in view,
And thunder loudens . . .

(CP, II, 235–6)

Campbell writes as if he took part in the attack, though it is certain that he did not. It is characteristic that he writes of the Nationalists as using horses rather than tanks, and that his weapon is the sabre rather than the rifle of his title:

But nearer yet, and we are in the storm
Before their battered rearguard can reform –
While running bolshies fall upon their face,
Some stop to fire, reloading as they race,
Suddenly doubling as you make their pace,
So where you thought to slash the bulging nape
It is a face you widen in its gape,
To whose fierce shock your jolted elbow rings
And like a tuning-fork, your sabre sings,
The numbing blow, in its collected force,
Trebled by the momentum of the horse.

(CP, II, 236)

There seems little point in trying to establish the degree of truth that lies behind Campbell's boasts of right-wing virtues, and his accusations against the Left. It is clear that he was willing to turn fact and fiction alike to use in glorifying the side he supported and vilifying the one he opposed. What is of interest is the simplicity of his belief that *Flowering Rifle* would aid Franco's cause. Shortly after its publication, he wrote to his mother,

The British Press has tried to make light of the book as it brings such heavy charges against them. But this time I have lots of good people to champion me, and the book spreads in England like fire. Several people like the Maxwell Scotts are never without a dozen copies, which they pass round to their friends. I think I told you how favourably the Spanish Royal Family were impressed with my book, and how they have had their gentlemen and ladies-in-waiting write to me, to thank me.[12]

Nothing better illustrates the feebleness of his grasp of the political feelings of his likely readers.

Critical reactions to *Flowering Rifle*, predictably, reflected the deep political division that split the literary world of the Thirties. Catholic papers such as *The Tablet* welcomed the poem as 'genuine Rabelais', asked 'why poetry or satire should not be inspired by Fascism as well as by Communism', and found in Campbell's style a resurrection of the style of the seventeenth century.[13] Arthur Bryant, in the *Illustrated London News*, rhapsodized, 'In the light of this magnificent epic of civil war, criticism is dumb, for poetry such as this has not been written in English since Julian Grenfell fell in battle . . .' At the other end of the political spectrum, Stephen Spender condemned the poem as 'ignoble sweepings of every kind of anti-Semitic and atrocity propaganda' and said that several passages in the book made him feel physically sick.[14] Few critics made even a pretence of trying to review the poem objectively.[15]

But those who welcomed the poem as a blow struck on behalf of Fascism were as wrong as those who condemned it for the same reason. Campbell was as incapable of perceiving the true nature of Fascism as, for instance, Spender and Arthur Koestler at the time were of seeing the true nature of Communism. And unlike them he, with his hatred of regimented groups, never joined a political party. Nor was he unaware of the close similarity between the methods used by the two sides in the Spanish struggle; in *Flowering Rifle* he draws a powerful picture of them as two indistinguishable fighting beasts:

> As if his soul into the flesh could strike,
> Each in the other conjures up his like;
> With rags of flesh upon their nails and teeth
> They wrestle now above and now beneath,
> And both so foul with blood and soot and dust,
> And one by hate, the other by disgust
> So unified, by smoke so densely screened,
> You scarce can tell the angel from the fiend.
>   (CP, II, 234–5)

When alarmed friends, including his brother in South Africa, wrote asking whether he was now a Fascist, Campbell strenuously denied the charge, writing long, confused letters trying to explain his position.

A considerable part of my attraction to the Right and aversion from the Left is due to the fact that there is more laughter and less grumbling among the soldierly people. . . . I believe in family life and religion and tolerance: and I find far more tolerance to Britain in Italy than I find tolerance of Fascism in England.[16]

Campbell proved to be an easy mark for Franco's propaganda for a number of purely personal reasons: his recent conversion to Catholicism, his anti-Semitism, his enmity towards left-wing writers, the horror engendered by his personal experience of the left-wing terror in Toledo, his observation that there was more bread to be had on Franco's side of the line, and so on. He was a political simpleton; but to term him a Fascist is to misjudge him. His violent fantasies were the nastiest thing about him, and there are few men of whom that could be truly said.

In the fortnight during which he composed the greater part of *Flowering Rifle*, Campbell worked like a man possessed. He lived on endless flasks of hot, sweet tea, and little else, and by the end of March 1938 he was very thin and strained. Partly from piety, partly as a relaxation after his labour, he undertook a pilgrimage to the shrine of Our Lady of Fatima, a Portuguese equivalent of Lourdes, in May. He travelled with Mary and with two Portuguese friends he had made, and before setting out he took his Spanish pigskin *bota* to a wine shop to be filled with a mixture of wine and water. When he took a drink later that day, he got a shock: the *bota* contained nothing but water. It was clear to Campbell what had happened: it was a miracle, a sign from the Virgin of Fatima, a reversal of Christ's miracle at Cana. Most other men would have gone angrily back to the wine shop. Instead, Campbell went on to the shrine and there took a solemn oath to remain teetotal until Franco had achieved victory. It says much for his faith that he kept his oath, though it nearly killed him to do so.

He lived very quietly at Estombar, doing a certain amount of fishing, and nursing the hip he had twisted in Talavera. Arthritis began to affect it, and he was in considerable pain. This was the beginning of the trouble that continued to plague him for the rest of his life. At Estombar too he began to elaborate his claims to have fought for Franco; the account grew with extraordinary speed. His technique from the beginning was to introduce his fantastic details with studied casualness into a perfectly credible account. He wrote to his brother George for instance, after a paragraph discussing photo-graphing lions,

I only take snaps, not good photos, but I got one fine one in the war when the Russians managed to break the door of their tank and are reeling like blotto guys in the heat. The Delegation of the Press gave me a fiver for the negative. I took the snap ten yards from the tank and shot the five men with the other hand with one of those new pistols (but they are fair terrors) they are machine-guns we call them pistolas-ametralladadoras. . . . The Russians are

Laurie Lee, Mary, and Campbell on the roof of the Campbells' first house in Toledo, with the towers of the Alcazar behind

Airosas 13, Toledo, 1936

Sergeant Campbell of the King's African Rifles, 1944

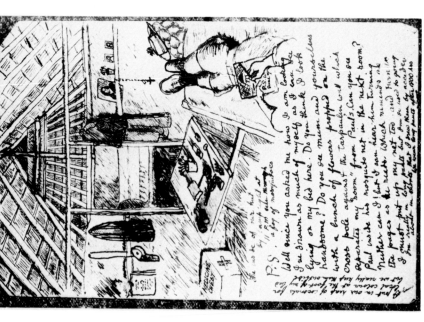

One page of a letter from Campbell to Tess, 13 September 1943

no more soldiers than a posse of coolies would be. They were only trained for cinema work.[17]

Like *Flowering Rifle* itself, this typically Campbellian yarn lacks any power to convince; George cannot have been taken in for a moment by the picture of Campbell wielding camera and machine-gun simultaneously. Yet it remains extraordinary how many of Campbell's contemporaries chose to believe such transparent tales, and to condemn their teller as a Fascist brute.

The condition of his hip continued to worsen, and he began to think of going to Italy to consult a specialist. It seems to have been his mother who provided the money to pay for this trip, for after having visited them in Altea in 1935 and been shocked by what she saw of their poverty, she had been more sensitive to their possible needs. In September 1938 they set out for Italy, Campbell and Mary taking the opportunity to visit Toledo on the way, travelling by train as usual.[18] It was an eerie experience. The front had hardly moved during the past year, and the city was still very much in the firing-line. The street-lamps had been painted blue for security against air raids, and outside each important building, in the weird submarine light, grim-faced guards were posted. General Franco was expected to visit the city at any time, and security was very tight; foreigners walking the streets were continually challenged and searched. The Campbells did not enjoy themselves. Their house had been occupied by Moors, and few of their possessions were undamaged.[19] After two days they were relieved to escape the tension of Toledo and hurry south to meet their daughters who had travelled to Seville. (Josephine Bosch, having at last traced her parents, who had been taking refuge with some poor relations in Catalonia, had been able to rejoin them as the Nationalist advance moved towards Barcelona.)[20]

By contrast with Toledo, Seville seemed a relaxed and cheerful place, full of handsome, wounded officers and pretty girls drinking coffee in the cafés. They spent a night there before taking the train to Gibraltar, where they embarked on the *Rex*, one of the huge luxurious liners Mussolini had built to symbolize the success of his regime. It was while exploring the Fascist ship, before sailing, that the Campbells saw one of the largest British battleships, HMS *Hood*, sailing into that most British of harbours. Campbell was struck forcibly by the sight: 'Look at the might of the British Empire', he told his daughters, his voice trembling; and they, looking at him, saw that his eyes were full of tears.[21] The scene epitomizes his divided loyalties.

Naples early in September 1938 was golden with the glow of
autumn; its cubist beauty, as seen from the deck of a liner approaching
the harbour, betrays nothing of the filth of the back-streets. They
spent a week there, making an expedition to Pompeii to see the
frescoes, before taking the train to Rome on 11 September. They had
determined to spend several months in Italy, and to wait in Rome for
Campbell's mother, who was on another of her world tours. Accordingly, they rented a flat in one of Mussolini's hideous new suburbs, in
a great apartment block on the Via Donatello.²² Campbell had always
had a deep love for Latin literature and for all things Roman; he
immensely enjoyed being a tourist in the city which was also the
centre of his new faith. Pope Pius XI died on 10 February 1939, and
the Campbells made a point of going to see his lying-in-state. They
spent the days sight-seeing; they visited all the churches and had their
photographs taken in the Colosseum. As he always did in a new city,
Campbell went round all the art-galleries and museums, spending
hours in each one. He also went regularly to the new hippodrome near
their flat, to watch the equestrian championship competitions.²³

The Munich crisis, which filled the British papers with panic, was
largely kept from the Italian public by censorship. Campbell, whose
dislike of the British Press had reached a peak, regarded this as
proving the value of Mussolini's 'strong rule', and wrote to Enslin du
Plessis, who was still working in Fleet Street, 'A censorship is far less
misleading: one is far nearer the news with amputated truth than with
fevered fancy. You can't have your cake and eat it too. . . . In
England you have Free Speech, Free love, Free thinking & Free Verse
(most of which are contradictions in terms) . . .'²⁴

They met several acquaintances in Rome, among them Douglas
Woodruff, editor of *The Tablet*. Woodruff's wife had aristocratic
Italian connections, and through her the Campbells gained entry into
the houses of many great Roman families – to Mary's delight.
Campbell was everywhere introduced as a poet and a man of 'sound
political views', and when *Flowering Rifle* was published in February
1939, he became a very popular guest. Night after night he and Mary
would go to cocktail parties or dinners in the great town-houses of the
Sforzas, the Colonnas, and the Respigliosi. Mary's pleasure was
marred a little by the fact that she possessed only one dress fit for such
occasions, but it is difficult to believe that Campbell did not feel
totally out of place in these formal gatherings of the rich and
powerful. Apart from anything else, they strained to the limit his
resolve not to take alcohol until the end of the Civil War. Occasionally

they would meet other English writers at these parties. At one luncheon engagement Mary found herself next to Hilaire Belloc, who was too deaf to hear a word she said all through the meal.[25] He had just come from Spain, where he had visited the front and met General Franco, and his energy and fire impressed Campbell. He had read *Flowering Rifle*, and told Campbell that he thought it 'a really good thing', adding that Campbell's other work would not count beside it in the long run. Campbell was delighted with this opinion; he wrote repeating it to his mother, adding, 'His word is worth more than the whole of Fleet Street'.[26]

He had been seeing an Italian doctor about his hip, and having a tooth X-rayed, and had been pronounced fit again, though the continued strain of doing without alcohol made him lose weight steadily. In the photographs of this period he is a gaunt, dark-eyed figure, his clothes hanging on a skeletal frame, deep lines of strain etched between his eyes. His mother, vigorous as ever, arrived to stay with them in early 1939, and in mid-January the Campbells set off for a trip with her through Italy, travelling in style, staying in good hotels, and enjoying themselves enormously. They journeyed slowly, spending weeks in Venice and Milan, and returned to Rome on 23 March. During February the Republicans had collapsed completely in Catalonia, and it was clear that the end of the Civil War was imminent; the Campbells decided to return to Toledo. Parting from Mrs Campbell in Rome, they travelled by train across France, entering Spain north of the Pyrenees because of the continuing confusion in Catalonia. At the border town St Jean-de-Luz they met the Marquess de Merry del Val (father of the Nationalist Press Officer) who had been the Spanish Ambassador to London in the early Thirties. When he heard that Campbell was the author of *Flowering Rifle*, he said, 'As a Spaniard, I thank you from the bottom of my heart for the fine work you have done for my country.' And at a word from him the Campbells were whisked through the border without formalities. Campbell commented to his mother, 'I was very touched indeed, for it is so little to have done for a country that saved my soul, and I would so willingly have given my carcase for the cause as so many and such much better men than me have done.'[27]

On Easter Sunday the Campbells attended High Mass in the cathedral of Avila, and the next day went on to Toledo. They found the city terribly changed by the years of war. The gap-toothed streets were choked with rubble; the churches had been desecrated, their paintings slashed and burned, their images broken; trees in the cool gardens had been chopped down; filth and graffiti were everywhere. There was very little food to be had. The rich of the city were dead, and the population seemed to creep, sad and aimless, among the ruins; only the stories they had to tell, of heroism, cruelty, and martyrdom, evoked the colour and the grandeur that had gone. The heaped rubble of the Alcazar, like an extinct volcano, hung over all.

The Campbells set about making their house habitable again and then turned their attention to the needs of the poor of the city, who seemed to be living mostly on bad potatoes. Mary in particular threw herself wholeheartedly into the work, and spent a great deal of time organizing the Toledo branch of Catholic Action and helping to run kitchens to feed the poor. It was at this time that she sold all her jewellery to refurbish a ruined chapel, and for nearly two years she wore the same brown dress every day, having, like Campbell, given away much of her clothing.[28] Campbell himself never cared what he wore. One day he collected from the Post Office a parcel of three silk shirts which his mother had sent him. He promptly put them all on, on top of the shirt he was wearing, and went off to a bar. (Since Franco's Victory Parade in Madrid on 19 May, he had been celebrating hard.) There, after a number of drinks, he collected four cronies, to each of whom he presently gave a shirt, returning home bare-chested that night to tell his resigned wife the story.[29]

He seems to have written little at this time, being content to rest and gain weight after the long struggle to live without the aid of alcohol. The Campbells spent two weeks, in May 1939, staying on a *dehesa* (ranch) outside Toledo; it belonged to one of the friends Mary had made while working for Catholic Action. The combination of farm food and exercise did wonders for Campbell's health. Six weeks after this, early in July, they revisited their old haunts in Altea, travelling by train through Madrid to Alicante, and then going on to Altea by bus, using the last of the money Campbell's mother had given him. They stayed in the Fonda Ronda, the same pension they had lived in when first they came to Altea, and spent a week seeing all the peasants they had known. They went back to Alicante then, and did a wide sweep by train to Segovia and Ávila. They loved Segovia, with its great castle; it reminded Campbell of a desert Scotland. The local delicacy was sucking-pig, and Campbell ate great meals of it and drank the local wine as if trying to make up for all the binges he had missed during the war.

Mary had decided that it was time Anna, by now thirteen, was put to school; the visit to Ávila had been planned so that they could leave her at a school run by the Teresian nuns on a hilltop outside the city. Tess returned to Toledo with them, and helped Mary to teach in the free night-school which Catholic Action had organized. Tess had been showing signs of mental disturbance ever since being sent away to school in England, briefly, in 1935;[30] at first these symptoms consisted merely in extreme nervousness, and a refusal to eat. Campbell was not much worried by this behaviour, ascribing it to puberty and the strains of war.

There was to be no release from these strains, for Europe was now sliding rapidly towards the universal conflict which Campbell had so long ago foreseen. The hoopoes were singing their foreboding song again in his garden. He wrote cheerfully enough about them to Edmund Blunden, describing them and the 'twenty horsepower nightingale' which also nested there,[31] but his poem 'The Hoopoe', begun at this time,[32] reflects his fears accurately:

> . . . round Toledo's shattered walls,
> Where, like a crater in the moon,
> The desecrated grandeur sprawls –
> Though out of season, pitch, and tune,
> All day the boding hoopoe calls.
>
> (CP, II, 33)

Franco had declared, during the Munich Crisis of 1938, that Spain would be neutral during any European war. But it seemed quite possible that Germany would be able to force Spain into the war on the Axis side; Hitler after all had a right to demand some return for his aid to Franco. Campbell therefore had to consider what his situation would be if Spain were to join in the coming war against Britain. It seems to have been at this time that he began his poem 'The Clock in Spain', inspired by an old clock he and Mary had bought. On its face was inscribed 'Birmingham, 1922' – the place and date of the Campbells' marriage, and this may have given him the idea of using it to symbolize his own feelings. The clock, he says, may have abandoned its habits of British accuracy under the seductive influence of Spain, but it is British at heart yet, and so is Campbell:

> . . . if the dreadful hour should chime
> For British blood, and steel as grim,
> My clock will wake, and tick the time,
> And slope his arms and march – and I'm
> The one to fall in step with him.
>
> (CP, II, 62)

The progress towards war was rapid, every retreat by British politicians giving Hitler greater confidence. The pace of events accelerated. Czechoslovakia was occupied by German troops on 15 March 1939, without resistance. Later the same month Lithuania bowed to German demands and handed over the city of Memel. On 5 April Mussolini, without warning, bombed Albanian towns and cities; in May came news of the German-Italian military pact. Chamberlain's appeasement policy was in tatters, and Britain continued to rearm hastily. At the same time, she rather half-heartedly conducted negotiations for a non-aggression pact with Stalin. At the end of August, however, came the astonishing news that Stalin had instead signed a non-aggression pact with Hitler; Britain and France were isolated. It seems to have been this event, more than any other, that clarified the issues for Campbell. When, during July 1939, it appeared that Britain might succeed in signing an agreement with Stalin, he had written bitterly to his mother, 'This alliance with Russia is the last degradation – only evil will come of it as it has come to everybody who ever meddled with Russia. It is like jumping into the river so as not to get wet.'[33] He had always regarded Communism as the chief enemy of the individual and Christian values he cherished. But once the two great systems of mass-thought and materialism, Fascism and Communism, were united in opposition to Britain, he was quite clear as to where his allegiance lay.

On 1 September came news that Germany had crossed the Polish frontier and bombed Warsaw, in defiance of the pact signed between Britain and Poland. On 3 September Chamberlain declared Britain at war. Campbell heard the news next day, and immediately took the train up to Madrid. There he presented himself at the British Consulate and offered his services. It was a quixotic action, for not only was he a South African living in a neutral country, but his age and family status made it extremely unlikely that he would ever be wanted. The British Consul quite naturally turned him down.[34] Campbell seems to have been relieved. He had no real wish to return to England; he might in any case fail the Army medical test, though his hip seemed to have healed. He returned to his beautiful house in Toledo, and began writing a history of the Civil War with the aim of vindicating Franco and the Nationalists. It was a slow task which he never finished.

The outbreak of the general conflict prevented Spain from building up its war-shattered economy by importing from abroad. Crops and livestock had been particularly hard hit during the Civil War, and for two years after its end there were severe food shortages throughout the country. Anna, suffering from the rigours of life at her spartan school in Ávila ('it was like Dotheboys Hall in *Nicholas Nickleby*', she was to say of it later)[35] had been brought home, and Mary decided that to ensure an adequate diet for the two girls they should be sent to an expensive school, the Assumption College in Madrid. Here Tess learned typing and shorthand, with vague ideas of taking a secretarial job. Anna, vivacious and intelligent, was already showing promise of extraordinary beauty. She was everywhere petted and made much of, and she made Tess feel very plain and plump by contrast. Throughout these early years of the war Tess, in reaction, subjected herself to crash diets in order to slim. These, combined with the shortage of food and the struggles of adolescence, put a continuing strain on her nerves.[36]

It was during this period of what American papers dubbed the Phoney War that Campbell became a British secret agent. The idea seems to have been his own; to be inactive in a time of war chafed him, as it had done during the First World War. Accordingly, he apparently visited the Madrid Consulate again, and there came across Tom Burns, the friend who had given him accreditation to *The Tablet* in 1937, now working as a Press Attaché. It must have seemed to Burns that Campbell might well be a useful gatherer of information: after all, he spoke Spanish fluently, moved about the country freely gathering information for his history of the Civil War, and was on good terms with a great many ordinary Spaniards. If nothing else, he would be able to keep his finger on the pulse of lower-class Spanish life. Accordingly, Burns seems to have hired Campbell on his own initiative to act as a gatherer of background information on the mood of Spain. It is difficult to see what other information he can have expected, for Campbell had no access to men of influence in the country.

Campbell was delighted with his new position. It gave him that feeling of direct participation in the struggle which was so necessary to his well-being. It also allowed him to hold up his head when writing home to South Africa, where several of his brothers had signed up as soon as war had been declared. He set about the task of being a British spy with gusto. His method of gathering information was original. He would settle into a bar, have a few drinks, and tell a few of the jokes and tall stories at which he excelled. In this way he would soon collect a circle of acquaintances, for whom he would buy drinks while his money or credit lasted. When the evening had progressed to the stage where they were all lifelong friends, he would lower his voice and quieten the rowdy circle before sharing with them a great secret, which they were to keep under their hats: he was a British spy. He was gathering information for his government. It was true, he swore to them. His government wanted information about anything suspicious – any troop movements or new military installations, any signs that Spain was breaking her neutrality. Had any of them seen anything suspicious lately?

Burns, not surprisingly, very quickly got wind of Campbell's revolutionary method of spying, and dismissed him; Campbell himself was later ruefully to admit that he had been a most un-secret agent.[37] These experiences, however, did allow him to write cryptically to his mother,

After the war I shall be able to tell you what I have been doing. But let it suffice that I have been on His Majesty's service since September 3 1939 and often on extremely dangerous work . . . . I hope my brothers don't think I have been slacking as I could not tell you what I was doing: but I never had such excitement even in the Spanish War.[38]

He wrote no original poetry at this time. But, prompted by Mary, he began translating the poems of St John of the Cross. St John attracted him because of his association with Toledo (the saint had for a time been imprisoned there), and because he had been a close associate of St Teresa of Ávila, to whom Mary had long felt a strong attraction. And, more importantly, Campbell associated St John with his own lucky escapes from death in Toledo in 1936, when he had saved the saint's papers from destruction in the Civil War. During 1940 Campbell also prepared a selection of poems from his volume *Adamastor*, at the request of Faber & Faber, for republication. He took the opportunity to drop 'The Theology of Bongwi' and 'Solo and Chorus from "The Conquistador"', both of which he now thought irreverent and unChristian. He changed entire verses in 'Mazeppa', 'The Albatross', and 'Poets in Africa', and made substantive changes to 'A Veld Eclogue', 'Resurrection', and 'Estocade'. But though he promised Faber's some entirely new poems,[39] he did not send any, and it seems likely that he had none to send. The reprinted poems appeared in 1941 under the title *Sons of the Mistral*, a phrase from 'Horses on the Camargue', suggested by Campbell himself.

During 1940 the Phoney War had ended abruptly with Hitler's invasion of Norway in April, and of Holland, Belgium, and France in May. By August Britain was totally isolated, and fighting for her life in the Battle of Britain, her only ally (apart from the countries of her Empire) being Greece. By September the Blitz on London was proceeding night after night, and the English papers the Campbells bought were full of stories of death and destruction. The Campbells read those papers with much the same feeling of isolation as they had read Spanish papers while staying on Wishart's estate at Binsted. Just as then, they were now deeply involved in a distant conflict, and the great mass of people around them were at best indifferent to its possible outcome. One afternoon a Spanish peasant came by their house with two hares he had just shot. 'Inglaterra!' he grinned, holding the little bloodstained bodies aloft: 'England!'[40] The Campbells began to feel that they must return to Britain.

In April 1941 came the German attack on British positions in North Africa, where Campbell's brothers George and Bruce were both serving. The German invasion of Yugoslavia followed, and then the assault on Greece, from which the British forces, greatly outnumbered, withdrew hastily. In June came Operation Barbarossa, Hitler's invasion of Russia. It was widely expected that Russia would capitulate within a fortnight.

Campbell could not bear to be on the sidelines with such events passing him by. Besides, conditions of life in Spain were deteriorating. The food shortages were severe, and what food there was was very expensive; the poor were reduced to eating acorns and thistle-tops. More important still, with the disruption of wartime mail his regular monthly income from South Africa was now getting through less and less frequently, and the Campbells were accordingly beginning to run into debt again. Mary was forced to remove Tess and Anna from their expensive school in Madrid, even though Tess had for some time been helping with the teaching there to pay some of the fees for her sister and herself.

Finding transport between Spain and England, with the French routes closed, was no easy matter. It was eventually arranged, through the British Consulate in Madrid, that they should travel to Portugal and leave for Britain from there. Campbell could travel by sea, but Mary, Tess, and Anna would follow by air when seats on the few remaining clipper flights became available. Until then, they would stay with their Portuguese friends the Caupers, who generously offered them an entire floor of their huge house on the Estrada da Luz in Lisbon. They travelled to Lisbon by sea, from Valencia, on 17 July 1941,[41] and having seen his family settled into the Caupers' house, Campbell travelled down on a small coaster to Gibraltar, on 2

August, to join a convoy to England. He was greatly impressed by the plentiful food to be had on Gibraltar – food was always the most powerful form of propaganda to him. It was in Gibraltar harbour that he saw HMS *Ark Royal*, badly hit in a raid against Sardinia, limping into port amid frenzied cheers. It was his first sight of Britain at war, and it lifted his heart as seeing HMS *Hood*, in this same harbour, had done in 1938. He later wrote of this moment as one of the great experiences of his life:

> The kick of my heart, like a punch on the rib
> To see the 'Ark Royal' returning to 'Gib'
> As that great swan of victory rippled the tide
> With a hole in her decks, and a list in her side . . .[42]
>   (CP, II, 114)

He was no longer merely observing the might of the Empire from the decks of a foreign ship; he was sailing to Britain to fight for Britain.

He arrived in London on 17 August, after a slow and dangerous voyage. On the boat he met many Jewish refugees, and several British soldiers who had failed to get off the Dunkirk beaches, and had travelled the length of France and Spain to reach Gibraltar.[43] On reaching London he was interviewed by the correspondent of a Durban paper, who asked him about conditions in Spain. Campbell seized on this opportunity to make it clear what side he was on. He spoke with feeling about the starvation in Spain, and contrasted it with the quantities of 'genuine white bread' he had seen on Gibraltar; he described Axis Europe as a 'desert', filled with secret police, prison camps, and artificial misery; and he remarked on the great change for the better he had noted in the English: 'This war has made the English greater, nobler, and better than ever before in history.'[44]

He had arrived in London penniless. There was nowhere to stay, for the city, after nearly a year of bombing, was full of homeless people sleeping on the platforms of Underground stations or anywhere else that seemed safe. He found few of his old friends still around, but one of them, Eve Kirk, who like the Campbells was a Catholic convert, lent him both money and a room until his mother was able to cable him £100 through Enslin du Plessis' newspaper.[45] With this he was able to rent a single room, at 8 Conway Street just off Fitzroy Square.

Now that he had arrived in London, he found it by no means easy to participate in the war effort as he wanted to do. He considered going into the Navy; he rather liked the idea of working on a minesweeper. But the Navy wanted proof that he had had sailing experience and he could produce none.[46] Eve Kirk was working as an Air Raid Precautions warden, and she soon persuaded Campbell to join her post as a full-time warden, while he looked around. He enjoyed wearing the blue uniform and steel helmet. The blitz had eased, for the Luftwaffe was concentrating its attentions on Russia, and he found what raids there were exciting rather than alarming. However, he had a fear of heights, and disliked crawling over crumbling brickwork eight storeys above the street.[47] He found firewatching an uncanny experience. From the roofs of the higher buildings, blacked-out London, silent under the moonlight, had the air of a vast necropolis; only the occasional flash of distant anti-aircraft fire showed that life existed still among the ruins. When the dawn came he could see vast areas of the city desolate and cratered – 'a lunar landscape blasted by fire and earthquake', as he described it.[48] It showed him vividly the terrible sufferings Londoners had undergone.

He began to explore old haunts and to see more of his old friends, but he found that *Flowering Rifle* had alienated many of them. Cecil Gray, whom he saw often, was friendly enough, but Augustus John, whom he had not seen for nearly five years, stared at him sardonically and then said coldly, 'A member of the Axis, I believe.'[49] Another night he was about to enter a pub when Nancy Cunard and Robert Nichols (a man whom Campbell had known well during his Oxford days) emerged. 'Hello, Nancy,' said Campbell shyly. 'Don't look, Nancy, it's Roy Campbell, that horrid Fascist,' said Nichols, and he and Nancy Cunard passed without a word and hurried into the darkness. A roar arose from the blacked-out street behind them: 'I'm not, I'm not a Fascist, Nancy! I'm a *requeté*!' But they did not look back.[50]

However, he was also making new friends. In his lodging-house in Conway Street he met a young Welshman and his beautiful wife, living in a single unheated room in extreme poverty. They were a noticeable couple, quarrelling fiercely and continuously, though they were very much in love. Campbell took to this young man at once. With his grubby clothes, his curls, and his pugnacious baby-face, he had a capacity for drink equal to Campbell's own, and he told Campbell that he wrote poetry too. His name was Dylan Thomas.

Thomas had been judged medically unfit for the Army, and he was desperately in need of money and a job. Campbell shared with the Thomases what money he had. One day when they were both penniless he and Thomas visited all the poets and writers they could

think of to borrow money. They got very little, though they fancied
they could hear the pocket-books of these men 'crackling with
bradburies', as Thomas put it.[51] They called on Harold Nicolson,
then a BBC Governor. Campbell wisely waited outside while Thomas
went in; he received a £1 note and a lecture on the evils of drink.[52]
They got a much better reception from T. S. Eliot who treated them
with great kindness and gave them enough money to save them from
anxiety for days.[53] It was at this time too, late in 1941, that Campbell
met Aimé Tschiffely, the horseman and biographer, and author of
Tschiffely's Ride. He was big, bluff, and practical, and Campbell at once
recognized him as a member of the mythical 'equestrian nation'; the
two were soon very good friends.

Campbell was still applying to join the armed services; he was keen
to play a more active role than that of air raid warden. He heard in
November 1941 that his younger brother Neil had been killed in
action in North Africa, and he was dazed by the news;[54] he badly
wanted to hit back at the Germans. Many of the duties of an air raid
warden seemed ignominious. In October, for instance, he had to take
part in a march to raise funds for Russia. He had never reconciled
himself to the idea that the Russians were now his gallant allies.
Having marched in pouring rain from St Pancras to Hampstead
Heath behind a band playing 'The Internationale', he came back
drenched and in a very bad temper.[55] He was not particularly pleased
either when his friends at the air raid post discovered that he was a
poet. On 2 October he was sweeping the floor of the post when, to
his astonishment, he heard Christopher Stone on the radio congratulating him on his fortieth birthday. He immediately acquired the
glamour of a celebrity: 'I have taken on the importance of the cat, our
mascot', he wrote wryly to his mother.[56]

He was finally turned down by the Navy, and by the Intelligence
section of the RAF; so, concealing his age, he applied to join the
Army. He had been offered a position in the Ministry of Information
(where so many men of letters found a haven during the war) but
spurned it as a 'counter-jumping existence'.[57]

Mary, Tess, and Anna meanwhile were still living with the
Caupers in Lisbon, waiting for seats on the flying-boat, though
Campbell had originally expected them to follow him to England
within a few days. Having waited four months, they were informed at
very short notice that seats were available. They flew to Shannon in
Ireland, and then travelled by bus, light plane, and train to London
which they reached just before Christmas. They arrived exhausted by

the journey to find sleet falling and the city bitingly cold. Campbell was not in his lodging-house when they reached there; they set out to look for him, slipping in slush and stumbling over fallen masonry in the black-out. By sheer chance they found him drinking with Eve Kirk in a nearby pub, the Windmill, and the surprise and joy of that meeting effaced the miseries of wartime London, even though they had to spend the night in Eve Kirk's bombed and windowless house.

XIII

War

1942–1944

CAMPBELL had been accepted by the Army Intelligence Corps, mainly because of his knowledge of languages, late in 1941, but he was kept on Deferred Embodiment for months. In the spring of 1942, however, he left his air raid unit and joined the Army as a private in the Royal Welch Fusiliers regiment, on 1 April.[1] He was sent by train to Brecon, in Wales, to undergo basic training. As soon as he gave his name at Brecon he was greeted enthusiastically by one of his officers, Andrew Cruikshank, who had for years been an admirer of his poetry. Campbell was not pleased to be known; he told Cruikshank that he had given up poetry completely, though he seemed touched when Cruikshank cried out, 'No no, you mustn't!'[2]

His work as an air raid warden had tired him; he was flabby and pale and but for his face might have been taken for an unemployed docker.[3] But he was determined to make a good soldier, and he threw himself wholeheartedly into the training, competing fiercely with men less than half his age. The man he most admired was Sergeant Davies, in charge of the 21st Intelligence Training Corps. From the start Campbell set out to emulate him, studying him closely. He reported to Mary,

. . . our Sergeant is the finest man here, and we are marvellously lucky to have him. He is a real comic too. He has all Mr King's[4] virtues with many more. His face and swagger are absolutely indescribable. But he is a magnificent soldier worth all the officers combined. He is ugly and handsome, naif and cunning, wise and simple, severe and kind – a sort of walking paradox.[5]

Campbell had fought hard and successfully against his bisexualism since leaving Oxford, and he did not relax now, but it is clear from his letters that he loved Sergeant Davies, and strove to model himself on him. He was to continue this pose for several years after the war ended.

He seems to have had a hard time reaching the standard of fitness required by the Army, for constant exposure to cold and damp brought on a recurrence of the sciatica which had affected his left hip in 1937. He was soon limping badly, and he was uncomfortably aware that this destroyed the unity of his platoon during drill. On the day of the drill competition towards the end of his basic training, therefore, he arranged that he should be made latrine orderly, and he was delighted when his platoon won.[6] Towards the end of his training course his group was sent into the Welsh mountains to a spot called Cwm Gwdi, to complete their weapons training under different NCOs. 'We have lost our adorable Sergeant Davies', he wrote gloomily to Mary.[7] He dreaded the cross-country runs and long marches of Cwm Gwdi, but he escaped them completely when he was made telephone orderly. During a storm the telephone was struck by lightning; Campbell, who was sitting nearby, was flung on to his back and was very lucky not to have been killed[8] – an incident which confirmed him in his lifelong hatred of telephones.

Because it was so foreign to his nature he struggled hard to be a neat and precise soldier, taking endless trouble with the petty tasks he hated. He proved to be a fair shot with bren-gun, rifle, and mortar, and he won the company swimming race across the Usk.[9] He loved the cameraderie which is the sole compensation for the essential horror of army life; he who had always been an outsider revelled in the sense of being a member of a strongly knit group. Yet even during his training there were times when he felt that he was serving in a foreign army; he spoke of the English as 'them': 'Somehow I don't feel that the British have even started to wake up yet: but it certainly does not pay to try to wake them up . . . . What one can do is to volunteer and serve and suffer with the lowest and poorest of them. That is what satisfies me, all other methods having failed.'[10]

Surprisingly, he was writing poetry under these very difficult conditions. Since 1939 he had been reading and translating the mystical Spanish poems of St John of the Cross, and it was while he was telephone orderly up at Cwm Gwdi that he wrote his fine sonnet, 'San Juan de la Cruz', presenting a copy of it to Lieutenant Cruickshank on his return to the Brecon camp.[11] On 13 June 1942 Mary came down to Brecon to see him, and stayed several nights; immediately after her return to London, he began his superb translation of St John of the Cross's 'En la Noche Oscura', completing it within a few days.[12] It is utterly astonishing that he should have been able to produce such poetry, which several critics rate among his very best work, under such circumstances.

His basic training over, he was moved in July to the Intelligence Corps Depot near Winchester, close enough for Mary, who was living near Petersfield, to visit him much more often. At Winchester his company was trained on motor cycles, which they learnt to ride across country in all conditions, crashing through the New Forest and jumping logs and ditches. Campbell hated every moment of it, and longed for Brecon: he had never understood even the simplest machinery. The motor cycle, he told Mary, confused him horribly. It took him days to learn how to change gears; he fell off repeatedly and sprained his ankle.[13] He was punished for his fumblings and made to wheel the 400-lb. motor cycle for miles, a task he later said was the hardest thing he had ever done.[14] In spite of this, he was enjoying barracks life more, for he was very popular with his fellows. 'Everybody calls me by my Christian name,' he wrote to Mary, 'including even the female cooks. It is quite a change for me after being so eminently unpopular as a writer. I only hope it lasts – and spreads!'[15]

At the end of October he was moved again, this time to Wentworth, near Rotherham in Yorkshire, for training in map-reading and orienteering. The Intelligence Corps here was housed in the stables of a stately home, a place so sumptuous that even the mangers were of marble. Campbell compared it to inhabiting an outhouse of the Escorial itself. He enjoyed patrolling the park of the huge building during night guard-duty, with rutting stags belling in the woods and the moonlit landscape crackling with frost.[16] He wrote almost daily to Mary, who was very unhappy; the monthly cheques from South Africa had been interrupted by the war, and she and Tess had had to become domestic servants, working as cook and chambermaid for a wealthy widow near Petersfield, Mrs Bridson.[17] This was a great strain for Mary, for she had never done even her own household work. Campbell's letters show that he felt her humiliation as deeply as she did. They show also that he was as deeply in love with her as he had ever been. 'I love you more tenderly and passionately every day of every year,' he wrote to her. 'We have grown up well together and there may be a time of great happiness together and a serene old age in peace, when all these trials are over. God bless you.'[18]

At the end of November he was moved again, to Matlock, a beautiful spa-town in Derbyshire. He was still being troubled by his hip, and drank the bathwater in the hope that it would cure his sciatica.[19]

He was given a week's leave early in December when his training was finished and, believing that he would very soon be sent abroad on active service, he steeled himself to part from Mary for several years. Instead, he was sent back to Wentworth, his embarkation having been delayed, and spent a glum Christmas in camp, the sole bright spot being a camp concert in which he gave an imitation of a Zulu buying horses from a Spaniard. It brought the house down.[20]

In February 1943 he was told that he was being sent out to East Africa. To his enormous pleasure he was promoted to sergeant. After a week's embarkation leave, and a period in a Lanarkshire transit camp, his draft set sail. Off the coast of Ireland the convoy ran into a tremendous storm, and Campbell's troop-ship, the *Antenor*, began having engine trouble. She lost speed, struggling along at the rear of the convoy for a time, and then broke down completely. Pitching and tossing in the storm, her funnels pouring smoke, she had to be abandoned by the convoy with its protecting aircraft-carrier and destroyers. For five days she wallowed helplessly, shunned by all other craft, a column of black smoke marking her as a sitting target for German submarines. The troops, herded like sheep and soaked to the skin, lived in their life-jackets; water, thick with vomit, washed continually through the mess-deck, pitching the men among floating buckets and kitbags.[21] Under such conditions Campbell and the two other sergeants had the utmost difficulty in getting the exhausted and terrified men to obey them. This was the experience that lay behind Campbell's fine poem 'One Transport Lost':

> Where, packed as tight as space can fit them
> The soldiers retch, and snore, and stink,
> It was no bunch of flowers that hit them
> And woke them up, that night, to drink.
>
> Dashing the bulkheads red with slaughter,
> In the steep wash that swept the hold,
> Men, corpses, kitbags, blood, and water,
> Colliding and commingling rolled.
>
> (CP, II, 63)

After five days the engineers got one engine working again, and the *Antenor* limped back to Glasgow. The men were promptly transferred to another ship, and by 24 March Campbell was at sea again.[22] He passed the voyage down to South Africa by reading Samuel Butler, Camoens, and Dante, and he gave talks to the officers' mess on bullfighting and the Spanish Civil War, and was rewarded with great quantities of whisky. He still had no firm idea of where he was being sent, but he prepared himself for death by attending Mass daily. He had much time to think during the voyage, and he looked back on his life with satisfaction. 'No accident of death could rob us now of what is between us', he wrote to Mary.[23]

His convoy reached Durban early in April 1943. It was sixteen years since he had last seen his birthplace and he had the great good luck to be given two weeks' leave, which he spent with his mother (now eighty) and his brother George. He later said that Field-Marshal Smuts intervened personally to get him off the troopship,[24] but it was in fact Sir Patrick Duncan, the Governor-General, whose wife was a friend of Campbell's mother. Campbell was immensely relieved to exchange the fetid troop-ship for two weeks at George's hut in the forest, fishing, swimming, and sunning himself; he enjoyed himself so much that he felt almost guilty.

From Durban on 18 April he began an extraordinary journey overland to East Africa. Africa, as always, exhilarated him, and the military trains seemed luxurious compared to the troop-ship. He travelled by rail to Johannesburg and on to Beit Bridge and Bulawayo. One morning he woke to see what appeared to be smoke rising from the plain; a distant roar grew in volume, and suddenly the train was on a bridge right over the chasm of the Victoria Falls, which he had never before seen.[25] When the train stopped at Livingstone, he used some of the money his mother had given him to hire a taxi and drive back to spend an hour at the Falls, which he thought the greatest natural spectacle he had seen.[26]

He went on by slow trains to Lusaka and Broken Hill, and from Elisabethville, in what was then the Belgian Congo, continued the trip by lorry. On the ferry across the Congo his kitbag with most of his possessions and all his money rolled into the water and sank, so that for the rest of the trip he was penniless.

A large party of African askaris returning from leave joined the convoy of trucks, and Campbell was put in charge of 400 of them. They were a wild group, many of them cannibals with teeth filed to needle-points, and earlobes pierced and stretched to take saucer-sized discs of wood or ivory. Though they were from several different tribes, they all spoke Swahili, and Campbell began picking up the language with his usual ease. They travelled by steamer up the length of Lake Tanganyika, and were taken by road to Lake Victoria and across it by boat, an experience that inspired 'Nyanza Moonrise', a cryptic poem about Mary. He completed the journey to Nairobi by train, arriving on 5 May 1943.

Campbell disliked Nairobi; it struck him as a dirty town full of superior officers, and it was tremendously expensive. He dubbed it 'Nairobbery' in his letters to Mary, and within a few days of arriving there produced 'Snapshot of Nairobi':

> With orange-peel the streets are strown
> And pips, beyond computing,
> On every shoulder save my own,
> That's fractured with saluting.[27]
>
> (CP, I, 282)

He was attached to the King's African Rifles and posted to a camp two miles out of Nairobi. He wore the great cockaded hat of the KARs with delight, but he was disgusted to find that he had been made a military censor. 'Any old woman of 80 could do this job I have got,' he wrote to Mary, 'and I cannot look an infantryman in the face.'[28] He began pestering his superiors to let him join a more active unit, for his sciatica had cleared up in the dry climate of East Africa.

His irritation and boredom at this sedentary job made him begin to wonder what he was fighting for: what sort of world would emerge after the war? The Beveridge Report had been published in November 1942, and its picture of the future shape of British society seemed to Campbell a profoundly depressing combination of socialist ideas, forecasting a colourless Woolworth-world, with all men ironed out to one drab egalitarian level. He sent a copy of his biting epigram 'The Beveridge Plan' to Mary on 11 June 1943, and it must have been about this time that he wrote in the deeply cynical poem 'Monologue',

> I'm fighting for a funkhole-warren
> Of bureaucrats, who've come to stay,
> Because I'd rather, than the foreign
> Equivalent, it should be they.
> We all become the thing we fight
> Till differing solely in the palms
> And fists that semaphore (to Right
> Or Left) their imbecile salaams.
>
> (CP, II, 68)

It was probably at this time too that he wrote the depressed 'Heartbreak Camp'.

On 1 June he heard to his delight that he had been transferred to the 12th Observation Unit of the commando force which General Wingate was training for jungle warfare against the Japanese in

Burma. The Observation Units were trained on motor cycles at the foot of Mount Kilimanjaro, in what is now northern Tanzania. They travelled there through a huge game park, the Athi Reserve. During the war years the animals had multiplied enormously; great herds of them were continually crossing the road. Campbell later said of this trip,

It seemed that the whole of Noah's Ark had been let loose: and I am afraid that it rather upset our sense of military dignity, for we were tempted to go after the animals on our motorbikes, and to show off what we had learned in the rough-riding school. We would stand on the footrests and race after a troop of zebras, or a lion, or a bunch of wildebeeste, with our claxons hooting. . . . But when we suddenly ran into the first herd of giraffes – I really thought they were exaggerating! Talk about 'dreaming spires'! It was like shunting into Oxford on a Sunday afternoon.[29]

It was this experience which inspired the finest of his war poems, 'Dreaming Spires', which he was to write in hospital in Mombasa a year later.[30]

He spent nearly two months on the slopes of Kilimanjaro, a period of hard training interrupted by his first attack of malaria, during which he spent some days in hospital in Moshi, the nearest town. It was almost certainly while he was in Moshi hospital that he wrote the first drafts of his two fine sonnets on Camoens, 'Luis de Camoens' and 'Imitation (and Endorsement) of the Famous Sonnet of Bocage', which he posted to Mary on rejoining Wingate's force. Late in July 1943, however, he injured, during a fall while training, the hip which had for so long been affected by sciatica. He could no longer disguise his lameness. He was sent back to hospital in Nairobi and finally certified unfit for active service. The doctors, on seeing the X-ray of his hip, told him that it was incredible that he could have done so much with it.[31] It was clear that he could never again hope to be a front-line soldier.

During this period of inactivity he met, each evening after dinner, a group of men who were interested in literature and who admired his work. With the exception of Major S. C. Mason (whom Campbell first met on 11 June 1943) they were all young Jews, most of them intelligent students from Palestine, kept out of the front line because of the unrest in that territory. The group talked about almost anything – the Talmud, the social purpose of art, Roman Catholicism. Campbell's vitality and erudition impressed them enormously; they called him 'Maestro', and literally sat at his feet.[32] For his part,

Campbell greatly enjoyed these lively evenings, and the hospitality of the Darevskys, the Jewish family in whose home they generally met, provided a very welcome relief from camp life.

Mary meanwhile had left her humiliating employment, and was living in a small, cheap cottage near Petersfield. Tess had joined the WRNS, which she hated; Anna was living with an English family in London and taking dancing lessons in the hope of becoming a ballerina. Their depressed letters made Campbell wonder whether it had been worth separating from them to be so ignominiously crippled in East Africa. Why should he not have taken one of the 'soft' jobs offered him in London? The thought began to obsess him, though he wrote encouragingly to Mary,

You will see in the end that it was worth it. There is only one kind of socialism that is not sheer self-seeking claptrap and boloney – and that is voluntarily to share the burdens of the very lowest conscript and all the burdens that are imposed on one's fellow men and women. We could easily have escaped separation if I had accepted the reserved jobs offered me on the B.B.C. and M.O.I. As a South African I was never liable to conscription or enlistment except as a volunteer. But it was the only thing for a Christian soldier to do, in a world where everyone is snarling for his rights . . .[33]

Now that he was less active he brooded more and more over the reflection that the left-wing poets of the Thirties, who during the Spanish Civil War had urged others to fight Fascism, had in 1939, when the opportunity came for them to do so themselves, either taken what Campbell called 'soft jobs' or fled to America. This thought became an obsession with him. Louis MacNeice, Spender, Auden, Day-Lewis – not one of them was on active service. Instead it was he, whose work had been boycotted because he had been labelled a Fascist, who was fighting Hitler. Spender, in his savage review of *Flowering Rifle*,[34] had called Campbell a 'talking bronco'; now Campbell proudly took the name to himself and struck back at the four left-wing poets, rolling them into the composite monster 'MacSpaunday':

> . . . joint MacSpaunday shuns the very strife
> He barked for loudest, when mere words were rife,
> When to proclaim his proletarian loyalties
> Paid well, was safe, raked in the heavy royalties,
> And made the Mealy Mouth and Bulging Purse
> The hallmark of Contemporary verse.
>
> (*Talking Bronco*, p. 79)

Now that he was disabled, it seemed that he might have to go back to a desk job; he tried to get an appointment as an Army farrier, but was pleased instead to be offered employment as a coast-watcher, looking out for German submarines. He was posted near Lamu, on the Kenya coast north of Mombasa, on 5 September 1943, where he lived in a flimsy thatched hut on a hill overlooking the sea, shaded by great baobabs and coconut palms. He wrote to Mary and his daughters almost daily, describing his Crusoe-existence with stories of his fellow watcher, Paul Duponsel (a French Madagascan) and the small incidents that served to lighten the long boredom of his days. After a month he came down with his second attack of malaria and spent three weeks in hospital in Mombasa (a city which reminded him poignantly of the back-quarters of Lisbon) before being sent to another coast-watching post a little further north. Various officers who admired his work had presented him, when he left Nairobi, with many books, so that he passed his days reading Dante, Homer, Shakespeare, Camoens, and an anthology of Spanish verse.[35] After less than a fortnight he had another attack of malaria, and then another; by 12 November he had had five bouts of it, and soon he lost count completely. 'It is a sort of jack-in-the-box existence,' he wrote humorously to Tess. 'Then out of bed & back to the C-W [Coast-Watching] post and then after a few weeks back to hospital again & so on.'[36]

He spent the Christmas of 1943 in Mombasa hospital, his depression relieved only by visits from two officers, Major Trevor and Captain Penman, both of them Cambridge dons and admirers of his work.[37] While he was recuperating in Mombasa he was given a light job with the native security police of the city, and from them he learned a great deal about the cosmopolitan population of the ancient port, Indian, African, and Arab. He was reading Camoens's *Lusiads* again, and wrote to Mary,

I could never have understood this masterpiece so well if I had not lived out here in contact with the unchanged populations of which Camoens writes and in the midst of the same racial and religious clashes which form so much of his theme. He stands out much more clearly and magnificently, from here, as one of the eight or nine greatest writers in all literature.[38]

He must have been briefly on board dhows in Mombasa harbour, where he would sit and smoke while watching the sunset, but his subsequent claims to have visited Madagascar and Goa, and to have been a coast-watcher at Cape Guardafui in Somalia are without foundation.

Sciatica was again affecting his hip, and it gave him great pain; even

when he recovered from malaria he was forced to spend the early
months of 1944 in Mombasa hospital. He wrote to assure Mary that
the bone was not diseased. 'It's more wear & tear through trying to
bluff it through route marches etc. when it was chipped and twisted,
and that ground it up. But they may be able to fix it up. ¿Quien
sabe?'³⁹ In fact there was no chance of 'fixing it up'; he was to limp
heavily for the rest of his life, and to suffer intermittent pain from the
affected joint until he died.

He published some of his most recent poems in the Army magazine
Jambo at the urging of its editor, Captain Tyfield, but he was not
proud of these poems, written in noisy bars or crowded hospital
wards.

He occupied himself with planning his life after the war. He
foresaw clearly that post-war life in England would not be pleasant,
and in his almost daily letters to Mary he suggested that they should
come out to South Africa or return to Spain, or go to live in Paraguay
or Ecuador (he had been reading travel books on South America).⁴⁰
But Mary, who after leaving Mrs Bridson had worked for a French
officer in Hans Road, Mayfair, had now found a house for the family
to live in – 17 Campden Grove, in Kensington. The monthly cheques
from South Africa were arriving again, and she was intent now on
settling down permanently in England for the first time in their
married life. She resisted all Campbell's romantic suggestions.

He was still preoccupied with the idea that the left-wing poets had
escaped the sufferings of war. Late in February 1944 he saw in *New
Writing* a poem by Day-Lewis (then employed by the Ministry of
Information) beginning 'Will it be so again?' – a poem which provoked
Campbell to write 'The Volunteer's Reply to the Poet' from his
hospital bed:⁴¹

> . . . Oh well may he weep for the soldier,
> Who weeps at a guinea a tear,
> For although his invention gets mouldier,
> It keeps him his job in the rear.
>   (CP, I, 287)

On 2 April 1944 he heard that he was to be sent home, since he
was no longer fit for active service. By an error he was sent by sea to
South Africa, where he spent four happy weeks with his mother in
Durban during May,⁴² hobbling about on two sticks, meeting old
friends and revisiting loved places, before sailing north again through
the Suez Canal on the hospital ship *Oranje*. He seems to have arrived

in Liverpool late in June 1944, and was sent to the Stepping Hill hospital in Stockport, from where he wrote to Mary to let her know he had arrived. The house at 17 Campden Grove had just been damaged for the second time by a flying-bomb, and was uninhabitable, so she and Campbell travelled independently to Oxford and met there, amid the crowds at Carfax, after a separation of sixteen months.

XIV

London

1944–1952

THEY found, with some difficulty, a room at number 44 Wellington Square, and spent the two weeks of Campbell's disembarkation leave there, simply enjoying being together again. During the day they wandered round Oxford looking for old friends and finding none. Edmund Blunden was in Kent writing a book on Shelley; Alan Porter was dead. They did meet C. S. Lewis briefly. Above all, however, they visited Campion Hall, making several good friends among the Jesuits there. It was at this time that they met the brilliant and cultured Father D'Arcy, around whom so many Catholic artists gathered; he and Campbell became very good friends. Campbell also met the South African poet Frank Prince (through Father Fortune, a young South African Jesuit); Prince and Campbell had corresponded during the Thirties, but had since lost contact.

This stay in Oxford was a curious experience for Campbell; he was eerily reminded of the past, and of his first view of the city as a scared boy in 1919. The old buildings seemed quite unchanged, and then, as now, the streets had been full of American soldiers – 'but this is a thirstier lot and they leave one less beer', he wrote wryly to Blunden.[1] The change that had taken place was in himself. In 1919 he had been healthy, brilliant, confident that the world lay before him to be taken and enjoyed. Now, in contrast, he dragged himself painfully through the old streets, a uniformed cripple learning how to use his sticks, and leaning on his wife every so often when he grew tired.

It must have been soon after his return to England that he wrote 'Reflections',[2] his most obviously introspective and self-critical poem. In it he holds up for scrutiny the worst and weakest sides of himself, with unswerving honesty. He even admits that he joined his air raid post originally with the idea of avoiding the Army:

> Of many selves that meet in me
> The meanest has the most persisted,

The one that joined the A.R.P.
When half humanity enlisted.
                                    (*Talking Bronco*, p. 49)

As he later explained to T. S. Eliot, who mistook this for a jibe at
Stephen Spender, 'As soon as the Blitz was over, I was sorely tempted
to remain on in that job. Every man has that side to his nature where
the poltroon and the hedonist (and the devil) all pull together against
his better Nature.'³

He spent several more weeks in a hospital near Oxford before being
allowed to go down to London to rejoin Mary in the Campden Grove
house, which was being repaired again. After various bureaucratic
delays he was discharged from the Army on 24 September 1944 and
given a partial disability pension. He did not find it easy to get back
into civilian life. The Army's womb of discipline had protected him
from alcoholism, money troubles and, above all, responsibility for
looking after his family. It had fed him, clothed him, kept him
occupied and yet given him leisure to write; no wonder he found
civilian life in wartime Britain a strain. The money from South Africa
was clearly going to be inadequate to support a family after the war,
and the paper shortage meant that it might be years before he could
publish the poems he had written in Africa. The greatest of his
troubles was Tess, who was now on the edge of insanity and
worsening rapidly. The strains of the Civil War had increased her
eccentricity, which had first shown itself in 1936, but it was her war
service in the WRNS which had finally tipped the balance. She had
spent months cleaning the spark-plugs of naval engines, and this
deadening task, the absence of her adored father, the unwelcome
attentions of American soldiers and the constant air raids had
combined to unhinge her already weakened mind; the flying-bomb
blast which wrecked 17 Campden Grove and nearly killed her and
Mary had been the last straw.⁴ After treatment at Guy's Hospital she
was sent first to a home near Oxford, and then to one run by nuns
near Epsom. Away from home her condition deteriorated further, and
she soon had to be confined, restrained, and kept under continual
observation.⁵ The care she required was very expensive. Campbell
began casting desperately about for a job. His frequently expressed
contempt for those who had taken 'soft jobs' at the BBC or at the MOI
kept him from doing so himself, though he must have longed to.

A public commission had been set up in 1941 to compensate
owners of houses damaged by war, and a representative of the

commission, Mr Plumb, called on the Campbells to inspect the repairs of their house. He knew Campbell's work, and when he heard that Campbell was trying to get employment as a lift-attendant, he arranged instead for him to be offered the post of Temporary Assistant on the War Damage Commission. Campbell began work on 13 November 1944, at an annual salary of under £300 a year.[6] His task was to write dozens of letters a day, explaining to enquiring householders how the War Damage Commission could help them. Each morning he rose early to take two buses to his work in Acton, where he would limp into the office in his demob suit, wearing the great slouch hat of the King's African Rifles incongruously above it. He would settle silently at his desk, resisting any well-intentioned efforts to get him to talk about poetry, and work glumly until it was time to go home again through the black-out. He made little impression on his fellow clerks, none of whom could remember him in later years. The fire seemed to have died in him; life was a weary round of drudgery, poverty, watery beer, and rationed food. Tormented by the pain of his hip and the thought of Tess, shut away in Epsom, he limped through the ruins of London, his cockaded hat a last defiant symbol of the life that had gone. 'I'm a civil servant now,' he wrote tiredly to his mother,[7] ' . . . and I'm far too glad to have the job to find any grouse with it.' It is a testimony to his basic humility, and to his lowness of spirit, that this poet, soldier, and traveller kept himself uncomplainingly to his miserable task for eight months.

His output of original verse had almost stopped under the strains of this way of life. He continued to work at translating the poems of St John of the Cross, and he also began translating the best work of the Spanish poet Garcia Lorca, who had been killed under mysterious circumstances during the Spanish Civil War. Meanwhile he pressed ahead preparing all the poems he had written since 1936 for publication by Faber & Faber. T. S. Eliot was the director with whom he negotiated the contract for this book, which he called *Talking Bronco*, and the two men saw a good deal of each other. Eliot seems to have found the negotiations tricky, for Campbell was determined to include a polemical preface violently critical of Mac-Neice, Spender, Auden, and Day-Lewis (all of whom published with Faber) as well as other writers such as Hugh MacDiarmid.[8] Eliot undertook the task of persuading Campbell to drop this attack, though he hinted broadly that he agreed with Campbell's opinion of much contemporary verse:

Of course I have the additional reason for never expressing an opinion about any modern poetry, that I am a publisher, and therefore not in a position to do so: but even if I wasn't, I should think twice about it, because if I said exactly what I think about a good deal of it, it would simply be put about that I was jealous and didn't want any younger men to be successful.

Incidentally, as for Auden, my sympathies are now rather on his side: for I have begun to suspect that some of his friends who have (more or less) faced the terrors of London, are now ready to cold-shoulder him – and it takes the form of depreciating his recent work. I don't think that anyone who has not actually gone and fought, or shown his readiness to, is in a position to adopt this attitude towards him.

So I don't know whether you can abbreviate this preface to what can be left, or prefer to scrap it altogether. I am not sure that it isn't better just to leave the volume to itself: and leave the vipers to be forgotten.

I enjoyed the evening very much, and I should like both to come again and to reciprocate: except that a London restaurant now is a very poor return for such hospitality.[9]

Campbell agreed that the preface should be dropped entirely, and his reply showed how little real substance he regarded his attacks on 'MacSpaunday' as having: 'Anyway it only shows how hard up we all are if we consider courage or patriotism as a criterion of poetry. (One might as well condemn the paintings of Cezanne because he deserted from the French army in the franco-prussian war!)'[10]

In spite of this admission and his abandonment of the preface, he was determined to print his poems on 'MacSpaunday'. However, he did agree to all but one of the changes Eliot proposed to make, softening particularly his attacks on Spender.[11]

He was gradually becoming accustomed to his job on the War Damage Commission, and it no longer left him exhausted at the end of each day. Through two South Africans with contacts in the BBC, Jacques Malan and John Swift,[12] he got an invitation to broadcast two talks on his experiences in East Africa, in July and September 1945. It seems to have been these talks which brought him to the attention of Desmond MacCarthy, who was then on the BBC's Literary Advisory Committee. MacCarthy was horrified to hear that Campbell was working as a government clerk. He promptly sent Campbell £40, and it was he who arranged for Campbell to be offered the post of Talks Producer on the BBC.[13] With great relief Campbell resigned his post at the War Damage Commission on 21 July 1945 and took a brief holiday, much of which he spent in hospital with a renewed attack of malaria, a disease he was never to shake off completely.

He became acquainted with the Sinhalese editor of *Poetry London*, Tambimuttu, who planned to publish several of Campbell's translations of Spanish poetry, and who, with R. M. Nadal, had the sole British rights in Lorca's work;[14] but the plan came to nothing. It was through Tambimuttu too, in December 1945, that he met the deaf South African poet David Wright, in a pub off the Tottenham Court Road. Wright was struck by Campbell's 'battered imperial face, cold eyes and cruel looking mouth under a cockaded felt hat';[15] he reacted coolly to Campbell's generous offer to recommend Wright's poems to F. C. Slater, an anthologist. (Campbell, not put off, recommended Wright anyway, together with another young South African, Anthony Delius.)[16] Wright had heard nothing but ill of Campbell and his work, and it took months for this prejudice to dissipate. The influence of *The Georgiad* and *Flowering Rifle* lingered, and many writers who had never met Campbell nursed a fierce antipathy towards him. In any case Wright never managed to lip-read Campbell, perhaps because of his heavy South African accent. Some months after this first meeting Campbell saw Wright in the street. Remembering that he was deaf, Campbell simply placed a hand for a moment on Wright's shoulder as if to say 'sorry we can't speak', and then after a moment walked on.[17] The incident recalls Campbell's instinctive sympathy with Aldous Huxley's blindness.

Campbell joined the BBC as a producer on the fledgling Third Programme, and was also appointed to the BBC's Literary Advisory Committee,[18] on 1 January 1946. In later years he loved to say that he had arrived at Bush House wearing all his medals, expecting to be made a commissionaire. This was the sort of self-depreciating story Campbell enjoyed, the obverse side of his boasting. He liked his work at the BBC, though for his first six months he was required to produce a very pedestrian programme called 'Can I Help You?' designed to aid the public in getting the greatest benefit out of the new machinery of the welfare state. In contrast to his job on the War Damage Commission, the BBC work brought him into contact with a great many people who interested him – poets, novelists, and playwrights, intellectuals of all kinds. He hated the regular hours the BBC imposed on him, but his highly efficient secretary, Daphne Chasmar, supplied his work with the order and method he lacked.

After a time he was asked to produce the talks on the Third Programme. This work he found both congenial and interesting. He would arrive each morning in the office he shared with another producer, Archie Gordon, and their two secretaries, and settle down at once to reading the pile of scripts on his desk, choosing one or more for future programmes and rejecting the rest. At about eleven, when the pubs opened, he would go out saying he had agreed to meet someone. He had no idea that his secretary knew where he went every morning, and once, when she telephoned him at the George (his favourite pub near Bush House) to remind him that he had an appointment, he was filled with astonishment and admiration.[19]

He found her efficiency alarming, and when she asked him what she should be doing, he would reply 'Oh, there's nothing to do! You go and have a coffee.' In fact, as she soon discovered, there was a great deal to be done; if letters were to be answered at all, she had not only to compose and type them for Campbell, but often to sign them on his behalf as well.[20] Nor did he find it easy to communicate by telephone. He had two on his desk, an internal and an external line, and when one rang he would invariably pick up the other and bellow into it as if trying to prove that the instrument was unnecessary.[21]

His failure to understand mechanical contrivances resulted in many ludicrous situations. One evening he had been drinking with Dylan Thomas in a large bar in the basement of a London working-man's club. Campbell and Thomas quarrelled and Campbell, in a rage, determined to leave. He limped into the lift and pressed the button; the lift rose and came to a stop, but the doors in front of Campbell remained closed. Irritated, he pushed more buttons; the lift went down and came up again, but still the doors remained closed. Then someone tapped him on the shoulder. He turned angrily – and saw that the exit door for the ground floor was on the opposite side.[22]

In many ways he was out of place at the BBC, in spite of the fact that he found the work and the company congenial. One small incident illustrates the point. Campbell and the other members of the Literary Advisory Committee (Desmond MacCarthy, Stephen Potter, and Geoffrey Grigson) used to meet in the Controller's office for a meal before their discussion; a secretary would bring up drinks and food from the BBC kitchens. On one occasion there was no bottle-opener on the drinks tray. 'Don't bother about an opener, man,' said Campbell, limping over to the Controller's finely veneered desk with a bottle of beer. He closed a drawer on the serrated metal cap of the bottle, and with a flourish jerked the bottle sharply downwards. With a crack, the cap scored a great gash in the veneer of the desk; there was a gasp of horror from the secretary and confused apologies from Campbell.[23] It is not surprising that he spent as little time as possible at the BBC, escaping whenever he could to go drinking with Dylan Thomas or Aimé Tschiffely.

The great advantage of his new job was that it provided him with the leisure and the stimulus to work seriously at his own poetry again. He was able to correct the proofs of *Talking Bronco*, and the volume was at last published on 10 May 1946. It got a mixed reception from the reviewers.

The Times praised it, while observing that Campbell would have done better to have concentrated more on his lyrics than on satire.[24] There was praise also from the *New English Review*,[25] and even Vita Sackville-West, in *The Observer*, called Campbell 'one of our most considerable living poets'.[26] *Poetry Review* was unreservedly enthusiastic.[27] However, the BBC's own magazine, *The Listener*, printed a review which hardly commented on the poems, but contained a sustained and violent personal attack on Campbell[28] – an attack which drew several letters of protest the following week, one of them from the Oxford historian A. L. Rowse.[29]

But it was Stephen Spender who responded most vigorously to *Talking Bronco*. Outraged that Campbell should have accused 'Mac-Spaunday' of writing Communist propaganda for financial gain, he wrote to Campbell accusing him of 'infamous slander' and calling him 'a liar, a gross slanderer, an empty-headed boaster, a coward, a bully and a Fascist'. He also promised to produce a copy of this letter when he thought it necessary on any occasion when Campbell's poetry was under discussion in literary circles.[30] He sent several strong letters of protest to Faber & Faber, and he reviewed *Talking Bronco* in *Time and Tide* under the title 'The Case of Roy Campbell'. He denied that 'MacSpaunday' had accepted money for their writings about Spain and he called Campbell 'a mixture of pretentiousness, violence, glamour, cruelty and ignobleness'. He quoted Campbell's lines

> The vultures on the cook-house nest
> Like poets on the BBC

and observed, twice, that Campbell should be happier now that he himself was roosting on the BBC.[31]

Campbell was generally pleased with the reviews – at least his work was no longer being ignored – and he was delighted by Spender's reaction to his satiric shafts. He sent a long reply to Spender's letter, rejecting the epithets 'coward' and 'Fascist' by a comparison between his own war service and his view of Spender's, in the most inflated terms:

For a disabled British Infantry N.C.O., wearing the King's medals for loyal service, and commended on his discharge sheet for 'excellent military conduct' – to be called a 'coward' by a 'chairborne' shock trooper of the Knife-and-Fork Brigade, one who dug himself in with his eating-irons in the rearguard of both wars . . . why to me that seems funny, not annoying![32]

Nevertheless, he found Spender's threat to blacken his name in literary circles alarmingly reminiscent of the boycott from which he had suffered so much before the war. These fears were strengthened when, in June 1946, Ewart Milne wrote to *Tribune* suggesting that measures should be taken to 'isolate' Campbell, who replied vigorously. The two of them carried on a warm correspondence in the paper's letter column for some weeks.[33] (Campbell, who had the last word, was publicly supported in this correspondence by William Empson, who wrote to deny that *Talking Bronco* showed any falling-off from the standard of Campbell's earlier work.)[34]

This support was symptomatic of growing public recognition of Campbell's writing; his reputation, having reached its lowest point after the publication of *Flowering Rifle*, was slowly rising again. In May 1947, for the first time, he was invited to Oxford to address a student poetry group – a task he greatly enjoyed despite his hatred of public speaking. Although he undoubtedly revelled in his literary quarrels, he was also pathetically pleased to be accepted and recognized, if only by a student society. Oxford, as always, reminded him of his own failure there, and he had little in common with the president of the poetry society, who on his arrival had offered him nothing but tea made with powdered milk. The talk itself was not entirely successful. Campbell came stumping into the hall in a duffle-coat, and read a number of his poems in his heavy South African accent, before explaining that he had cribbed them all from French poets. It was after this talk that he met Geoffrey Dutton, the Australian writer, then a student at Oxford. Campbell seized his hand with relief: 'Man, thank God to see another colonial amongst all these bloody Pommies! Come and let's have a drink, quick, before the pubs close.'[35]

He was drinking as much as ever, and growing stouter as a result, for his lameness meant that he could take no exercise. He saw a great deal of Dylan Thomas; the two of them used to meet for drinking-bouts at the Catherine Wheel, the pub nearest Campbell's house in Campden Grove – bouts so heroic that over thirty years later several of the aged 'regulars' of the Catherine Wheel could remember the two poets eating a bunch of daffodils whole, flowers, leaves, and stems, for

From the left: Alan Paton, Laurens van der Post, Enslin du Plessis, Roy Campbell, Uys Krige.
London, 1952

Tess's wedding-party in the sitting-room at Bochechos, 7 August 1954. From the left: Anna, Rob Lyle,
Mary, Tess, Ignatius Custodio, Campbell. At Tess's feet, unidentified, Anna's daughter Frances

In the George, 1953

a bet on St David's Day.[36] At the George, near the BBC, he and Louis MacNeice one day quarrelled and traded light blows, MacNeice actually drawing blood from Campbell's nose, before they made it up very amicably, with Campbell buying MacNeice a drink.[37] After this encounter in 1946, Campbell would defend MacNeice steadfastly when he heard him criticized by others. [38]

He made several other new friends at this time. In 1947 he met Alister Kershaw, a young Australian poet, who had just arrived in England. Kershaw was a friend of Geoffrey Dutton who had arranged for him to meet Campbell. They had a few drinks in the George with Cecil Gray and Parry Jones the singer, and when Campbell heard that Kershaw had landed in England penniless, he at once suggested that Kershaw should do a talk for the BBC. Kershaw was struck by this act of generosity, for Campbell had no idea whether Kershaw had any ability as a writer or broadcaster. During the rehearsal of his talk, Kershaw saw Campbell in the control-booth talking to the engineer and obviously not listening to a word of the talk. When Kershaw finished, Campbell was roused by the sudden silence and said over the talk-back, 'Man, you read that like an angel!'[39]

In fact the broadcast went very well; Campbell arranged a repeat and it was printed in *The Listener*. Kershaw was paid a sizeable amount as a result, and he used it to fly to Paris to meet another writer he admired, the novelist and biographer Richard Aldington. He talked about Campbell to Aldington, who sent Campbell a copy of a limited edition of his article on Charles Waterton; Campbell wrote back, and the lively correspondence thus begun continued until the end of Campbell's life. In December 1947, Aldington sent the Campbells a huge Christmas turkey, by airmail – a bird Campbell described as being the size of a baby Austin.[40] Aldington's generosity, and the food itself, lifted the spirits of Campbell's family; they depended very much at this bleak time on the food parcels they got irregularly from friends (especially the faithful C. J. Sibbett in Cape Town) to supplement their rationed diets.

Another acquaintance was the sculptor Hugh Oloff de Wet. Like the Campbells, he was a great lover of Spain, though his political allegiances were diametrically opposed to Campbell's; during the Civil War de Wet had volunteered to fly for the Air Force of the Spanish Republic. In spite of this he and Campbell became great friends. He made portrait heads, in bronze, of both Campbell and Mary, that of Mary being much the better. The head of Campbell is now in the Durban City Library.

Most significant of all the people Campbell met at this time, however, was the poet Rob Lyle, who was to become his closest friend and his patron. Early in 1947 Lyle sent Campbell a satirical poem he had written and shortly afterwards Campbell rang him and arranged to meet him, in February 1947, in the Catherine Wheel for a drink.[41] Though Lyle was at this time twenty-seven, and Campbell forty-five, the two men took to each other at once. Campbell discovered that Lyle had been a Staff-Captain of the Intelligence Corps camp at Rotherham where he had himself trained, and though they had not been there at the same time, he would often hereafter introduce Lyle as 'my Commanding Officer'. Lyle, a very shy man, admired Campbell not only for his poetry but for his complete lack of self-consciousness and reserve. For a time the two men met once a week in the evenings, and then began to meet for lunch as well, at Campbell's suggestion. They would go to a nearby fish and chip shop, or, occasionally, to Pagani's restaurant.[42] By June they were meeting daily. Campbell helped Lyle with his poetry, and Lyle, for his part, began to look for more ways of helping Campbell financially.

Campbell's letters at this time make it plain that his continuing money worries made it difficult for him to write original poetry.

. . . I have been converted into a breadwinning machine and never have a minute outside my job for anything except sleep without which, in my present crippled condition, I couldn't keep or continue my job. I haven't written a line of poetry for over a year . . .

he wrote to Sibbett.[43] Tess's treatment was still costing a great deal of money; Campbell used to go down to see her in the home near Epsom at weekends. She was a little better and wanted to come home, but Campbell feared that looking after her would put too much of a strain on Mary and Anna. Anna herself had had a minor breakdown, in June 1948, as a result of her dancing increasingly difficult roles. Campbell's lifelong fear of going mad himself also made him inclined to distance himself from Tess. Her slow improvement, however, made it possible for Mary to stay with her in a country cottage they rented near Winchelsea, and eventually to bring her home to Campden Grove, where for a time she seemed almost well.

Campbell himself was plagued during 1948 by recurring bouts of the malaria he had contracted in East Africa. Sweating and shaking, he would take to his bed for weeks at a stretch. He continued working on his translations of Spanish poems, and he also corrected the proofs of the first volume of his *Collected Poems*. He lost interest in it, however, when the publisher insisted on dividing the poems into 'lyrics' and 'satires', rather than printing them chronologically, and the volume, when it eventually appeared in 1946, published by the Bodley Head, was full of misprints. Campbell complained bitterly that such satirical pieces as 'A Veld Eclogue' were printed among the 'lyrics', while 'St Peter of the Three Canals' was classed as a satire. None the less the book got good reviews (including a full page in the *Times Literary Supplement*)[44] and it sold steadily.

On 6 October 1948[45] Campbell travelled with Rob Lyle to Spain to give a lecture on modern English writers at the Ateneo in Barcelona, where he had been recommended by Charles Ley, a man whom Campbell had met before the war, when Ley had been working for the British Council in Madrid. Ley had a great many literary friends in Spain, and it was through his influence that Campbell got this and subsequent invitations to lecture in Spain. Campbell and Lyle spent a week in Barcelona, and Campbell drank continually during the days before and after his lecture, which he delivered in Spanish. Throughout his life he prepared his lectures with meticulous care beforehand; but on reaching the podium, he would invariably throw aside his notes and improvise, filling his talk with the mixture of humour, violent invective, and curious learning that was typical of him.

During this Barcelona trip his relations with Lyle warmed. Lyle found him an essentially solitary man in need of someone to share his solitude.[46] It was in Barcelona, while they were drinking at a pavement café, that Campbell gave an account of his political beliefs:

I don't believe in anything. At heart I'm a complete anarchist. I fought in the Spanish War because I was disgusted with the crimes of the Reds and the humbug of the liberals. I joined the British Army in 1939 [*sic*] because I couldn't sit at home while my comrades went out to fight. I didn't believe in democracy or in any of the 'causes' for which we were supposed to be fighting: but I believe in comradeship and in standing shoulder to shoulder with my fellow-men.

When Lyle repeated this to a sober Campbell, the next morning, he exclaimed that he must have been drunk;[47] but there is much truth in his self-analysis.

It was the very fact that he had no theoretical political convictions that made him so sensitive to the charge of Fascism levelled against him by Stephen Spender. Early in April 1949 he heard that Spender would be reading his verse for the Poetry Society in the crypt of the

Ethical Church in Bayswater, and he decided to go along and denounce Spender before Spender could denounce him. Accordingly, having had enough beer beforehand to work up his feelings, he went along to the Ethical Church on the night of 14 April, with Mary and Anna, as well as Lyle, Tschiffely, John Gawsworth, and Charles Mulvey, a Canadian soldier and hunter who was one of Campbell's most faithful drinking companions. None of them seems to have known what Campbell was planning.

They stood patiently at the back of the hall while a large soprano sang *lieder* to warm up the audience, until Spender was introduced. He stepped to the podium, coughed, and began to speak. At once Campbell lurched into action. 'I wish to protest on behalf of the Sergeants' Mess of the King's African Rifles,' he bellowed in his best parade-ground voice, stumping down the aisle with his knotty stick. The audience, dumb, swivelled its collective head to watch his progress. Yelling curses at Spender, Campbell threw open a door which he imagined led on to the stage and limped inside, to find himself in a passage leading to the lavatory. The audience was still paralysed, and Spender leaned on his lectern as if hypnotized. Campbell reappeared in a moment and climbed on to the stage. He limped heavily across it and, leaning on his stick, swung a clumsy, right-handed blow that connected lightly with Spender's nose, which promptly began to bleed. As if the blow had tripped a switch, the hall awoke into uproar.

The Chairman of the Poetry Society, Robert Armstrong, leaped on to the stage and bundled Campbell off it, and Gawsworth, Lyle, and Mulvey got him outside. Wet handkerchiefs were applied to Spender's nose, but when Armstrong and others offered to call the police, Spender quietly declined. 'He is a great poet; he is a great poet. We must try to understand,' he said, and he insisted on continuing his reading. However, someone had already summoned the police, and Tschiffely and Anna, who had fled at the first sign of trouble, met them outside the church. When the policeman demanded to know what was going on, Tschiffely replied, 'Nothing, officer, just a couple of poets having a row.'[48]

This was easily the most highly publicized of any of Campbell's personal clashes, and most of the richly embroidered versions which later circulated were put about by Campbell himself, as if he were proud of his conduct. In fact, it seems likely that he had gone along to the hall with the idea of doing nothing more than heckling from the back; drink and his sense of grievance had taken over when he got there. He was ashamed of himself when he sobered up, as his subsequent letter of apology to the organizers of the reading shows clearly enough.[49]

It was at this time too that he quarrelled with Geoffrey Grigson, who had published a critical review of Edith Sitwell's work, and though Campbell had not seen her for years, he sprang to her defence, writing letters to such magazines as *Poetry Review*. When Grigson, in a radio broadcast, also attacked Desmond MacCarthy, to whom Campbell owed his BBC job, Campbell decided to take action. Meeting Grigson in the Aldwych one morning at the end of 1949, Campbell advanced threateningly upon the younger man, stick raised. Grigson, a slight, short-sighted man, was later to maintain that he stood his ground,[50] while Campbell insisted that he had fled into a cake shop;[51] whatever the truth of the matter, the story went to bolster Campbell's reputation as an iron-fisted persecutor of his juniors. Campbell delighted in this reputation; as his hip rendered him less and less active, he boasted increasingly of his fighting ability. Age and alcohol were catching up on him, and he clung to the ghost of his vigorous youth by every possible means.

As a result of his intervention on her behalf, Edith Sitwell wrote to Campbell in August 1949, inviting him and Mary to lunch with herself and William Walton, another friend whom Campbell had not seen since his Oxford days. In her disregard for conventions, Edith Sitwell was rather like Campbell; both of them hated the smallness and greyness of post-war English life, and loved grand and heroic gestures. Even in their eccentricities of dress they were similar, her sweeping robes and oversized jewellery expressing the same facet of character as his broad-brimmed hats and carved sticks. After this meeting in September 1949 they continued to see each other regularly, and the Campbells' Catholicism influenced Edith Sitwell profoundly. When she was received into the Roman Catholic Church herself, in August 1955, she asked them to be two of her godparents. For his part, Campbell became devoted to her; in many of these literary quarrels, she provided him with what he needed – a cause for which to fight. He treated her, as he treated all women, from BBC secretaries to Spanish *condesas*, with fantastic courtesy. At one party at Lyle's house, in 1949, he knelt at her feet, kissed her hand, and announced solemnly, 'Edith my darling, you are a great lady! I will be your knight and fight your battles for you!'[52] Both of them enjoyed such displays. And when he attacked Grigson on her behalf, she would write him delighted letters thanking him and egging him on.

She was not the only one to be impressed by the obvious depth and sincerity of Campbell's Christian faith. Rob Lyle was also deeply influenced by his contact with Campbell and Mary. One day, when they were lunching at Pagani's together, Mary began to scold Campbell for not attending Mass often enough. (She went herself every morning, while Campbell communicated only on occasional Sundays.) Campbell rejected her rebuke with a rare show of independence. 'Look kid, you worship in your way and I'll worship in mine,' he said firmly. And he told Lyle, 'Ninety per cent of Christian doctrine you can throw away. But what means something to me is that that man hung on the Cross for me. That's what I hold on to.'[53] Partly as a result of Campbell's influence, Lyle was himself converted to Roman Catholicism, and Campbell was his godfather.

Lyle was now playing a much larger part in the Campbells' lives. Knowing that Campbell's work at the BBC, though as congenial as such work could possibly be, was still preventing him from writing original verse, Lyle found a way to support Campbell without offending him. For some time Lyle had been toying with the idea of starting a literary political magazine. From the beginning of 1949 he began organizing seriously, and in April 1949 the first slim issue, in brilliant scarlet, appeared. Lyle called it *The Catacomb*, and as its name suggested, it was intended to be the voice of what Lyle saw as the Catholic, conservative, classical forces of Europe, driven underground by the triumphant tide of socialism, but surviving.

Lyle asked Campbell to contribute to the magazine, and paid him for doing so. After a few months Lyle asked Campbell to be the full-time editor. Campbell, in spite of his memories of *Voorslag*, agreed unhesitatingly. He resigned from the BBC in September 1949, and began work with Lyle, immensely relieved to escape at last the regular hours he had so hated. Running *The Catacomb* took up very little of his time, for Lyle did most of the work and wrote many of the articles, under a variety of names. Campbell himself contributed odd articles attacking Spender[54] or Grigson;[55] and he also contributed many of the translations he was making at this time, of Lorca, Rimbaud, Baudelaire, Apollinaire, and Aurelio Valls. But he published very little of the original verse Lyle hoped he would write when freed from the BBC.

Instead, late in 1949, he began work on a second autobiography which, at Lyle's suggestion, he called *Light on a Dark Horse*. In private letters he expressed his dislike of all prose writing by calling the book 'my autobuggeroffery'. It is not clear why he wrote it at all. Although he called it 'a potboiler' he did not write it for money, for his salary from *The Catacomb*, together with his monthly cheque from South Africa, was enough to support his family; yet he did not enjoy writing it. 'I have to be locked in like a wild beast or a felon, because I keep on procrastinating and have to make up for lost time in long bursts of feverish hard work, otherwise the wretched thing would never get done . . .', he wrote to Edith Sitwell.[56]

Even more than *Broken Record*, *Light on a Dark Horse* was the product of imagination. He drew upon his former autobiography, retelling the tales and embroidering them until they bore scarcely any resemblance to the original event. Many of the chapters were so quickly written that in them he threw grammar and syntax to the winds; but others, particularly the chapters about France, he worked at with great care. His narrative method was carefully designed to appear artless – a story leading into a digression, that into another digression, and yet another, in an interwoven maze Laurence Sterne might have admired. He gave himself a heroic role in all the stories, boasting in such a way that not even the most credulous reader would believe him.

Why did he not occupy his time by writing poetry instead, as Lyle hoped he would, and as he himself longed to do? The answer seems to be that the fountain of inspiration had partially dried up. He had never been able to write well in England; although he loved London, it did not produce those fertile periods he had had in South Africa, France, and Spain, and even Wales. Moreover, poetry had always been 'the sweat of other activities' for him – and he had fewer and fewer activities.

It was not simply that his leg increasingly prevented him from getting about freely; he was growing more and more lethargic, and getting steadily heavier. His acute eyesight was deteriorating, and he was forced to start wearing National Health spectacles for reading; he hated them and refused to be photographed wearing them. What was left of his hair was grey. He was now forty-eight, and looked at least ten years older. Mary, by contrast, seemed as beautiful and vivacious as ever, and Campbell was intensely aware of this. It was at this time that he produced what in the context of his feelings of inadequacy is his most heart-rending poem – 'Counsel', freely translated from a Portuguese original by Manuel Bandeira:

> The world is pitiless and lewdly jeers
> All tragedy. Anticipate your loss.
> Weep silently, in secret. Hide your tears,
> So to become accustomed to your cross.

Alone grief can ennoble us. She only
Is grand and pure. Then learn to love her now –
To be your muse, when you are left and lonely . . .

(CP, II, 118)

One sorrow, at least, was lessened: Tess, after a suicide attempt in
1948, was showing signs of slow recovery from her mental illness.
She was gradually eating a little more, and showing more interest in
the world, and less fear of it. Lyle gave her a job getting *The Catacomb*
ready for posting each month, and the simple, repetitive labour gave
her an activity she could cope with. Early in 1950 a Polish doctor
came to see her, a slim nervous man who was a friend of one of the
Campbells' neighbours. Instead of probing into her past, he asked her,
'What do you want most in the world?' 'To go to France or Spain,'
said Tess unhesitatingly, and the Pole, after talking to her for some
time, recommended that she should if possible be given a holiday in a
Latin country. Campbell himself had been longing to get back to
France or Spain; now he began making plans to spend some months
staying near Richard Aldington in the village of Bormes in the south
of France.

He delivered several books almost simultaneously to the publishers
early in 1950 – four volumes of translations of Lorca, which Eliot
wanted for Faber & Faber; his translation of the poems of St John of
the Cross, on which he had now been working for eleven years; and
the manuscript of *Light on a Dark Horse*. With the advances for these,
and some help from Lyle, Campbell was able to leave for France with
Tess on 11 May 1950.[57] Mary did not accompany them, and Anna
was staying for a few months with Mary's sister Helen, who lived in
Italy, having married an Italian professor after the death during the
war of her first husband, 'Grandpère'.

Campbell and Tess spent two quiet weeks staying in the village of
St Jacut de la Mer, in Brittany, to accustom Tess to the change; then,
by easy stages, they travelled south through Paris, where they spent
an afternoon, and on to Bormes, a beautiful place, high in the
pinewoods, overlooking Hyères and the Côte d'Azur. There Campbell rented rooms at a garage,[58] about six miles from Aldington's villa.
He and Aldington took to each other after some initial suspicion.
They were both big, bluff, no-nonsense men – in appearance at least –
and Aldington liked a drink and a good story as much as Campbell
did. He was nine years older than Campbell, who at first treated him
with care.

He seems a bit like W. L. [Wyndham Lewis] in the way that most of his reactions are hostile. He is a recluse and seems anti-everything. For him everybody is a 'Jew' – including Eliot, Lewis and Pound. He is unlike Lewis however in that he is goodnaturedly 'anti' – there is no real rancour in what he says . . .

he wrote to Peter Russell.[59] Once having sized one another up, however, the two men began meeting every day, Aldington sending his big car to fetch Campbell in the afternoons.

The sunlight, the natural beauty, the food, and the simple life of the Mediterranean had an immediate effect upon Tess. Her recovery from this time on was rapid; she smiled for the first time in several years, and she began gaining weight. The effect on Campbell was almost as beneficial: he began writing poetry again. It was at Bormes, in June 1950, that he completed a poem he had begun in hospital in London in 1945, 'Rhapsody of the Man in Hospital Blues'. In it, for the first time, he came to terms with his lameness:

> From Notting Hill to Prince's Gate
> I'd started breaking-in my stick
> And of my new, three-legged gait
> Acquired the quaint arithmetic.
>
> No more to canter, trot or trippel,
> Where dandies prance along the Row,
> I coaxed the strange unwieldy cripple
> I had become yet feared to know . . .
>   (CP, II, 100)

Light on a Dark Horse was giving him trouble. His old friend Tom Burns, who was preparing the manuscript for publication by Hollis & Carter, had given it to a reader, Lewis Hastings, who suggested many changes. Burns therefore asked Campbell to travel to St Jacut again, to meet Hastings and work on the book. Campbell arrived there penniless on 20 July, [60] to find the town so full that there was no hotel room to be had; he was forced to spend the first night in the bracken by the main road, and got soaked to the skin.[61] He agreed to revise the book completely, and after two days returned to Bormes to work on it, his sciatica very much worse.

He saw a lot of Augustus John, who was spending the summer in a nearby village, and who was also finishing work on an autobiography, *Chiaroscuro*. He planned to reproduce in it his 1920 portrait of Campbell, but was unable to find a photograph of it, and his plan to paint a fresh portrait of Campbell came to nothing.[62] Mary and Anna arrived in July, and stayed for two months. Campbell spent the summer in a pleasant whirl of activity, finishing *Light on a Dark Horse*, revising *Adamastor* for republication by a South African publisher, Paul Koston, drinking and talking with Aldington, and revisiting his old haunts in Provence.

Late in September 1950 he returned with the family to London. The condition of his hip had so deteriorated that he was bedridden for over a month, in November and December. He spent the time correcting the proofs of his translations of St John of the Cross, and finishing a story for children, *The Mamba's Precipice*, a powerful evocation of Natal as it had been in his privileged childhood. In an attempt to improve his health, he tried substituting tea for beer, and worked at a furious pace on prose and translations; meanwhile he sent doleful letters to his South African friends, telling them that he was to have his leg amputated at the hip.[63]

By May 1951 he was well enough to make another trip to Spain, to lecture at the Ateneo in Madrid, again at the invitation of Charles Ley. He was also being invited regularly to address student literary groups at Oxford and Cambridge, and even various Scottish universities, including St Andrews; he often accepted these invitations. Generally he began his talks by reading some of his poems, and he would then launch into wide-ranging discussions of modern literature, praising his friends (Eliot, Dylan Thomas, and Edith Sitwell) and damning his and their enemies. In the course of one of these good-humoured diatribes, at Oxford, when he had been defending Dylan Thomas against 'MacSpaunday', he stopped in mid-sentence, left the lectern, and began stalking some invisible object round the stage, his knotty stick raised, while the audience stared in puzzled fascination. Suddenly the stick came down with a crash: a cloud of dust arose, Campbell straightened up and grinned. 'Got him!' he said. 'I can't bear spiders!' Then he went back to his talk about 'MacSpaunday'. The audience took the point.[64] Much of the success of his talks lay in such carefully planned gestures and jokes.

His translations of St John of the Cross were published by Harvill in June 1951, and the book was given a more enthusiastic reception than anything he had written since *Adamastor*. Its sales quickly surpassed those of any of his other works. The book was widely and enthusiastically reviewed, and many critics made the point that the translations were fine poems in their own right. An anonymous *TLS* reviewer commented on 15 June 1951, in the course of a long article, 'The translations from St John of the Cross are . . . among the most pure and lucid of English mystical poems.' Edwin Muir, in *The Observer*, (2 June 1951) called the work 'a triumph'; and Kathleen Raine's review in the *New Statesman* (16 June 1951) is representative of comments that appeared in most major newspapers:

Of all living English poets Roy Campbell is the most masterly in his use of rhyme, and he is able to use metre so as to convey a sense of intense passion. He has reproduced the Spanish rhymes and metres as closely as possible, and yet his English versions have the freshness of original poems.

Campbell richly deserved this success, for he had spent eleven years in writing and polishing these poems, though he was later to claim that he had written them in a couple of months, inspired by the saint himself. 'Were I superstitious I should say that San Juan brought me luck,' he said. 'Not being superstitious, I say that he wrought a miracle.'[65] In a sense, these translations he made after the war are a natural extension of his habit, beginning with his juvenile verse attempts, of using the work of other poets as a springboard for his own inspiration.[66] The great success of *The Poems of St John of the Cross* made him better known than he had been since the early Thirties, and the book also won him the Foyle Prize for Poetry. To Campbell's great amusement Stephen Spender was chosen to award the prize, after an excellent lunch in the Dorchester, on 17 January 1952. Spender had not known until shortly before who the recipient was to be, but the two men shook hands with the utmost cordiality, in marked contrast to their previous encounter.[67]

Campbell was no longer feeling so isolated in the literary world. His circle of friends was distinguished and astonishingly wide. Painters, policemen, ex-soldiers, diplomats, bullfighters, butchers, and sculptors rubbed shoulders at the rowdy and hilarious parties he and Mary gave in the basement of their Campden Grove house. The aritificial or real barriers that divide men simply did not exist for Campbell. Among the regular or occasional visitors were Augustus John, the Spanish Ambassador, and the South African High Commissioner (an old school-friend of Campbell's), the local butcher Jack Russell, T. S. Eliot, Father D'Arcy, the bullfighter Mario Cabré, the Provençal writer Charles de Richter, Evelyn Waugh, the Australian horseman and film actor Chips Rafferty, Sir Ronald Storrs, and the sculptor Oloff de Wet. They were all welcomed with open arms, plied with drinks and Campbell's hilarious stories, given unconventional dinners in the kitchen, and (according to Rob Lyle) 'more often than not assisted off the premises'.[68] Campbell seldom talked about poetry at these gatherings; he would reserve such 'shop-talk' for his solitary evenings with Lyle.

His fame grew as his output of original poetry declined. His much-revised *Light on a Dark Horse*, 'this often beautiful and always bee-loud autobiography', as Dylan Thomas called it,[69] was published on 7 December 1951, to a mixed reception, scattered reviews, and disappointing sales. Before its publication Harold Nicolson had written to protest against Campbell's account of his stay at Long Barn, and Hollis & Carter agreed to alter the passage [70] – though in fact the original account had been both restrained and tactful. Campbell complained that Lewis Hastings had bowdlerized the book, and he announced angrily that he was rewriting it, complete with the excised sections, under the title *As You Were*. He did not get very far with the project, and the few pages of his uncompleted manuscript which survive suggest that he was wise not to continue with it.

In October 1951 he was once again invited to lecture in Spain, this time at the Universities of Salamanca and Madrid. He took Tess with him, and stayed two months, from 7 October until 15 December. As usual he drank a great deal and found the lectures a tremendous strain. In Salamanca he delivered his lecture, on Camoens and Ercilla, to the Faculty of Philosophy and Letters, from the seat of Unamuno, the great philosopher and former Rector of the University, who had died under house arrest in Nationalist hands in 1936. Campbell was shaking and sweating with drink and nerves; he told the worried Rector that he was suffering from malaria, and was promptly dosed with quinine. As he later wrote to Lyle,

I prayed like Hell, and went on, absolutely trembling. For the first minute my voice trembled but from then on I was raising murmurs of academic applause like 'Olé's' heard about half a mile away, alternating with hearty laughter. It was finished with a storm of clapping. When I got back to the Hotel I fainted clean out on the floor – not passed out – fainted for the first time in my life. Fortunately there was a thick carpet, red, and it not only saved me from splitting my nose but from colouring it with my blood.[71]

He had some idea of riding as a picador for the bullfighter Ortega y Gasset, whom he had met and impressed with his knowledge of bullfighting. But Ortega's performance came to an end shortly after Campbell arrived, 'which is perhaps as well for me', Campbell wrote frankly to Lyle. With Tess vainly trying to moderate his drinking, he went on to lecture in the *ateneos* of Granada and Barcelona. At a great banquet just before he left for England, the many Spanish friends he had made presented him with a golden torero's outfit, a *traje de torear*, to his huge delight. The Spanish trip had been such a strain that on his return to London he took to his bed for over a month.[72]

His visit to Spain, however, had convinced him more than ever that he would like to live there permanently. The publication, within two years, of his *Collected Poems*, *Light on a Dark Horse*, and *St John of the Cross* brought him more money than he had ever earned before. To increase his financial independence further, Lyle gave him a house in London which brought in a rent of £1,000 a year.[73] He was therefore able, for the first time since the war, to consider moving back to Spain, renting out the house in Campden Grove.

The circulation of *The Catacomb*, which had never risen above 200 copies, had been declining for nearly a year. In the summer of 1950 Lyle had turned it from a monthly into a quarterly, and prefaced the new series with an encouraging letter from T. S. Eliot,[74] but the decline had continued. Though the magazine had printed not only Campbell's work, but contributions by Richard Church, Peter Russell, John Heath-Stubbs, Bernard Bergonzi, Charles Causley, Charles Tomlinson, and Sacheverell Sitwell, its mixture of poetry and Catholic conservatism had not proved popular. Even Wyndham Lewis refused to contribute to it, though Ezra Pound, from his mental home, wrote to Campbell praising the magazine and urging him to persuade Lewis to write for it.[75] In December 1951 Lyle decided to suspend publication. He was therefore free to leave England with Campbell.

One morning Campbell showed Lyle a paper which reported that a man who had ill-treated a dog had been jailed for three months, while a bus conductor who had punched a woman in the stomach, causing a miscarriage, had been fined £5.[76] It seemed a final piece of evidence that there was something seriously wrong with English values.

The two men determined to rent a small farm in a Latin country, and after considering Spain, Cyprus, and Mozambique, they decided on Portugal. Campbell now recalled that in 1937, while living at Cezimbra, he and Mary had visited the beautiful resort town of Sintra in the hills north-west of Lisbon. He suggested to Lyle that they should begin the search for a new home there. Accordingly Campbell, with Lyle's wife, flew to Portugal in March 1952, and Mary and Lyle followed soon afterwards. After a search they rented a beautiful smallholding in the hills at Galamares, near Sintra. It was called Quinta dos Bochechos ('Gurgling Farm') and Campbell, who hoped to produce wine there, liked the sound of the name. He loved the pace of life in Portugal, the sunshine and the food. He would wander for hours through the streets of Lisbon munching olives, nuts, and salted cod's-tongues, a huge limping figure under a Spanish sombrero, just watching the crowds as he ambled from one *adega* (bar) to another. One evening he and Lyle went to hear Portuguese *fados* sung. Campbell, who normally took care to avoid all but the lightest of music-hall tunes, was moved beyond control by these most melancholy of folk-songs. Rising from his seat, he knelt unsteadily in front of the singer, crossed himself and kissed her feet, tears streaming down his cheeks. Lyle was intensely embarrassed by this open display of emotion, but the Portuguese audience tactfully took no notice.[77] They returned to England on 24 March to prepare for the final move to Portugal.

Campbell's beautiful younger daughter Anna was by now married. In August 1951 she had met a Spanish nobleman, Viscount Jaime Cavero de Carondelet, in Paris. He was the handsome younger son of the Duke of Bailén, and she discovered that he had spent his childhood in Toledo, as she had. He swept her off her feet. She returned to England in 1951, and Jaime subsequently joined her and married her; their daughter Frances was born the following year. The marriage was unhappy from the start, and caused Campbell great anxiety, but he was delighted by the first of his grandchildren, whom he called 'Impi' or 'Cuca' as the mood took him.

Early in May 1952 Campbell met Alan Paton, whose novel *Cry the Beloved Country* had been published to great acclaim in 1948. Campbell, Paton, Laurens van der Post, Enslin du Plessis, and Uys Krige had lunch together, and signed an open letter to the South African government, protesting against the plans to remove voters of mixed race from the electoral roll. The letter, which was published in several South African newspapers, had little effect. Paton was immensely impressed by Campbell; he said afterwards that Campbell's conversation had seemed to light up the luncheon-table like a flare.

During the last weeks in England, before his return to Portugal, Campbell worked at tremendous speed on a translation of the poems of Baudelaire, which the great success of *The Poems of St John of the Cross* had encouraged him to attempt. He made translations of seventeen of the poems in a single night, limping weary and ink-stained into a pub the next day to show them to Lyle.[78] On 9 May 1952 Campbell, Tess, and Felicia Lyle flew once more to Portugal to begin the work of settling into the big pink farmhouse on Quinta dos

Bochechos. Lyle and Mary stayed on in England, planning to come on together by car to Portugal once they had found tenants for the house in Campden Grove. Campbell began learning Portuguese with his usual speed, and he thought the Portuguese peasants, slow of speech and strong as oxen, much better companions than English men of letters.[79] If he suffered unhappiness its chief cause was his separation from Mary.

XV

The Last Years

1952–1957

WHILE he waited for the books and furniture to arrive, and for the arrival too of Mary and Lyle, Campbell kept his mind occupied by working hard at his translations. When his rheumatism would let him, he limped into Sintra to buy wine, or explore the town. At last, a month after his own arrival in Portugal, he heard that Lyle and Mary had crossed the Channel and were motoring across France and Spain. The day of their planned arrival came and went; day succeeded day with no sign of them. But Lyle and Mary finally appeared, more than two weeks late; their car had broken an axle in the Pyrenees, and they had been forced to wait while it was replaced in Pamplona. With their arrival the task of moving into the big house began in earnest. Great crates of books and furniture shipped from England had to be moved in, and the farm, which was very neglected and overgrown, had to be taken in hand. Lyle hired four peasants in addition to the full-time labourer on the quinta, and with Mary as overseer, the planting of tomatoes and potatoes and the rearing of pigs began. Campbell took no part in this activity; though he liked to talk of himself as a farmer, he did nothing other than setting lines to catch eels in the stream that ran beneath the house. Having arranged his rods on the bank, he would retire to his study to work, watching from his window for any movement that would tell him he had a bite.

He worked tremendously hard during these years; though there was no obvious financial pressure on him now, he worked as he had never worked before. He was planning to move to Spain and rent a farm of his own, leaving Lyle to run Bochechos,[1] and it seems clear that in these years he was labouring to achieve complete financial independence. He finished his translation of Baudelaire (too hastily)[2] and he corrected the proofs of a remarkably scholarly book of criticism he had written on Garcia Lorca for the Cambridge publishers Bowes & Bowes,[3] filling it with his fine translations of Lorca's poems, which Faber & Faber had been unable to print because of copyright difficulties.[4] In addition, during the rest of 1952, he laboured at a translation of a Portuguese novel, *Cousin Basilio*, by Eça de Queirós. His Portuguese was still very imperfect, and he had to use a dictionary constantly. While he worked at it, he gave up drink for several months, becoming bad-tempered as a result.[5] The work so obsessed Campbell that he could talk of nothing else; for months the characters in the novel seemed as real as his own family, and they were all very relieved when he finished the work and these ghostly companions haunted them no more.[6] He promptly continued writing a book about bulls, a project he had first considered seriously in 1932, at the suggestion of Faber & Faber. He filled this 'Bull-book', appropriately enough, with nonsensical stories and myths, and paraded in it all his favourite prejudices; the publishers reacted by rejecting it and demanding the return of the advance they had paid him.[7]

During these early years in Portugal, he resumed the eccentric work-style that the regular hours imposed by the BBC had kept him from. He might wake at lunchtime and go back to bed at five in the afternoon; wake at midnight and, having eaten everything he could find in the larder, work for twenty-four hours before falling dead asleep again. At other times he would keep almost 'normal' hours; he was always unpredictable, and his family had long since learned to expect anything.

In the evenings he and Lyle would sit up long after the others had gone to bed, drinking wine, sharing jokes, and talking about poetry. Often they would read verse – their own, if either of them had completed anything that day, or the work of Marlowe, Shakespeare, Keats, Shelley, and Byron, or such French poets as Victor Hugo, Vigny, and Baudelaire. Campbell's reading was extraordinarily wide; he directed Lyle to innumerable works the younger man would otherwise have overlooked, ranging from medieval Provençal poets to modern South American writers. During these sessions too Campbell would suggest improvements to Lyle's poems, his advice and encouragement being directed always to increasing the clarity and energy of the lines. He was the most unobtrusive and humble of teachers; his criticisms were usually offered as suggestions, and if Lyle offered any suggestions about Campbell's own work, he would adopt them with alarming promptness.[8] On other evenings, as the wine circulated, Campbell would sing songs by the hour – Scots Border ballads which he had learned from his mother, or the ragtime songs of the Twenties, or such South African songs as 'Ferreira' or 'Sarie Marais'.

This pleasant existence was interrupted in 1952 only by a Poetry Congress which he attended in Segovia, in June; and early in March 1953 he lectured in Salamanca and Madrid, again in Spanish to the *ateneos*. As usual the taste and smell of Spain made him yearn to live there again. 'After Spain dear little Portugal seems like a quiet pond after the sea', he wrote to Richard Aldington.[9] He longed to be able to buy a smallholding near Ciudad Rodrigo. But in March 1953 Lyle had to return to England with his wife, who had come to dislike living in Portugal.

Mary determined to continue running Bochechos by herself, and Campbell gave up the thought of moving to Spain, though he continued to visit the country whenever he could. The Campbells found Bochechos expensive to run once the Lyles had left; the rent was 2,500 escudos a month. In good years the smallholding's crop of fruit and vegetables could be sold at a small profit, but it was an undependable source of livelihood. Campbell continued his translation work, and began to make plans to go on a lecture tour of North America.

He had for some months been corresponding with the Canadian poet John Sutherland, editor of the Montreal literary magazine *Northern Review*, and it was Sutherland who had suggested and arranged the schedule for the lecture tour, from which Campbell hoped to make $2,000. He sailed from Lisbon on the *Vulcania* in October 1953. As so often before, the wildness of wind and wave moved him to ecstasy; at 2 a.m. in mid-Atlantic he stood in the prow of the ship, under a full moon, reciting Byron and one of Rob Lyle's poems, 'Atlantica', to the surging darkness.[10] He arrived in Halifax on 20 October, delighted with the beauty of the autumnal woods, red maples flaming among the conifers. His first lecture was at a Roman Catholic university, St Francis Xavier in Antigonish, Nova Scotia; from there he moved by train to Sackville, New Brunswick. He was very anxious to like the Canadians and be liked by them, and (at this early stage in his tour) very much on his best behaviour. He impressed those who met him by his tentativeness, his humility, and his vulnerability to criticism. He was nervous and awkward, and though the weather was mild he dripped with sweat. He obviously wanted reassurance; he inspired immense liking and protectiveness, an impression curiously at odds with the effect produced by his heavy, slurred accent, his great bulk and battered, stevedore's face. The Canadians were not at all sure what to make of this 'tamed lion balancing a teacup in his paw',[11] as one of them subsequently described him.

Campbell, unused to the American lecture circuit, was enormously impressed by the size of the audiences who turned up to hear him. His lectures were generally humorous, and he framed the readings of his African poems with the vigorous stories at which he excelled. The effect was muffled, however, by his thick Natal accent which seemed to strengthen as he aged; it struck his rather bemused audiences, most of whom had never before heard a South African, as a kind of Cockney with a German flavour. After the lectures he would enquire anxiously of his host how it had gone, and ask how he could improve his performance, taking careful note of the replies.[12] It was in the small informal gatherings after the lectures that Campbell, tired and relieved, really shone; he gulped gallons of beer ('The best in the world, man') and talked until late in the night. Inevitably, drink and lack of sleep, combined with the daily journeys across a continent, sapped his strength. He was so nervous of being late for his trains in the morning that he stayed awake at night; after three days he bought a cheap wrist-watch, and thereafter woke only at intervals to check the time before rolling over.[13] He used his energy to the limit. Observing his drinking, more than one of his hosts felt a pang of guilt; it was obvious that no man could go on at this pace and live long.

In two months he lectured in twenty-seven cities in North America, from Nova Scotia to British Columbia, and from California to New Jersey. He loved the vastness of North America, and he loved the people he met; every place seemed to him more friendly than the last. On 4 November, in Toronto, he met Marshall McLuhan, Professor of English at St Michael's College. McLuhan had befriended Wyndham Lewis in Canada during the war, and he and Campbell liked each other at sight. Campbell, who loved all children, fascinated McLuhan's sons with his endless stories and Zulu songs. He was greatly taken, too, by the poet Ned Pratt, whose work Sutherland had sent him in Portugal. At the University of Washington he met the poet Theodore Roethke, who introduced him to bourbon whisky. Campbell claimed never to have encountered it before. He quickly got to know it well, and was never quite sober during his stay in Seattle. Flying down to California he found himself sitting next to Eleanor Roosevelt whom he thought delightful: 'we almost fell for each other', he wrote to Mary.[14] During his lecture at Santa Barbara College, on 13 November, he spotted in the audience an old flame, Iris Tree, whom he had last seen in the late Twenties; he waved to her in the middle of his lecture, and afterwards embarrassed her further by kneeling at her feet to kiss her hand.[15]

The pressures of his tour gradually told on him; cities passed in a blur before his eyes; his drinking increased. In Seattle in mid-November he was shocked to hear that Dylan Thomas had just died in New York. He wrote at once to Caitlin Thomas, who had been left destitute, offering to adopt one of her children. 'Dylan was killed by American hospitality,' he told his alarmed hosts, helping himself liberally to the whisky.[16] His own drinking habit frightened him, but though he tried, in Cincinnati, to avoid alcohol, the pressures of the trip forced him to drink. He could more readily do without food than alcohol. When he arrived in Chicago, to be met at the station by Henry Regnery, his American publisher, he had been drinking steadily on the train, and the two salesmen he had met on the journey insisted on having 'one more drink with Roy'. 'We'll never meet a man like this again in our lives,' they told the protesting Regnery. In the station bar they challenged Campbell to tests of strength, which ended in his throwing them both to the floor. Regnery was forced to cancel the talk Campbell was to have given that afternoon.[17] During this week in Chicago, Campbell met the poet Robert Lowell, Antony Kerrigan, and Mrs Adlai Stevenson, whom Campbell described admiringly to Lyle as 'breath-taking – a mother-of-pearl tank!'[18]

In New York he was delighted to come across Gene Tunney, former world champion heavyweight boxer, whom he met by chance on a station platform. Tunney knew Campbell's great friend Aimé Tschiffely, and Tschiffely had asked Campbell to give Tunney his regards if they should meet in America. The two men talked for a time about Tschiffely as they waited for trains, unaware that he was at that moment dangerously ill. He was to die within a fortnight, and it was this meeting with Tunney that Campbell recalled when he wrote his poem in memory of Tschiffely, three months later:

> Only a week before you died, we stood,
> Gene Tunney and myself, on Stanford Station
> And voted it was worth a celebration
> To drink the health of one so great and good:
> We did not know how near to death you lay,
> And as the train rolled onward through New York,
> Each from his memories drew forth the cork
> To which you are the vintage and bouquet . . .[19]

But such pleasant encounters were like oases in a desert.

He was very relieved to sail from New York, on 10 December 1953, exhausted but triumphant, aboard the American liner *Constitu-*

tion. When it docked at Gibraltar he hitched a ride in a cattle-truck to Lisbon, from where Mary drove him home. Financially the tour had been something of a disappointment; instead of the $2,000 he had hoped to make, he brought back less than $500,[20] having spent money wildly in America. But once he had recovered from his exertions, he thought the trip well worth while.

He had barely arrived home when he heard that the University of Natal intended to confer an honorary doctorate on him. This belated recognition from his home country delighted him, and he wrote at once to accept the honour, and began making plans for the trip. He intended going by sea, but because he procrastinated buying the ticket, and because he and Mary made a brief trip to London in February 1954,[21] he missed the last sailing and had to fly to South Africa instead. He travelled by air to Rome on 10 March, to catch the South African Airways flight to Johannesburg, and ran into trouble almost at once when the need for an expensive yellow fever vaccination held him up for four days, so that hotel bills consumed all his money. He had not even enough for a tip. 'I walk around the hotel avoiding waiters,' he wrote dolefully to Mary.[22] However, once on the plane he discovered that the Afrikaans air hostess, Sonia Groenewald, had been a refugee on the *Maine* with him in 1936, and she not only lent him money at Khartoum, but gave him a letter to her family in Johannesburg.[23]

He arrived in Durban in his blue serge suit and Spanish hat, on 18 March, to a tremendous welcome. He was met at the airport by a group which included his brother George, Geoffrey Dutton, and his old schoolmaster, Bill Payn; they carried him off at once to a rowdy party.[24] He stayed for a few days before and after the degree ceremony with his mother, now ninety-two years old, and he delighted in the beauty of her house, Carndonagh, overlooking the Valley of a Thousand Hills; all his love for South Africa returned.

He had been asked to deliver the address at the degree ceremony on 20 March, and as usual he prepared his speech with great care. He was determined to shine: all his old friends would be there, and every member of his family still in South Africa. But when he stood up to speak he abandoned his notes almost at once. Instead of the dignified discussion of poetry his audience expected, he trotted out all his political hobby-horses. Though he knew well enough that English-speaking Natal intellectuals detested Prime Minister Malan's racial policies, and were proud of being part of the British Empire, Campbell opened his speech with an apparent defence of apartheid, and a vigorous attack on England. (He was not a supporter of apartheid, but his reference later in the speech to 'the dangerous and suicidal plight of our country' went almost unnoticed.) He referred to Churchill as 'a valiant but superannuated Beefeater', he called Roosevelt 'a tittering zombie', he denounced 'the Yalta boobytrap', he sneered at England for 'hanging around for Marshall Aid, in other words "tips"', and he praised Franco's Spain. Into this diatribe he sandwiched attacks on such diverse targets as poetic obscurity, bureaucratic government, Geoffrey Grigson and Stephen Spender, Romanticism, William Morris, Aldous Huxley, and the United Nations;[25] he ended by condemning 'academical pedants'. He seems to have been appalled himself at the effect this characteristic whirl of prejudices had on his dumbfounded academic audience; but once he had begun he had no choice but to go on desperately, sweat pouring down his face.[26] 'The inspiring crash of dropping bricks echoed through the Pietermaritzburg City Hall,' reported the *Natal Witness* drily.[27] The applause when he sat down was markedly unenthusiastic and he was very glad to get away from the banquet that followed. 'The doctoring went off with a tremendous bang,' he wrote to Mary, '. . . it was like a bullfight with the gold scarlet gowns.'[28] The comparison says a good deal.

He had intended returning to Europe overland with Geoffrey Dutton and his wife, but decided against it with great regret when he saw how small their Fiat was, and heard that the trip might take four months.[29] Mary, alone in Portugal, was begging him to return quickly. 'All I know is that I have had enough of being quite alone here, and I am *longing* for you to come back,' she wrote,[30] and he replied prophetically, 'I am longing to see you beloved – but this is the last time I will ever set eyes on my beloved country (How I love it!) so let me take in all I can before I finish with it.'[31]

He spent a week fishing with his brother on the wild coast south of Port Edward, but had to cut the trip short early in April because of the death of his sister Ethel, who had been ill for a long time.[32] A week after the funeral he set off again, this time travelling north in a Land Rover with his younger brother Bruce and George's son Hamish. They travelled through the Hluhluwe game reserve, where Campbell's attempt to secure a photograph of himself 'toreadoring' a black rhinoceros with his duffle-coat ended in the infuriated animal charging their vehicle and tearing off a number plate.[33] They travelled through Swaziland to Mozambique on 29 April and after staying for a time in the plush Hotel Polana, returned to Durban by the same route. Campbell enjoyed this trip enormously; he ate almost as much as he drank, and acquired a mahogany tan. And as always, Africa stimulated his Muse; although he wrote nothing at the time, it was the memory of this trip that he poured into one of his last poems, 'The Singing Hawk', written in February 1955.[34]

He flew back to Portugal (through central and west Africa) on 14 May. Tess, who had by now completely recovered her health, had, in May, fallen in love with and proposed to a Portuguese companion of the poet Antonio Porto, one of Campbell's many Portuguese friends. Campbell liked the young man, Ignatius Custódio, and agreed that Tess should marry him; the wedding took place on 7 August. Ignatius was handsome, ambitious, and anticlerical, and he bitterly resented Tess's insistence that they should be married in a Catholic church. Partly as a result, this match, like that of Anna, was unhappy from the start; Ignatius deserted Tess for a wealthy Swiss woman after a fortnight, to Campbell's fury and sorrow. He threatened Ignatius by letter with a hiding, to little effect.[35] In March 1955 Tess gave birth to a son whom she named Francis.

Campbell had become reinfected with malaria in Mozambique, and he spent weeks in bed during June and July 1954, making translations of another of Eça de Queirós's novels, *The City and the Mountains*, and of plays by Lope de Vega, Calderón de la Barca, Lorca, and Tirso de Molina, for the BBC.[36] He was too ill to accept an invitation to be crowned a 'Soci' of the Felibrige (a society of Provençal poets) in Avignon, and he was glad to get a long and very funny account of the proceedings from Richard Aldington.[37] His illness, however, did not affect his love for a fight. When the publication of Aldington's book on Norman Douglas, *Pinorman*, evoked a storm of protest from Graham Greene, Nancy Cunard, and others in June 1954, Campbell joined the fray at Aldington's side with delight; but his letters to the English papers were too violent to be printed. Two months later, when Aldington's next book, on T. E. Lawrence, was also greeted with fierce criticism, Campbell and Lyle planned to publish a pamphlet entitled 'What Next' in defence of him. 'Well my dear Roberto, once again into battle,' Campbell wrote joyously. 'It feels fine. One has to do it. You can't lie down in servitude like these bloody Saxons are doing. I bet it will make a shindy.'[38] The project, like so many others Campbell engaged in, came to nothing because of the danger of a libel suit.

In September Campbell's American publisher Henry Regnery, with his wife and daughter, arrived by sea from Chicago to stay with

Campbell and Mary for three days. Regnery was impressed by the extraordinary confusion of Campbell's workroom (he was translating forty pages a day of Eça de Queirós's *The City and the Mountains*), and by the small boy, grandson of the cook, whose sole task in life seemed to be to trundle great flagons of wine to Campbell in a small wagon, and then haul the empties away.[39] When the Regnerys flew on to Madrid, Campbell and Mary followed by road in their old Triumph on 1 October 1954.[40] Campbell and Regnery, an admirer of Franco, had hoped to meet the Spanish leader in Madrid, and even hired morning suits for the occasion, but at the last minute the audience was cancelled. Campbell was very disappointed, chiefly because he had so looked forward to wearing the frock coat and striped trousers. They travelled together to Segovia and to Toledo where they had lunch in the Campbells' old house, now a smart hotel. For Campbell, this was an opportunity to say goodbye to the city he loved most in the world, as he had said goodbye to South Africa. He conducted the Regnerys round Toledo, trying to revisit all the places he had known, and constantly being greeted by old friends who recognized him and rushed up to embrace him.[41] He and Mary drove home again on 23 October, after Campbell had delivered a single lecture at the *ateneo* in Salamanca. As usual, Spain made him dissatisfied with Portugal and he and Mary revived their plans to leave Bochechos and move to Ciudad Rodrigo.

But he was losing energy. When he and Mary travelled to England on 11 October he was feeling increasingly unwell. Throughout his life, though he talked ceaselessly about a host of imaginary and deadly diseases he believed he had contracted, and took drugs of all kinds for them, he seldom mentioned his real illnesses. He would drink until his heart palpitated and take sedatives to calm it, followed by powerful stimulants to even the balance, but he very seldom mentioned the continual pain he suffered from his hip. When he arrived in London, however, he was clearly ill; he complained to Lyle of being old and tired, and talked often of death. On 20 December he roused himself to deliver an oration at the ceremony held at the Argentine Embassy to honour his friend Tschiffely, whose ashes had been interred in Buenos Aires. He was convinced that he himself was dying. One morning he failed to appear at the Catherine Wheel, where he had arranged to meet Lyle; after waiting for a time Lyle went to the house in Campden Grove, to find Campbell sitting in a rocking chair, a book on his knees, looking blankly at the wall. Lyle felt a dreadful premonition and persuaded Campbell to see his doctor, who diagnosed a mild form of diabetes, brought on by excessive drinking. Once the treatment began, Campbell recovered his spirits; to know that he was genuinely ill made him feel important, and he was fascinated by the tests and medicines.

He was warned to moderate his drinking, but he was quite unable to take heed. When the South African poet Guy Butler telephoned to arrange a meeting with him in January 1955, Campbell responded with an invitation to 'meet me in my pub at 11.30 for a quick one before lunch'. And in the Catherine Wheel he drank beer by the quart, resisting the attempts of Mary and Anna to get him home for lunch. While he drank he talked of his love for Dylan and his loathing for Spender, of the beards grown in South Africa by the Nationalist supporters of the Voortrekker celebrations ('the only crop ever grown in my country without a government subsidy'), of Somerset Maugham's short stories, of rugby, of his translations of Lope de Vega. But the sparkle had gone out of his conversation; he struck Butler as a sick, defeated, and frightened man, frightened by his own drinking habit and by the horror of life. At 2.30 Campbell finished his last quart and said, 'Well Butler, I don't think we'll bother about lunch, do you?' 'Mr Campbell,' said Butler woozily, 'I am quite incapable of bothering about anything.'[42]

Campbell and Mary flew back to Portugal on 20 January 1955, and Campbell put himself to bed for a month to finish his translations of Spanish plays for the BBC; he was working on Calderón de la Barca's *Love After Death*. A selection of his poems was published in the United States by Henry Regnery in March, and the *New York Times* printed a hostile review of it by the poet Randall Jarrell. The attack stung Campbell particularly because Jarrell quoted a phrase of Edith Sitwell's out of context, in such a way as to make her seem to denigrate Campbell's work. Though Edith Sitwell wrote at once to reject Jarrell's misuse of her phrase,[43] Campbell brooded over the attack for days: adverse reviews hurt him more as he grew older. Not until he had written eight epigrams on Jarrell could he recover his composure; the last of them ran,

> These verses have prohibited to you
> (Ere you could vanish down some friendly drain)
> The damp oblivion that was your due.
> Posterity will have to pull the chain.[44]

Financially, Campbell seemed at this time to be in a happy position. Living on Bochechos was cheap, since the smallholding, though it ran at a small loss, provided almost all the food he and Mary needed. His translation work brought in a steady income, and in addition to Lyle's continued support, the Campbells had the income from their two houses in London. Early in 1955, however, the position changed dramatically for the worse. The labourer who helped Mary run the smallholding, José Mel, was pruning a tree one morning in March when his ladder broke. Though he had been only three feet above the ground, his right leg and ankle were badly broken, and he was taken to hospital in Lisbon. There, after long delays, it was found necessary to operate on his leg to reset it; the operation was unsuccessful, and over the next six months two further operations were carried out. These also were unsuccessful, and it gradually became clear that the man was permanently crippled. The Campbells had neglected to insure him against accidents, and under Portuguese law they were not only responsible for his very large hospital bills, but for paying an amount equal to two-thirds of his monthly wage for the rest of his life. This was a crushing blow, though Campbell put a brave face on it in his letters; it demolished his financial security at a stroke, and at a time when he badly needed to be able to rest.

He and Mary sold the lease on their Campden Grove house in June[45] to pay the immediate costs of medical treatment, and they gave up all thought of either buying Bochechos outright or moving to Spain. Campbell revived a project he had had in mind for some time of writing a book on Portugal, and he also began making hasty plans for another lecture tour of North America in the autumn.

He secured the support of the Portuguese government for his book on the country. In the interests of tourist promotion he was given a grant to tour Portugal, and passes that allowed him and Mary to stay at certain *pousadas* (inns) at government expense. During July and August Mary drove him around the areas of northern and central Portugal which he had not previously visited, and with the aid of the Portuguese grant they also visited their beloved Spain, for two separate periods of a week each.[46]

The trip had to be cut short, however, when Campbell fell ill with what he described as both malaria and diabetes. It may well have been diabetes, for he refused to take insulin; instead he believed firmly in a peasant remedy involving drinking cupfuls of an infusion of the wild periwinkle plant, which Tess would gather and boil for him.[47]

He had barely recovered when, on 9 October, he sailed for Canada again, on the *Saturnia*, for his second lecture tour. It was not a success. John Sutherland, who had arranged his tour in 1953, was dying of tuberculosis and Campbell's lectures were organized by a Catholic agency, the Alma Savage Lecture Service. In consequence, all his engagements were at Catholic girls' colleges or seminaries; it is difficult to imagine audiences less suited to appreciate Campbell's particular blend of talents. And he was so ill, and so poisoned with drink and drugs, that he was quite incapable of looking after himself.

There was confusion from the beginning. He had embarked with virtually no money, and he landed at Halifax vaguely and mistakenly expecting to be met on the dockside. His first lecture was in Toronto, nearly a thousand miles away, in three days' time, and he had no way of getting there. He telegraphed wildly to Canadian acquaintances, begging for money, and in his confusion left his luggage on board the *Saturnia*, which sailed next day for New York, taking with it not only his clothes, but all his lecture notes.[48] The Canadian winter had come early, and he wandered round Halifax docks dazed with cold, lacking even a jacket. He was rescued from this appalling situation by Professor Bennett of Dalhousie University, who managed to raise the money for part of his fare to Toronto, and by a Canadian air hostess whom he had met on the ship, who arranged with a friend for him to be smuggled on board the next flight west. There were no spare seats on the aircraft, and Campbell had a most uncomfortable time in the baggage-hold. He wrote jokingly to Bill Payn later,

I nearly kicked the bucket from claustrophobia . . . We ran into a hurricane and the suitcases on which I was supposed to be lying started jumping around and trying to lie on me. It was quite grim and the hostess number two said she wondered if I was still alive. After having to box for three hours with flying trunks and suitcases I was black with bruises, but I got to Toronto and gave a speech that night . . .[49]

In Toronto he was able to borrow an overcoat from John Sutherland, and wearing this and his leather chaps (the leggings worn by Portuguese cattlemen) he was ready to brave the cold. He travelled by train to New York, intending to seek out one of Mary's sisters-in-law, who had married an actor, Rollo Gamble, and was staying in New York. On the train to New York the mixture of drugs he was taking indiscriminately combined with alcohol to produce a near stupor; he arrived in New York in a blinding snowstorm, unable to remember who he was or where he was going. After wandering about for a time he sat down in a doorway on 47th Street and dozed off. By chance, which Campbell later thought a miracle, Gamble passed by and noticed the huge unconscious figure. After walking on a hundred yards he realized there could not be two men in New York in such chaps and such a hat and walked back.[50] The Gambles and Tambimuttu, who was also in New York, took Campbell to a doctor, who diagnosed an overdose of bromides. As usual, while he was under medical care, Campbell recovered quickly; he was able to continue his tour, and in Kentucky even went racoon hunting with a negro taxi-driver he met in Bardstown.[51] At Kenyon College, in Ohio, where he gave the most successful lecture of the tour, he struck up a warm friendship with the poet John Crowe Ransom. But his magnificent constitution was at last breaking down. Many of his lectures were rambling, and his accent so thick that he was difficult to hear; though he rested often he was perpetually tired. He lost money as fast as he earned it; in Rochester, New York, he left not only his earnings but his passport in a taxi, and was lucky to recover them.[52]

By the end of November, when he had delivered fifteen lectures, it became clear that he could not continue; cutting short the tour, he returned to Portugal aboard the *Andrea Doria* on 19 December, and Mary put him to bed at once. The trip had been a total failure financially, and he was never to visit North America again. He spent weeks on his bed, making verse translations of five further Spanish plays for a volume to be edited by the critic Eric Bentley,[53] and he also began gathering his work together for the second volume of his *Collected Poems*.[54]

In March 1956, when the Campbells' plans to leave Bochechos and live in a small rented house in the nearby village of Linhó were well advanced, their financial crisis resolved itself as suddenly as it had arisen. Campbell's mother, after a protracted illness, had died in January at the age of ninety-three, and in March Campbell heard that she had left him £6,000.[55] The money was a godsend, for they were able to persuade the crippled José Mel to accept a lump sum in lieu of the lifetime monthly payments. They had already sold many of their possessions in preparation for leaving Bochechos, and on 29 April they moved into the Linhó house, which was modern and comfortable but so small that it could barely hold Campbell's books.[56] 'Still it's an ill wind that blows no good,' he wrote to Edith Sitwell; 'the climate here is so dry and bracing that I do not suffer a tenth what I did on our misty, damp farm which racked us both with rheumatism.'[57] He was plagued, however, by a neighbour's large dog, which barked all night while he was writing his book *Portugal* and strengthened his dislike of the animals.[58] He managed to give up drink for nearly three months, from June to September. Even when he began again he drank moderately. He would be accompanied on his daily trips to the village inn by his granddaughter Frances and a crowd of the village children for whom he always bought sweets.

Mary had meanwhile found a plot of land for sale on a hillside a mile out of the village. It was rocky and brush-covered, but it was cheap, and it had superb views across the coastal plain to Cascais seven miles away, with the Atlantic shining beyond. They bought the two hectares with what was left of Campbell's inheritance, and began building a house – the first home they had ever owned.[59] Campbell hired a local peasant to divine water, and they sank a well. A rocky track was smoothed to allow their little Fiat (which had replaced the ageing Triumph) to reach the building site.

This was in many ways a very happy period for Campbell. Anna and Tess had taken a flat in Cascais, so that Campbell and Mary were alone together for the first time since 1922. Campbell's almost obsessive urge to travel constantly, as if fleeing from himself, had eased; he lived quietly and soberly, going to Mass at the nearby convent each morning with Mary, and saying the rosary with her each night. 'We have to say one fifth for the bolshies' conversion,' he told Edith Sitwell. 'I would sooner be fighting them – but the Holy Father knows best.'[60]

He was still suffering stoically from sciatica; a walk of more than a hundred yards was a severe struggle, and he grew very fat. His face in photographs taken during the last months of 1956 is as puffed and pale as a blister. He took drugs to make himself sleep, and drugs to keep awake. He looked towards death without fear or regret. The last-written of his published poems, 'November Nights', has a serenity seldom found in his earlier verse, a serenity accentuated by its long lines and gentle, subdued rhythm:

> Now peasants shun the muddy fields, and fisherfolk the shores.
> It is the time the weather finds the wounds of bygone wars,
> And never to a charger did I take as I have done
> To cantering the rocking-chair, my Pegasus, indoors,
> For my olives have been gathered and my grapes are in the tun.
>
> (CP, II, 121)

He spent a quiet religious Christmas in Portugal with Mary, his daughters, and his two grandchildren. In several of the Christmas letters he sent to old friends there is a quietly resigned and prophetic note. He wrote to Daphne Collins, his BBC secretary, with whom he had corresponded since 1950, 'I am rather ill; maybe I shall not write to you again, but I send my respectful affection, as from the first day that you so kindly worked with me.'[61] He was signing off.

In January 1957 he finished correcting the proofs of his second volume of *Collected Poems* for the Bodley Head, and dispatched the completed manuscript of *Portugal*.[62] At intervals he would take up again the project of writing a history of the Spanish War ('to correct the Kremlin-crazy liars in England') which he had begun in 1939, but he had not the energy to continue with it.

On 5 April he and Mary set off in the tiny Fiat 600 for Spain, intending to take part in the Holy Week ceremonies in Seville. They spent several days in Toledo, 'this heavenly place which means more than all the world to me', as Campbell wrote to Vernon Watkins,[63] and then went on to Seville. Campbell's great weight in the passenger seat helped to puncture the right-hand front tyre, and they were forced to replace it with the spare, which was badly worn.

Throughout the week of the processions in Seville Campbell was strangely quiet; the jokes and laughter that usually filled his conversation with Mary had stopped. He was unusually serious in his devotions, and Mary responded to his changed mood. On 23 April they drove back, crossing the border after lunch. By four in the afternoon they were just south of Setúbal, travelling down the long pine avenues that line the roads of southern Portugal. 'Count the miles, will you?' Mary said to Campbell, who had the map. 'Do you think we can get home in time for tea?' At that moment the worn front tyre burst, the car swerved violently off the road and smashed into a tree. The Portuguese policeman in the next car to pass by dragged them out of the smoking wreck for fear it should burst into flames. Mary was unconscious, her foot crushed, her arm, ribs, and front teeth broken; but Campbell's neck was fractured. He breathed for a little time, sighed twice and then lay still. For him the long journey was over.

POSTSCRIPT

CAMPBELL was buried in the cemetery of Sao Pedro, near Sintra, on 27 April 1957. Lyle and Anna had flown back from London on hearing the news, and Tess was there; but Mary was too badly injured to leave the Setúbal hospital. The South African Ambassador sent a representative, and many Portuguese friends, ranging from aristocrats[1] to the peasants who had been building the house he would never occupy, followed the coffin to the hillside cemetery.

Mary Campbell lived on in the new house for another twenty-two years, enduring poverty and increasing age with courage. She continued to paint, and made some money by selling her paintings; she delighted in music and developed a passion for Mozart, and she continued her ceaseless work for Catholic charitable organizations, even though at times she and Tess were forced to live on soup made of fish-heads. Above all she kept alive the memory of her husband. She loved to talk to visitors about him, and the room would ring with her silvery laughter as she recalled his exploits, real and imaginary. 'Oh, old Roy,' she would say, rocking, 'you never stopped laughing when he was around, never.' The remains of her beauty were still discernible in her eightieth year.

She died suddenly of a stroke on 27 February 1979, within two weeks of her eighty-first birthday, and was buried in Campbell's grave.

SELECT BIBLIOGRAPHY

Campbell's principal works referred to:

POETRY

The Flaming Terrapin, (London, Jonathan Cape, 1924)
The Wayzgoose, (London, Jonathan Cape, 1928)
Poems, (Paris, The Hours Press, 1930)
Adamastor, (London, Faber & Faber, 1930)
The Gum Trees, (London, Faber & Faber, 1930)
The Georgiad, (London, Boriswood, 1931)
Nineteen Poems, (London, Ernest Benn, 1931)
Choosing A Mast, (London, Faber & Faber, 1931)
Pomegranates, (London, Boriswood, 1932)
Flowering Reeds, (London, Boriswood, 1933)
Mithraic Emblems, (London, Boriswood, 1936)
Flowering Rifle, (London, Longmans, 1939)
Sons of the Mistral, (London, Faber & Faber, 1941)
Talking Bronco, (London, Faber & Faber, 1946)
Nativity, (London, Faber & Faber, 1954)
Collected Poems, (3 vols., London, The Bodley Head, 1949, 1957, 1960)

PROSE

Taurine Provence, (London, Desmond Harmsworth, 1932)
Broken Record, (London, Boriswood, 1934)
Light on a Dark Horse, (London, Hollis & Carter, 1951)
Lorca, (Cambridge, Bowes & Bowes, 1952)
The Mamba's Precipice, (London, Frederick Muller, 1953)
Portugal, (London, Max Reinhardt, 1957)

TRANSLATIONS

Helge Krog, *Three Plays* (London, Boriswood, 1934)
The Poems of St John of the Cross (London, Harvill Press, 1951)
Baudelaire, *Poems: A Translation of Les Fleurs du Mal* (London, Harvill Press, 1952)
Eça de Queirós, *Cousin Basilio* (London, Max Reinhardt, 1953)
Eça de Queirós, *The City and the Mountains* (London, Max Reinhardt, 1955)

Eric Bentley (ed.), *The Classic Theatre: Six Spanish Plays*, Vol. III (New York, Doubleday, 1959)

Paco d'Arcos, *Nostalgia, a Collection of Poems* (London, Sylvan Press, 1960)

Campbell's articles referred to:

'The Significance of Turbott Wolfe', *Voorslag*, No 1 (June 1926)

Review of *The Worship of Nature*, *Voorslag*, No 1 (June 1926)

'Fetish Worship in South Africa', *Voorslag*, No 2 (July 1926)

'Eunuch Arden' and 'Kynoch Arden', *Voorslag*, No 2 (July 1926)

'White Laughter', *New Statesman*, (20 July 1929)

'Reviewer's Preface' and 'A Rejected Review', *Satire and Fiction* (1930)

'Moo! Moo! Or Ye Olde Newe Awareness', *Poetry Review*, Vol. XL, No. 4 (Aug-Sept. 1949)

'Epitaph on the Thirties', *Nine*, No 5 (1950)

'A Note on W. L.', *Shenandoah*, Vol. IV, Nos. 2–3 (1953)

'Poetry and Experience', *Theoria*, No 6 (1954)

Other works:

L. Abrahams, 'Roy Campbell: Conquistador-Refugee', *Theoria*, No. 8 (1954)

Anon., 'The Poetry of Statement', *Times Literary Supplement* (24 March 1950), p. 184.

J. Paco d'Arcos, 'Roy Campbell: The Man and the Poet', *Modern Age*, Vol. 13, No. 4 (1969)

S. Bedford, *Aldous Huxley* (London, Chatto & Windus, 1973)

B. Bergonzi, *The Turn of a Century* (London, Macmillan, 1973)

H. Bolitho, *My Restless Years* (London, Max Parrish, 1962)

J. Bond, *They Were South Africans* (London, Oxford University Press, 1956)

G. Brenan, *The Spanish Labyrinth* (Cambridge, Cambridge University Press, 1943)

G. Butler (ed.), *A Book of South African Verse* (London, Oxford University Press, 1959)

L. V. Camoens, *The Lusiads*, (London, Penguin Books, 1952)

E. Campbell, *Sam Campbell: A Story of Natal* (Durban, privately printed, 1949)

A. E. Coppard, *It's Me, O Lord!* (London, Methuen & Co., 1957)

H. Crichton (trans.), *Mistral's Mereille* (London, Macmillan, 1968)

F. Cumont, *The Mysteries of Mithra* (London, Kegan Paul, 1903)

R. N. Currey, *Poets of the 1939–1945 War* (London, Longmans, Green & Co., 1960)

G. Dutton, *Africa in Black and White* (London, Chapman & Hall, 1956)

T. S. Eliot, *Selected Essays* (London, Faber & Faber, 1932)

H. D. Ford, *A Poets' War* (Philadelphia, University of Pennsylvania Press, 1965)

G. S. Fraser, *The Modern Writer and His World* (London, Derek Verschoyle, 1953)

J. G. Fraser, *The Golden Bough* (London, Macmillan, 1922)

H. Gardner, (ed.), *The Metaphysical Poets* (London, Penguin Books, 1957)

W. H. Gardner, 'Voltage of Delight!', *The Month*, Vol. 19, No. 3 (Jan.-March 1958)

E. Gillett, 'Two Poets: Campbell and Auden', *National and English Review*, Vol. 135 (1950)

G. Gilpatrick, *The Compleat Goggler* (London, The Bodley Head, 1939)

G. Gittings, (ed.), *The Letters of John Keats* (London, Oxford University Press, 1970)

P. Guggenheim, *Out of This Century* (New York, Dial Press, 1946)

A. Hamilton, *The Appeal of Fascism* (London, Anthony Blond, 1971)

N. Hamnet, *Laughing Torso* (London, Constable & Co., 1932)

T. Hardy, *Collected Poems* (London, Macmillan & Co., 1930)

C. J. D. Harvey, 'The Poetry of Roy Campbell', *Standpunte* (Oct. 1950)

K. Hewitt, *The Only Paradise* (London, Jarrolds, 1945)

T. Hillier, *Leda and the Goose* (London, Longmans, Green & Co., 1954)

M. Holroyd, *Lytton Strachey and the Bloomsbury Group* (London, Penguin Books, 1971)

G. Hough, *The Last Romantics* (London, Gerald Duckworth, 1947)

P. Howarth, *Squire: Most Generous of Men* (London, Hutchinson, 1963)

A. John, *Chiaroscuro* (London, Jonathan Cape, 1952)

R. John, *The Seventh Child* (London, Heinemann, 1932)

U. Krige, 'Roy Campbell as Lyrical Poet', *English Studies in Africa*, Vol. I, No. 2 (Sept. 1958)

U. Krige, 'First Meeting with Roy Campbell', *Theoria*, No. 12 (1959)

L. Lee, *As I Walked Out One Midsummer Morning* (London, André Deutsch, 1969)

J. Lees-Milne, *Harold Nicolson: A Biography*, Vol. I (London, Chatto & Windus, 1980)

W. Lewis, *The Apes of God* (London, Eyre & Spottiswoode, 1930)

W. Lewis, *Hitler* (London, Chatto & Windus, 1931)

W. Lewis, *Snooty Baronet* (London, Cassell & Co., 1932)

W. Lewis, *One Way Song* (London, Faber & Faber, 1932)

W. Lewis, *Men Without Art* (London, Cassell & Co., 1934)

W. Lewis, *The Revenge for Love* (London, Methuen & Co., 1937)

W. Lewis, *Blasting and Bombardiering* (London, Eyre & Spottiswoode, 1937)

W. Lewis, *Rotting Hill* (Chicago, Henry Regnery, 1952)

The Letters of Wyndham Lewis (ed. W. K. Rose) (London, Methuen & Co., 1963)

J. Lindsay, *Meetings with Poets* (London, Frederick Muller, 1968)

F. L. Lucas, *Authors Living and Dead* (London, Chatto & Windus, 1926)

R. Lyle, *Halcyon* (Aldington, Hand & Flower Press, 1953)

R. Lyle, *Mistral* (Cambridge, Bowes & Bowes, 1953)

R. Lyle, *Poems from Limbo* (London, The Bodley Head, 1960)

H. MacDiarmid, *The Battle Continues* (Edinburgh, privately printed, 1957)

J. S. McClelland, *The French Right* (London, Jonathan Cape, 1970)

G. McNeill-Moss, *The Epic of the Alcazar* (London, Rich & Cowan, 1937)

L. de Maria, *Marinetti e il Futurismo* (Rome, Arnoldo Mondadori, 1937)

F. Miller, *First Line and Title Index to the Poetry of Roy Campbell* (University of the Witwatersrand School of Librarianship, 1961)

G. M. Miller and H. Sergeant, *A Critical Survey of South African Poetry in English* (Cape Town, A. A. Balkema, 1959)

S. G. Millin, *An Artist in the Family* (London, Constable & Co., 1928)

F. Morrow, *Revolution and Counter-Revolution in Spain* (London, New Park Publications, 1938)

N. Nicolson, *Portrait of a Marriage* (London, Weidenfeld & Nicolson, 1973)

N. Nicolson, (ed.), *The Letters of Virginia Woolf* (London, The Hogarth Press, 1975–7)

F. W. Nietzsche, *Thus Spake Zarathustra* (London, J. M. Dent & Sons, 1933)

J. F. Nims, 'Roy Campbell's St John of the Cross', *Poetry*, Vol. 8, No. 3 (June 1952)

G. Orwell, *Homage to Catalonia* (London, Secker & Warburg, 1938)

A. Paton, 'Roy Campbell: Poet and Man', *Theoria*, No. 9 (1957)

R. Pattee, *This is Spain* (Milwaukee, Bruce Publishing Co., 1951)

R. Payne, *The Civil War in Spain* (London, Secker & Warburg, 1963)

W. Plomer, *Turbott Wolfe* (London, The Hogarth Press, 1925)

W. Plomer, *Double Lives* (London, Jonathan Cape, 1943)

W. Plomer, 'Voorslag Days', *London Magazine*, Vol. 6, No. 9 (July 1959)

W. Plomer, *Collected Poems* (London, Jonathan Cape, 1960)

J. Povey, *Roy Campbell* (New York, Twayne Publishers, 1977)

E. Rickword, *Collected Poems* (London, The Bodley Head, 1947)

M. Rosenthal, *Poetry of the Spanish Civil War* (New York, New York University Press, 1975)

M. L. Rosenthal, *The New Poets* (New York, Oxford University Press, 1967)

P. Russell, 'The Poetry of Roy Campbell', *Nine*, No. 3 (1950)

V. Sackville-West, *King's Daughter* (London, The Hogarth Press, 1929)

V. Sackville-West, *Collected Poems* (London, The Hogarth Press, 1933)

O. Schreiner, *The Story of an African Farm* (London, T. Fisher Unwin, 1883)

R. W. Service, *Collected Verse* (London, Ernest Benn, 1930)

E. Sitwell, 'Roy Campbell', *Poetry*, No. 92 (April 1958)

E. Sitwell, *Taken Care Of* (London, Hutchinson, 1965)

Edith Sitwell's *Selected Letters* (ed. Lehmann and Parker) (London, Macmillan, 1970)

O. Sitwell, *Those were the Days* (London, Macmillan, 1938)

O. Sitwell, *Left Hand, Right Hand* (London, Macmillan, 1945)

O. Sitwell, *Laughter in the Next Room* (London, Macmillan, 1949)

R. Smith, 'Roy Campbell and his French Sources', *Comparative Literature*, Vol. XXII, No. 1 (1970)

R. Smith, *Lyric and Polemic* (Montreal, MacGill/Queen's University Press, 1973)

S. Spender, *World Within World* (London, Hamish Hamilton, 1951)

J. Squire, *Selected Poems* (London, Oliver Moxon, 1948)

L. A. G. Strong, *Green Memory* (London, Methuen & Co., 1961)

F.-J. Temple, (ed.), *Hommage à Roy Campbell* (Paris, Éditions de la Licorne, 1958)

H. Thomas, *The Spanish Civil War* (London, Eyre & Spottiswoode, 1961)

H. Thomas, (ed.), *José Antonio Primo de Rivera* (London, Jonathan Cape, 1972)

L. Trotsky, *The Spanish Revolution* (New York, Pathfinder Press, 1973)

L. van der Post, *The Heart of the Hunter* (London, Penguin Books, 1965)

M. J. Vermaseren, *Mithras, the Secret God* (London, Chatto & Windus, 1963)

W. S. Vines, *Movements in Modern English Poetry and Prose* (London, Humphrey Milford, 1927)

G. Wagner, *Wyndham Lewis* (Westport, Greenwood Press, 1957)

B. Wall, *Headlong Into Change* (London, Harvill Press, 1969)

J. C. Weightman, 'Pedant Finds Fault', *Twentieth Century*, No. 153 (1953)

R. West, *The Meaning of Treason* (London, Macmillan, 1949)

M. Wishart, *High Diver* (London, Blond & Briggs, 1977)

D. Wright, *Roy Campbell* (London, Longmans, Green & Co., 1961)

W. B. Yeats, *Collected Poems* (London, Macmillan, 1933)

NOTES

Abbreviations

I have indicated the location (at the time of writing) of the letters and other documentary material on which I have drawn for information, by the following abbreviations, placed in brackets after every reference in the notes to a documentary source:

A	In the possession of the author
BH	In the possession of Dr Basil Holt
Bodley	In the possession of The Bodley Head Ltd.
CP, I, II, III	*Collected Poems* (see Select Bibliography)
CUL	Cornell University Library
DC	In the possession of Mrs Daphne Collins
DUL	Durham University Library
EduP	In the possession of Mr Enslin du Plessis
F&F	In the possession of Faber & Faber Ltd.
HRC	Humanities Research Center, University of Texas at Austin
HSRC	W. H. Gardner Collection, Human Sciences Research Council, Pretoria
JPL	Johannesburg Public Library
KCL	Killie Campbell Library, Durban
L	In the possession of Mr Lockwood
LvdP	In the possession of Sir Laurens van der Post
MC	In the possession of Mary Campbell
SANL	South African National Library
SUL	Saskatchewan University Library
TC	In the possession of Teresa Campbell
VE	In the possession of Mrs T. S. Eliot
WHG	From a copy made by Professor W. H. Gardner; I have not been able to trace the original

Campbell very seldom dated his letters. Accordingly, where I have made reference to these letters in the notes, I have whenever possible supplied a date. My dating is enclosed in square brackets to distinguish it from Campbell's own. He occasionally dated his letters with the month only, giving neither the day nor the year; in such cases the supplied information appears thus: [6] May [1947].

I. THE MAKING OF A POET

1. On 29 March 1850. I have drawn, for this account of William Campbell's voyage to South Africa, on Ethel Campbell's *Sam Campbell*, p. 164.
2. Ethel Campbell, p. 164.
3. J. Bond, *They Were South Africans*, p. 96.
4. For these and other details of William Campbell's achievements see Bond, *They Were South Africans* and Ethel Campbell, *Sam Campbell*.
5. Roy Campbell (henceforth referred to in notes as RC), *Light on a Dark Horse*, pp. 17–18. I have drawn further details from Ethel Campbell, pp. 176–9.
6. Statement made by Mrs S. G. Campbell to B. Holt (undated). (BH)
7. *Light on a Dark Horse*, p. 84. The story was confirmed for me by George Campbell, the poet's brother (interview, Durban, 14 July 1974). But RC was a young child at the time, and did not witness the feat he describes. This is a good example of his appropriating to himself the stories of others.
8. He left £41,000 when he died in 1926.
9. J. Dunnachie to Mrs S. G. Campbell, 19 Dec. 1901. Quoted in Ethel Campbell, p. 195.
10. Interview with George Campbell, Durban, 16 July 1975.
11. *Light on a Dark Horse*, pp. 29–30; confirmed by George Campbell.
12. As his description in *Light on a Dark Horse*, pp. 45–6 shows.
13. Interview with George Campbell, Durban, 16 July 1975.
14. *Light on a Dark Horse*, p. 119.
15. Interview with George Campbell, Durban, 14 July 1974.
16. Ethel Campbell, p. 195.
17. J. Dunnachie to RC, quoted in Ethel Campbell, p. 196.
18. Quoted in B. Holt's unpublished *Outrageous Poet*, Ch. 1, pp. 13–14. (BH)
19. *Light on a Dark Horse*, p. 33.
20. *Light on a Dark Horse*, p. 80.
21. *Light on a Dark Horse*, pp. 68 ff.
22. 'To A Pet Cobra': RC's *Collected Poems*, Vol.I (hereafter referred to as 'CP, I') p.31.
23. *Light on a Dark Horse*, p. 68.
24. *Light on a Dark Horse*, p. 69.
25. Unpublished early poem. (A)
26. Quoted by Ethel Campbell, p. 321.
27. *Light on a Dark Horse*, pp. 73–4.
28. KCL.
29. Unpublished letter, Mrs S. G. Campbell to B. Holt, 30 August 1947. (BH)
30. Unpublished poem. (A)
31. Unpublished poem. (KCL)
32. Unpublished poem. (KCL)
33. Unpublished poem. (KCL)
34. Unpublished poem, 'Dreams'. (A)
35. This resolve lasted until the end of the war. Unpublished letter, RC to Joan Tatham, 6 Aug. [1918]. (HSRC)

Natal University College register, 27 February 1918.

37. Unpublished portion of Chapter 4 of *Light on a Dark Horse*. (A)
38. Unpublished portion of Chapter 4 of *Light on a Dark Horse*. (A)
39. Unpublished letter, RC to Joan Tatham [Sept/Oct. 1918]. (HSRC)
40. Unpublished letter, RC to Joan Tatham, 6 Aug. [1918]. (HSRC)
41. Unpublished section of *Light on a Dark Horse*. (A)
42. See, for example, 'The Sisters', 'The Zebras', and the Rounding the Horn and Antarctic passages in *The Flaming Terrapin*. Frost was only gradually ousted by the sun in his image-store.
43. Referred to in letters to his parents from England: e.g., RC to his mother [1923], quoted by Ethel Campbell, p. 356.
44. This sense of being, culturally speaking, children of a broken home, is common to many English-speaking South African writers. It is a theme that runs strongly through much South African verse. See for instance Nortje's *Dead Roots*, or Guy Butler's *Stranger to Europe*.
45. *Light on a Dark Horse*, p. 3.

II. OXFORD AND AFTER

1. *Light on a Dark Horse*, p. 173.
2. *Light on a Dark Horse*, pp. 174–5.
3. *Light on a Dark Horse*, p. 176.
4. Number 136.
5. He eventually became a Professor of History at Rhodes University, South Africa.
6. *Broken Record*, p. 38. (This book was RC's first autobiography, published in 1934.)
7. *Broken Record*, p. 32.
8. See Rousseau's article on RC in the *Cape Argus*, 24 June 1933.
9. *Light on a Dark Horse*, pp. 181–2.
10. See his long and sincere tribute to Walton, *Light on a Dark Horse*, pp. 181–2.
11. Sir William Walton's answers to W. H. Gardner's undated questionnaire. (HSRC)
12. Unpublished letter, Sir William Walton to the writer, 24 June 1978. (A)
13. Rob Lyle, RC's closest friend in later years, to W. H. Gardner, unpublished letter, June 1958; also interview with Mary Campbell, Portugal, 3 Jan. 1975.
14. Sir William Walton's reply to Gardner's questionnaire. (HSRC)
15 After the war, however, the Sitwells came to be among Campbell's greatest friends.
16. See L. A. G. Strong, *Green Memory*, p. 179, for a description of Earp at this time.
17. *Light on a Dark Horse*, p. 183.
18. Strong, *Green Memory*, p. 226.
19. Interview with Edgell Rickword, London, 13 Feb. 1975.
20. Interview with Edgell Rickword, London, 13 Feb. 1975.
21. RC to his father [Aug. 1919]: quoted by Ethel Campbell, p. 355.
22. A disturbing portent. All his life Campbell embraced views or policies because people he liked embraced them – or because people he disliked opposed them. His naivety led him repeatedly into untenable positions.

23. RC to his mother [late 1919]: quoted by Ethel Campbell, p. 355.

24. Unpublished letter, Mary Campbell to W. H. Gardner, 9 May 1958. (HSRC)

25. *Broken Record*, pp. 40–1.

26. *Broken Record*, p. 37.

27. Referred to in unpublished letter, RC to William Plomer [May 1927]. (DUL)

28. Wyndham Lewis, *The Apes of God*, Part II, p. 78.

29. A. E. Coppard, *It's Me, O Lord!* pp. 189–190.

30. It is characteristic of him that he could at the same time ignore the Futurist Manifesto's glorification of militarism and patriotism, which he despised.

31. Undated letter, RC to his father: quoted by Ethel Campbell, p. 355.

32. Undated letter, RC to his father: quoted by Ethel Campbell, p. 355.

33. Augustus John in the London *Sunday Times*, 12 October 1958.

34. London *Sunday Times*, 12 October 1958.

35. *Light on a Dark Horse*, p. 184.

36. Unpublished letter, Mary Campbell to W. H. Gardner, 24 Sept. 1959. (HSRC)

37. *Light on a Dark Horse*, pp. 187–8. Nelson was a painter.

38. *Broken Record*, p. 39.

39. RC to his mother [1923]: quoted by Ethel Campbell, p. 356.

40. *Broken Record*, p. 39.

41. *Broken Record*, p. 129.

42. *Broken Record*, p. 129.

43. *Light on a Dark Horse*, pp. 194 and 214–15.

44. RC to his mother [July 1921]. (BH)

45. RC to his mother [July/Aug. 1921], quoted by Ethel Campbell, p. 356.

46. RC to his mother, unpublished letter [Sept. 1921]. (BH)

47. RC gives the date in his letter to Mary of 5 Sept. 1943. (SUL)

48. Campbell described the circumstances of their meeting in *Light on a Dark Horse*, p. 238. There are at least four other versions of this meeting but Campbell's memory was reliable when he cared to consult it, and he had no obvious reason for inventing these circumstances.

49. Interview with Mary Campbell, Portugal, 2 Jan. 1975.

50. Interview with Mary Campbell, Portugal, 2 Jan. 1975.

51. Interview with Mary Campbell, Portugal, 2 Jan. 1975.

52. Number 13, Regent Square.

53. Interview with Lady Kathleen Epstein, London, 27 April 1978.

54. Unpublished letter, RC to Mary Campbell, 5 Sept. 1943. (SUL)

55. *Light on a Dark Horse*, p. 238.

56. Unpublished letter, Mary Campbell to W. H. Gardner, 18 Sept. 1958. (HSRC)

57. Interview with Lady Kathleen Epstein, London, 27 April 1978.

58. Interview with Mary Campbell, Portugal, 4 Jan. 1975.

59. *Sunday Times*, 12 Oct. 1958.

60. Interview with Mary Campbell, Portugal, 4 Jan. 1975.

61. Wyndham Lewis, *Blasting and Bombardiering*, Part 4, Ch. 4, pp. 222–3.

62. Interview with Mary Campbell, Portugal, 5 Jan. 1975.

63. Interview with Mary Campbell, Portugal, 5 Jan. 1975.

64. Interview with Lady Kathleen Epstein, London, 27 April 1978.

65. Unpublished letter, Mary Campbell to W. H. Gardner, 28 Jan. 1958. (HSRC)
66. Romilly John, *The Seventh Child*, pp. 211–13.
67. *Light on a Dark Horse*, p. 253.
68. Interview with Mrs Martin, Aberdaron, Wales, 20 Sept. 1974.
69. Unpublished letter, A. Hughes to W. H. Gardner, 13 May 1961. (HSRC)
70. Interview, Portugal, 5 Jan. 1975.
71. Interview with Mary Campbell, Portugal, 5 Jan. 1975.
72. Unpublished letter, Edgell Rickword to RC, 9 Sept. 1922. (MC)
73. Unpublished letter, RC to his mother [mid-Sept. 1922]. (BH)
74. Augustus John, *Chiaroscuro*, p. 77; also unpublished letter, Jonathan Cape to W. H. Gardner, 29 April 1959. (HSRC)

III. THE FLAMING TERRAPIN

1. By the Dial Press.
2. Richard Hughes in the *Spectator*, 23 Aug. 1924.
3. Hamish Miles in the *Dial*, Nov. 1924.
4. Hamish Miles in the *Dial*, Nov. 1924.
5. Unpublished letter to RC, 28 Feb. 1923. (MC)
6. RC to his parents, undated. Ethel Campbell, pp. 356–7.
7. Garnett wrote of it, 'It is obvious that it was not planned originally as an ordered whole, but that it is a piecing together of diverse fragments sustained by a loose general argument.' *(Nation and Athenaeum*, 7 June 1924.) And see Morgan's view in the *Outlook*, 28 June 1924.
8. A method he followed all his life. Interview with Mary Campbell, Portugal, 4 Jan. 1975.
9.   As a fierce train, maned like a ramping lion
   With smoke and fire, thunders on rolling iron
   Pounding grim tunes, and grinds with flashing wheel
   Rockets of flame from parallels of steel,
   And, as the rails curve, shoots from flanks of brass
   Tangents of flame to singe the whiskered grass . . . (CP, I, 84)
10. CP, I, 60.
11. Marinetti had announced in the 'Futurist Manifesto', 'Noi affermiamo che la magnificenza del mondo si é arrichita di una bellezza nuova: la bellezza della volocitá . . . un automobile ruggente, che sembra correre sulla mitraglia, é píu bello della Vittoria de Samotracia'. Quoted by de Maria, *Marinetti e il Futurismo*, p. 6.
12.   Let squinting guns command the fairest views,
   And giant mills, the temples of despair,
   Reared to dull Vulcan and to brutish Mars,
   Wolfind huge coals with iron jaws aflare,
   Roll their grim smoke to choke the trembling stars! (CP, I, 76–7)
13. CP, I, 63.
14. *Broken Record*, p. 143.
15. In the *South African Pictorial*, 25 April 1925, p. 11.
16. RC to his parents [1920], Ethel Campbell, pp. 356–7.

17. CP, I, 66.
18. Unpublished letter, Jonathan Cape to W H. Gardner, 29 April 1959. (HSRC)
19. RC to his mother [Oct. 1923]: Ethel Campbell, p. 356.
20. Less than £50 in 1924. Cape to W. H. Gardner, 29 April 1959. (HSRC).
21. Interview with Mary Campbell, Portugal, 3 Jan. 1975.
22. Unpublished letter to Mary Campbell [late May 1924]. (MC)

IV. VOORSLAG

1. Unpublished letter to Mary Campbell [early June 1924]. (MC)
2. Unpublished letter, RC to Mary Campbell [July 1924]. (MC)
3. Unpublished letter, RC to Mary Campbell [July/Aug. 1924]. (MC)
4. Unpublished letter, RC to Mary Campbell [20 June 1924]. (MC)
5. Unpublished letter, RC to Edward Garnett [Oct. 1924]. (HRC)
6. W. B.Yeats, 'In Memory of Major Robert Gregory'.
7. *Light on a Dark Horse*, p. 101.
8. Interview with Laurens van der Post, London, 4 Dec. 1977.
9. Unpublished letter, Edward Roworth to W.H. Gardner, 23 Jan. 1959. (HSRC)
10. Recounted in RC's unpublished letter to Edward Garnett [late 1925]. (HRC)
11. Interview with Mary Campbell, Portugal, 3 Jan. 1975, and with Laurens van der Post, London, 3 Dec. 1977.
12. Unpublished letter, RC to Edward Roworth [20 April 1925]. (SANL)
13. Unpublished letter, RC to Edward Garnett [June 1925]. (HRC)
14. *Natal Advertiser*, 5 May 1925. Campbell never changed his opinion on this matter. Nearly thirty years later one finds him writing a very similar passage in *Light on a Dark Horse*, pp. 153–4.
15. Interview with Laurens van der Post, London, 3 Dec. 1977.
16. Interview with Laurens van der Post, London, 3 Dec. 1977.
17. Unpublished letter, William Plomer to W. H. Gardner, 26 June 1958. (HSRC)
18. Unpublished letter, RC to Edward Garnett [Sept. 1925]. (HRC)
19. Unpublished letter, RC to William Plomer [12 Oct. 1925]. (DUL)
20. Interview with Mary Campbell, Portugal, 4 Jan. 1975.
21. Dating Campbell's poetry is extremely difficult. But 'The Zebras' was certainly written in South Africa at this time (as an unpublished note from RC to B. Holt, 21 May 1947, makes clear) and 'The Sisters' is so closely linked with it that I believe they were both written in 1925, probably within a few days of one another.
22. *Light on a Dark Horse* p. 67.
23. And unites them in a way that looks forward extraordinarily to the central themes of Peter Shaffer's play *Equus*.
24. Interview with Laurens van der Post, London, 3 Dec. 1977.
25. *Natal Advertiser*, 19 March 1926.
26. *Natal Advertiser*, 19 March 1926.
27. Unpublished memorandum, RC to William Plomer [Aug. 1926]. (DUL)
28. Unpublished letter, Mary Campbell to William Plomer [10 March 1926]. (DUL]

29. *Voorslag*, No. 1 (June 1926), p. 39.
30. *Voorslag*, No. 1, p. 60.
31. *Broken Record*, p. 50.
32. Interview with Dona Anna Cavero de Carondelet (RC's younger daughter), Portugal, 2 Jan. 1975.
33. *Voorslag*, No. 2 (July 1926), p. 11.
34. *Voorslag*, No. 2, p. 13.
35. Unpublished letter, Edward Roworth to W. H. Gardner, 23 Jan. 1959. (HSRC)
36. Interview with Laurens van der Post, London, 4 Dec. 1977.
37. Unpublished memorandum, RC to William Plomer [Aug. 1926]. (DUL)
38. Laurens van der Post's introduction to Plomer's *Turbott Wolfe* (1965 edn), p. 27.

V. SOUTH AFRICAN POEMS

1. William Plomer, 'Voorslag Days', *London Magazine*, Vol. 6, No. 1, pp. 49–50.
2. Interview with Mary Campbell, Portugal, 3 Jan. 1975.
3. Unpublished note, RC to Basil Holt, 21 May 1947. (BH)
4. *Broken Record*, p. 21.
5. RC to his father: Ethel Campbell, p. 355.
6. See for instance his letter to William Plomer [17 Jan. 1926]. (DUL)
7. Nietzsche, *Thus Spake Zarathustra* – 'Of the Rabble'.
8. *Voorslag*, No. 2 (July 1926), p. 5.
9. Unpublished letter, William Plomer to W. H. Gardner, 3 Feb. 1958. (HSRC)
10. Unpublished letter, RC to C. J. Sibbett [4 Dec. 1926]. (SANL]
11. He read it in 1925: unpublished letter to Edward Garnett [20 Nov. 1925]. (HRC)
12. Though it was originally from a Hottentot legend: see Laurens van der Post's *The Heart of the Hunter*, p. 167.
13. Olive Schreiner, *The Story of an African Farm*, pp. 158–69.
14. William Plomer, 'Voorslag Days', *London Magazine*, Vol. 6, No. 1, p. 50.
15. Unpublished memorandum, J. R. Gillie to W. H. Gardner, 16 Nov. 1960. (HSRC)
16. *Broken Record*, p. 126.
17. Unpublished letter, RC to T. S. Eliot [Aug. 1928]. (VE)
18. Smith, *Lyric and Polemic*, pp. 54–5.
19. Interview with Laurens van der Post, London, 3 Dec. 1977.
20. William Plomer, 'Voorslag Days', *London Magazine*, Vol 6, No. 1, p. 50.
21. See for instance *Light on a Dark Horse*, pp. 44–6.
22. Unpublished letter, RC to Edward Garnett [20 Nov. 1925]. (HRC)
23. For example, *Ilanga Lase*, 14 January 1916, and March 1926.
24. Interview with Laurens van der Post, London, 3 Dec. 1977.
25. Unpublished letter, RC to Edward Garnett [20 Nov. 1925]. (HRC)
26. William Plomer, *Collected Poems*, pp. 18–19.
27. It is worth noting that the lines

    While her sharp nails, in slow caresses ruled,
    Prowl through his hair with sharp electric clicks,

are an echo both of Rimbaud's 'Les Chercheuses de Poux' (as Rowland Smith has shown) and of Campbell's own poem 'The Sisters'.
28. Interview with Laurens van der Post, 3 Dec. 1977.
29. Interview with Laurens van der Post, London, 3 Dec. 1977.
30. Interview with Laurens van der Post, London, 2 Dec. 1977.
31. Unpublished letter, RC to C. J. Sibbett [17 Aug. 1926]. (SANL)
32. Unpublished letter, Mary Campbell to W. H. Gardner, 23 May 1958. (HSRC)
33. William Plomer, 'Voorslag Days', *London Magazine*, Vol. 6, No. 1.
34. Unpublished letter, RC to C. J. Sibbett [28 July 1926]. (SANL)
35. *Broken Record*, p. 53.
36. Unpublished letter, RC to Herbert Palmer [Oct. 1927]. (HRC)
37. Unpublished letter, RC to William Plomer [12 Oct. 1925]. (DUL)
38. Unpublished letter, Mary Campbell to William Plomer, 19 Sept. 1926. (DUL)
39. Unpublished letter, RC to C. J. Sibbett [4 Dec. 1926]. (SANL)
40. 'ZZ' had criticized Campbell and Plomer in the Johannesburg *Star*. Edward Roworth to W. H. Gardner, 31 Jan. 1959. (HSRC)
41. Unpublished letter, Edward Roworth to W. H. Gardner, 23 Jan. 1959. (HSRC)
42. Unpublished letter, RC to C. J. Sibbett [7 Aug. 1926]. (SANL)
43. Unpublished letter, RC to William Plomer [26 Dec. 1926]. (DUL)
44. Unpublished letter, RC to C. J. Sibbett [4 Dec. 1926]. (SANL)
45. Published by Constable, London, 1928.
46. Unpublished letter, RC to C. J. Sibbett [April 1952]. (SANL)
46. Unpublished letter, RC to C. J. Sibbett [April 1952]. (SANL)
47. Camoens, *The Lusiads* (Penguin Edition) pp. 131–2.

VI. ENGLAND

1. Unpublished letter, Mary Campbell to W. H. Gardner, 24 March [1959]. (HSRC)
2. Interview with Mary Campbell, Portugal, 3 Jan. 1975.
3. Interview with Mary Campbell, Portugal, 3 Jan. 1975.
4. RC to William Plomer [26 Dec. 1926]. (DUL)
5. For evidence of her determination not to return to South Africa, see her unpublished letter to William Plomer [Feb. 1927]. (DUL)
6. (DUL)
7. Interview with Mary Campbell, Portugal, 2 Jan. 1975; also Harold Nicolson's letter to W. H. Gardner, 7 May 1958.
8. Unpublished letter, Mary Campbell to W. H. Gardner, 24 March [1959]. (HSRC)
9. Unpublished letter, RC to L. A. G. Strong [May 1927]. (HRC)
10. Harold Nicolson's reply to W. H. Gardner's questionnaire, 7 May 1958. (HSRC)
11. Harold Nicolson's unpublished diary, 23 May 1927.
12. Harold Nicolson's unpublished diary, 28 May 1927.
13. Harold Nicolson's unpublished diary, 10 June 1927.

14. Unpublished letter, RC to C. J. Sibbett [Oct. 1927]. (SANL)
15. Unpublished letter, RC to C. J. Sibbett [Oct. 1927]. (SANL)
16. Unpublished letter, Mary Campbell to William Plomer, 7 May 1927. (DUL)
17. Unpublished letter, Mary Campbell to William Plomer, July 1927. (DUL)
18. Harold Nicolson's replies to W. H. Gardner's questionnaire, 7 May 1958. (HSRC)
19. Harold Nicolson's replies to W. H. Gardner's questionnaire, 7 May 1958. (HSRC)
20. For an account of this unusual match, in some ways so much like the Campbells' own, see Nigel Nicolson, *Portrait of a Marriage*.
21. In 1929.
22. Harold Nicolson's unpublished diary.
23. Unpublished letter, RC to C. J. Sibbett [Oct. 1927]. (SANL)
24. Interview with Mary Campbell, Portugal, 3 Jan. 1975.
25. Vita Sackville-West's unpublished diary, 6 Nov. 1927.
26. Interview with Rob Lyle (Campbell's closest friend and confidant in later years), Portugal, 7 Jan. 1975.
27. The poetess of whom Yeats thought so highly.
28. Unpublished letter, Rob Lyle to W. H. Gardner, June 1958. (HSRC) In 'Orpheus', a poem written years later, RC alluded to this night:

> Gin-soaked, a shot-gun in her clutches,
> the Fury was a future duchess
>   whom Hell had posted for a sentry,
>   and who, though in her periwig
> the vipers, hissing vague alarm,
> like neckties on a hawker's arm
>   were faintly fluttered by my entry,
>   continued snoring like a pig. (CP, II, 129–30)

29. Vita's unpublished diary, 7 Nov. 1927.
30. Unpublished letter, Vita to Harold Nicolson, 7 Nov. 1927.
31. Letter in *Contrast* 38, (Jan. 1976), Vol. 10, No. 2, p. 75.
32. Interview with Laurens van der Post, London, 4 Dec. 1977.
33. Interview with Laurens van der Post, London, 4 Dec. 1977.
34. Interview with Laurens van der Post, London, 4 Dec. 1977.

VII. THE GEORGIAD

1. Interview with Mary Campbell, Portugal, 2 Jan. 1975.
2. As the third volume of her letters (ed. Nigel Nicolson, 1978) clearly shows.
3. Private information: Vita Sackville-West's Diary.
4. Unpublished letter, RC to C. J. Sibbett [July 1928]. (SANL)
5. Vita's diary, and private information.
6. Unpublished correspondence, Mary Campbell to Vita Sackville-West.
7. See for instance the 'Dedication' to *Adamastor*, and 'Silence' in the same volume.
8. An image Campbell had used in the last stanzas of 'The Festivals of Flight' and in 'Mazeppa'.
9. Private information.

10. Unpublished portion of *Light on a Dark Horse*, Vol II, p. 179. (JPL)
11. As Rowland Smith has noted, *Lyric and Polemic*, pp. 80–2.
12. *The Georgiad*, p. 239.
13. For example, Rowland Smith, *Lyric and Polemic*, pp. 80–3.
14. Unpublished letter to Herbert Palmer [Oct. 1927]. (HRC)
15. For example, CP, I 224–5.
16. The idea of a poet weeping for rivers half an hour's travel away, or of dogs saluting a monument with raised legs, was lifted from *The Wayzgoose*, as was the mockery of self-praise.
17. Compare CP, I, 205:

> But this put all such trifles in the shade,
> And beggared Bloomsbury of half its trade . . .

   with CP, I, 221:

> Then, Humbert, I may put you in the shade
> And beggar you of more than half your trade.

18. Michael Holroyd, *Lytton Strachey and the Bloomsbury group*, (Penguin edition) p. 41.
19. In *Te Deum*. See Holroyd, p. 41.
20. Unpublished letter, RC to Wyndham Lewis [1931]. (CUL)
21. Vita Sackville-West, *Collected Poems*, p. 15.
22. Patrick Howarth, *Squire, Most Generous of Men*, p. 20.
23. Nigel Nicolson, *Portrait of a Marriage*, p. 188.
24. *Light on a Dark Horse* pp. 58–9.
25. See his unpublished letter to Wyndham Lewis from Sevenoaks [1928]. (CUL)
26. RC's review of *The Apes of God*; Wyndham Lewis's 'Enemy Pamphlet No. 1', p. 16.
27. Unpublished letter, RC to Wyndham Lewis [late 1930]. (CUL)
28. *New Statesman*, 16 Aug. 1930.
29. Unpublished letter. (CUL)
30. Unpublished letter, RC to Herbert Palmer [June 1931]. (HRC)
31. Unpublished letter, RC to Wyndham Lewis. (CUL)
32. Humbert Wolfe's *The Ranciad*, which Rowland Smith (*Lyric and Polemic*, pp. 70–1) suggests is a reply to *The Georgiad*, in fact appeared four months before Campbell's poem, which was published in October 1931.
33. Gilbert Highet in the *Scottish Educational Journal*, 4 March 1932.
34. *Library Review*, Spring 1932.
35. Harold Nicolson, unpublished letter to W. H. Gardner, 27 March 1958.
36. CP, I, 241.

VIII. PROVENCE

1. The boat inspired one of Campbell's poems, 'La Clemence'. CP, I, 106.
2. The daughter resulting from this union was eventually to marry Laurie Lee.
3. Unpublished letter, RC to Herbert Palmer [May] 1929. (HRC)
4. *Light on a Dark Horse*, p. 271.
5. *Light on a Dark Horse*, pp. 208–9.
6. RC's unpublished note to B. Holt, 21 May 1947. (BH)

7. A good example of the closeness of RC's observation of natural detail, apparent, too, in his 'African' poems. A windblown olive-tree appears to go grey as the silvery undersides of the leaves are exposed.

8. Unpublished note, RC to B. Holt, 21 May 1947. (BH)

9. Unpublished letter, Mary Campbell to William Plomer, June 1929. (DUL)

10. *Broken Record*, pp. 188–9.

11. *Broken Record*, p. 178.

12. 'The Zebras' and 'The Sisters'.

13. *Light on a Dark Horse*, pp. 27–8.

14. *Light on a Dark Horse*, pp 306–7.

15. See Smith's *Lyric and Polemic*, p. 94. Campbell freely acknowledged his 'borrowings' to anyone who cared to question him. Interview with Rob Lyle, Portugal, 6 Jan. 1975. I have also drawn upon Lyle's unpublished *Herdsman of Apollo*. (HSRC)

16. J. T. Samat, author of *Sangar*.

17. *Light on a Dark Horse*, p. 306.

18. Unpublished letter, William Plomer to W. H. Gardner, 20 April 1958. (WHG)

19. Wyndham Lewis, *Rotting Hill*, p. 260.

20. Unpublished letter, RC to C. J. Sibbett [14 April 1931]. (SANL)

21. Sybille Bedford, *Aldous Huxley*, Vol. I, pp. 233–4.

22. Interview with Mary Campbell, Portugal, 4 Jan. 1975.

23. David Wright's notes of RC's conversation, 11 July 1949. (A)

24. Unpublished letter, RC to Enslin du Plessis [June/July 1929]. (EduP)

25. Unpublished letter, RC to Wyndham Lewis [June 1929]. (CUL)

26. Teresa Campbell: unpublished memoir of her father. (TC) On at least one other occasion Campbell was beaten in a fight, by his brother-in-law Douglas Garman, in a passageway of the Eiffel Tower restaurant: interview with Edgell Rickword, London, 13 Feb. 1975.

27. It was through Campbell that Plomer met Lewis.

28. Unpublished letter, Mary Campbell to William Plomer [June] 1929.(DUL)

29. Unpublished letter, RC to William Plomer [14 June 1929]. (DUL)

30. Unpublished letters, RC to Laurens van der Post [May 1930] (LvdP), and RC to Enslin du Plessis [April 1930]. (EduP)

31. Unpublished letter, RC to William Plomer [4 May 193]. (DUL)

32. Unpublished postcards, RC to William Plomer [3 Sept. 1930] (DUL) and [4 Oct 1930]. (WHG).

33. Only an unpublished draft of this letter survives (SANL). It may never have been sent.

34. Unpublished letter, William Plomer to W. H. Gardner, 26 Jan. 1958. (HSRC).

35. He parted from Uys Krige, for example, under circumstances in many ways similar.

36. Unpublished letter, RC to C. J. Sibbett [June 1929]. (SANL)

37. Unpublished postcard to C. J. Sibbett [21 June 1929]. (SANL)

38. Unpublished postcard to Wyndham Lewis [7 Sept. 1929]. (CUL)

39. Unpublished letter, RC to Laurens van der Post [May 1930]. (LvdP)

40. Interview with George Campbell, Durban, 16 July 1975, and with Teresa

Campbell, Portugal, 5 Jan. 1975.

41. *Light on a Dark Horse*, p. 282.
42. *Light on a Dark Horse*, p. 294.
43. Desmond MacCarthy in *The Sunday Times*, 20 April 1930.
44. Arnold Bennett in the *Evening Standard*, 24 April 1930.
45. Unpublished letter, RC to T. S. Eliot [early 1930]. (VE)
46. Unpublished letter, RC to E. du Plessis [May 1930]. (EduP)
47. *Light on a Dark Horse*, p. 294, and interview with Mary and Teresa Campbell, Portugal, Jan. 1975.
48. With the exception of one inferior poem, the whole of *Poems* (from which Campbell made £200 in 1930) is reprinted in *Flowering Reeds*.
49. *Light on a Dark Horse*, pp. 152–3.
50. Published in 1932.
51. Interview with Anna Cavero de Carondelet, Portugal, 2 Jan. 1975.
52. Wyndham Lewis, *Snooty Baronet*, p. 182. Such statements by Lewis show that the similarity of *The Georgiad*'s themes to those of *The Apes of God* cannot with justice be attributed simply to Lewis's influence on Campbell.
53. Wyndham Lewis to RC, 6 April 1930. (Rose, *Letters of Wyndham Lewis*, pp. 205–6.)
54. RC to C. J. Sibbett, unpublished letter [14 March 1931]. (SANL)
55. Unpublished letter, RC to Enslin du Plessis [June] 1930. (EduP)
56. Unpublished letter, RC to Lewis [Nov 1931] (CUL). The cheap edition of *The Apes of God* and *The Georgiad* appeared within a week of each other in November 1931.
57. 'First Meeting with Roy Campbell', *Theoria*, No. 12 (1954), pp. 25–6.
58. Interview with Teresa Campbell, Portugal, 6 Jan. 1975.
59. Laurens van der Post, Introduction to Plomer's *Turbott Wolfe*, 1965 edn., pp. 24–5.
60. Unpublished letter, RC to T. S. Eliot [Sept, 1928]. (VE)
61. Unpublished letter, RC to Wyndham Lewis [late 1932]. (CUL)
62. *Light on a Dark Horse*, pp. 313–14.

IX. FLOWERING REEDS

1. Unpublished letter [January 1933]. (SANL)
2. Unpublished *Memoir* of RC by Teresa Campbell. (TC)
3. Unpublished letter, RC to C.J. Sibbett [14 March 1931]. (SANL)
4. Unpublished questionnaire, Mary Campbell to W. H. Gardner, 1959. (HSRC)
5. Unpublished postcard, RC to Mary Campbell (in London) [1932]. (WHG) The stresses are RC's own.
6. Unpublished letter, Mary Campbell to the writer, 22 July 1976. (A)
7. Unpublished letter, RC to Mary Campbell (in London) [1932]. (WHG) It should be said that the dating of Campbell's letters at this period poses unusual problems.
8. Unpublished letter, Mary Campbell to the writer, 22 July 1976. (A)
9. Unpublished letter, RC to Mary Campbell [1932]. (WHG)
10. See *Light on a Dark Horse*, pp. 243–4 and p. 248.

11. Unpublished letter, RC to C. J. Sibbett [July 1933]. (SANL)
12. 'Overtime' draws upon two Baudelaire poems, 'Le Squelette Laboureur' and 'Une Gravure Fantastique' (Smith, *Lyric and Polemic* pp. 104 ff.)
13. *New Statesman*, 18 March 1933.
14. Geoffrey West, *Adelphi*, May 1933.
15. *TLS*, 27 April 1933.
16. Unpublished letter, RC to his mother [Sept. 1933] (A)
17. Unpublished letter, Uys Krige to W. H. Gardner, 19 Jan. 1959. (HSRC)
18. Interview with Mary Campbell, Portugal, 4 Jan. 1975.
19. Unpublished letter, RC to C. J. Sibbett [early Oct. 1933]. (SANL)
20. 'The worst part of the "revolution" was in this and the adjoining street. Machine guns were posted at every corner and we had to keep indoors after dark. One bomb exploded about 200 yards away . . . ' Unpublished letter, RC to C. J. Sibbett [Jan./Feb. 1934]. (SANL)
21. Unpublished letter, RC to Greenwood [late Nov. 1933]. (WHG)

X. SPAIN

1. Unpublished letter, RC to Greenwood [26 Jan. 1934]. (WHG)
2. Interview with George Campbell, Durban, 16 July 1975.
3. Interview with Mrs Martin, Aberdaron, Wales, 20 Sept. 1974.
4. *Broken Record*, p. 48.
5. Unpublished letter, RC to C. J. Sibbett [Jan./Feb. 1934]. (SANL)
6. Sybille Bedford, *Aldous Huxley*, Vol. I, p. 280; and interview with Mary Campbell, Portugal, 4 Jan. 1975.
7. Unpublished letter, RC to C. J. Sibbett [Jan./Feb. 1934]. (SANL)
8. Cumont, *The Mysteries of Mithra*. It appeared in an English translation in 1903. Campbell's daughter Teresa recalls that her father owned 'a book on Mithras' at this period.
9. *Broken Record*, p. 129.
10. Cumont, *The Mysteries of Mithra*, pp. 141–2.
11. He gives instructions on where to find one such sculpture in *Taurine Provence*, p. 14n, and the dust-cover of *Mithraic Emblems* carried a photograph of another.
12. I have kept to Cumont's version of the myth, since this is almost certainly the only one Campbell knew. For other views on the subject works by Zaehner, Vermaseren, and Patterson may be consulted.
13. J. G. Frazer's *The Golden Bough* was, like Gibbon's work, a book which Campbell read again and again throughout his life.
14. *Broken Record*, p. 69.
15. See his defence of this idea against Lewis in *Broken Record*, pp. 70–1.
16. Cumont, *The Mysteries of Mithra*, pp. 191–3.
17. *Taurine Provence*, p. 15.
18. Cumont, *The Mysteries of Mithra*, pp. 190–1.
19. Author's Note, *Mithraic Emblems*, p. 39.
20. In his CP, I (1949) Campbell altered 'The Sixth Sword' considerably to accentuate his love for Franco's Spain.
21. As Smith has pointed out: *Lyric and Polemic*, pp. 129–30.

22. Such images abound in southern Europe. A particularly good example stood in the old church in Altea, where the Campbells worshipped while they lived there during 1934–5. Interview with Teresa Campbell, Portugal, 3 Jan. 1975.
23. Campbell may also have known that one card in the Tarot pack depicts a heart transfixed by three swords. I am grateful to Prof. B. K. Martin for drawing my attention to this possibility.
24. Unpublished letter, RC to G. Faber [July 1936]. (F&F)
25. See Campbell's note to this sonnet in *Mithraic Emblems*, p. 174.
26. *Light on a Dark Horse*, p. 297.
27. *Light on a Dark Horse*, pp. 298–9.
28. As Smith has pointed out *(Lyric and Polemic*, p. 130) Campbell's closing lines about the cyprus are adapted from Apollinaire's

> C'est un cyprès sur un tombeau . . .
> Et chaque nuit c'est un Flambeau.

29. Campbell's holograph MS. of the Sword poems [early 1933]. (SANL) He used this ending (with minor alterations) for the poem in the *New Statesman* in 1933, and in *Mithraic Emblems* three years later.
30. On 26 Jan. 1934, Campbell refers (in a letter to his publisher Greenwood) to 'Mithraic Emblems' as a poem of 'only 14 half-pages'; and the only MS of the poem I have been able to trace (SANL) has only the first fourteen poems.
31. Unpublished letter, Greenwood to Mary Campbell, 16 July 1936. (L)
32. *Taurine Provence*, p. 20.
33. *Broken Record*, pp. 188–9.
34. *Broken Record*, p. 202.
35. W. Lewis, *Hitler*, p. 28, and the whole of Chapter 3. It is worth noticing too the reference to a 'a mere bagatelle of a *Judenfrage*' (p. 42).
36. *Broken Record*, p. 43.
37. W. Lewis, *Blasting and Bombardiering*, p. 221.
38. Its genesis can be dated from fragments of it written on the back of a draft letter to Plomer [Aug. 1933]. (SANL)
39. Unpublished letter, Mary Campbell to Greenwood, 12 July [1936]. (WHG)
40. 'The Serf' (written 1926), CP, I, 30.
41. *Broken Record*, p. 198.
42. W. Lewis, *One Way Song*, p. 104.
43. W. Lewis, *One Way Song*, p. 117.
44. Unpublished letter, RC to Lewis [Nov. 1933]. (CUL)
45. Quoted in RC's unpublished letter to Greenwood [mid-1934]. (WHG)
46. W. Lewis, *One Way Song*, p. 86.
47. For details of the steady drift to war, see Thomas's *The Spanish Civil War*, pp. 74 ff. Pattee, Payn, Morrow and others may also be consulted.
48. *Light on a Dark Horse*, p. 317, and interviews with Mary Campbell.
49. Unpublished letter, Mary Campbell to W. H. Gardner, 24 September 1959. (HSRC)
50. *Light on a Dark Horse*, p. 318.
51. Interview with Teresa Campbell, Portugal, 5 Jan. 1975.
52. *Light on a Dark Horse*, p. 318.
53. Quintanas 32, Altea.
54. Interview with Mary Campbell, Portugal, 4 Jan. 1975. Very few letters of this

period survive; I have drawn heavily for this account on interviews with Mary Campbell and her daughters.

55. Unpublished postcard, RC to W. Lewis [1934]. (CUL)
56. Interview with Mary Campbell, Portugal, 4 Jan. 1975.
57. He found the image of the fight, and part of its application, in Apollinaire's poem 'Les Collines'. (Smith, *Lyric and Polemic*, p. 183.)
58. Unpublished letter, RC to Enslin du Plessis [1934]. (EduP)
59. Unpublished letter, RC to Greenwood [end May 1934]. (L)
60. *Light on a Dark Horse*, pp. 320–1.
61. Unpublished letter, RC to Enslin du Plessis [June 1934]. (EduP)
62. Unpublished letter, Mary Campbell to Greenwood, 2 Sept. 1934. (WHG)
63. *Light on a Dark Horse*, p. 327.
64. Unpublished letter, RC to W. Lewis [1934]. (CUL)
65. Unpublished letter, W. Lewis to RC, 13 April 1936. (A)
66. Unpublished letter, RC to Greenwood [June/July 1934]. (WHG)
67. Interview with Teresa and Mary Campbell, Portugal, 4 Jan. 1975.
68. Unpublished postcard, RC to E. du Plessis [21 June 1935]. (EduP)
69. Unpublished letter, RC to E. du Plessis [25 June 1935]. (EduP)
70. Unpublished letter, RC to E. du Plessis [25 June 1935]. (EduP)

XI. TOLEDO

1. L. Lee, *As I Walked Out One Midsummer Morning*, p. 145–6.
2. Unpublished letter, RC to Greenwood [early 1936]. (WHG)
3. Interview with Mary Campbell, Portugal, 4 Jan. 1975.
4. CP, I, 155 and 157.
5. Reprinted in CP, II, 22 as 'Driving Cattle to Casas Buenas'.
6. CP. I, 158.
7. *Light on a Dark Horse*, p. 339.
8. *Light on a Dark Horse*, p. 326.
9. *Light on a Dark Horse*, pp. 342 ff., and interview with Mary Campbell, Portugal, 5 Jan. 1975.
10. So entitled in *Mithraic Emblems*, p. 99; considerably revised and republished as 'In Memoriam of "Mosquito"', CP, II, 23.
11. Unpublished letter, RC to W. Lewis [Dec. 1933]. (CUL)
12. Unpublished letter, RC to Greenwood [9 July 1936]. (WHG)
13. Unpublished letter, RC to Greenwood [April 1936]. (WHG)
14. Interview with Mary Campbell, Portugal, 6 Jan. 1975.
15. Interview with Mary Campbell, Portugal, 6 Jan. 1975.
16. I have drawn the following account of events mainly from McNeill-Moss's *The Epic of the Alcazar*, the most detailed study of the events in Toledo, and from interviews with Mary and Teresa Campbell.
17. Interviews with Mary and Teresa Campbell; and I have drawn on Campbell's unpublished 'Synopsis' of the (never written) second volume of *Light on a Dark Horse*. (A)
18. CP, I, 153.
19. Evidence of Anna Cavero de Carondelet (Campbell's younger daughter) quoted

in R. Lyle's unpublished *Herdsman of Apollo*. (HSRC)
20. Campbell's unpublished 'Synopsis'. (A)
21. Interview with Teresa and Mary Campbell, Portugal, 4 Jan. 1975.
22. Campbell's unpublished 'Synopsis'. (A)
23. Interview with Teresa Campbell, Portugal, 4 Jan. 1975.
24. Unpublished letter, RC to Mary Campbell [28 June 1937]. (A)
25. D. Wright: 'A Poet and His Dragons', *Telegraph Sunday Magazine*, May 1979. Laura Riding cannot now recall the incident.
26. Marsh Farm, Binsted, Arundel, Sussex.
27. London *Daily Express*, 12 Aug. 1936.
28. Unpublished letter, W. Lewis to RC [Aug 1936]. (WHG)
29. RC's 'Synopsis'. (A)
30. Unpublished letter, G. Faber to RC, 19 June 1936. (F&F)
31. *The Tablet*, 21 Nov. 1936.
32. *New Statesman and Nation*, 26 Dec. 1936.
33. *Sunday Times*, 17 Jan. 1937.
34. *Sunday Times*, 17 Jan. 1937.
35. *New Statesman and Nation*, 26 Dec. 1936.
36. Unpublished letter, S. Spender to W. H. Gardner, 26 June 1958. (HSRC)
37. In her memoirs, *Out of This Century*, Peggy Guggenheim calls Douglas Garman 'Sherman' and Wishart 'Brad'.
38. Unpublished letter, RC to W. Lewis [1936]. (CUL)
39. Unpublished letter, RC to W. Lewis [1936]. (CUL)
40. Interview with R. Lyle, Portugal, 7 Jan. 1975, and unpublished letter, RC to Edith Sitwell [July 1955]. (HRC)
41. Interview with Mary Campbell, Portugal, 5 Jan. 1975.
42. Unpublished letter, RC to F. C. Slater [Sept. 1936]. (WHG)
43. Interview with Teresa Campbell, Portugal, 5 Jan. 1975.

XII. WANDERINGS

1. Interview with Teresa Campbell, Portugal, 5 Jan. 1975.
2. Interview with Mary Campbell, Portugal, 4 Jan. 1975.
3. Unpublished letter, Teresa Campbell to the writer, 24. March 1978. (A)
4. Unpublished letter, RC to Mary Campbell, [25 June 1937]. (WHG)
5. Unpublished postcard, RC to Mary Campbell, 27 June 1937. (WHG)
6. Interview with Mary Campbell, Portugal, 3 Jan. 1975.
7. Unpublished letter, RC to Mary Campbell, 28 June 1937. (A)
8. It must be said, however, that it sold well enough for Longman's to bring out a second cheap edition, on 21 July 1941.
9. Unpublished letter, RC to F. C. Slater [Nov./Dec. 1938] (WHG)
10. This is the main point he makes in defence of his views in a long letter printed in the *TLS* of 25 Feb. 1939.
11. CP, II, 53. Campbell revised *Flowering Rifle* for his *Collected Poems*, and he then printed Book I of the poem as 'A letter from the San Mateo Front'. (CP, II, 38)
12. Unpublished letter, RC to his mother, [April 1939] (KCL)

13. 'Viator' in *The Tablet*, 11 Feb. 1939.
14. Spender in the *New Statesman and Nation*, 11 March 1939.
15. Among those who did were Edmund Blunden, who wrote privately to Campbell, 'I have tried for many years now to keep a cool mind in sorting out Continental affairs, but even that attitude does not satisfy the wild neurotics here . . .' E. Blunden to RC, unpublished letter, 30 June 1939. (KCL)
16. Unpublished letter, RC to E. du Plessis [Nov./Dec. 1938] (WHG)
17. Unpublished letter, RC to George Campbell [June 1938) (A)
18. Interview with Mary Campbell, Portugal, 5 Jan. 1975.
19. Interview with Mary Campbell, Portugal, 5 Jan. 1975.
20. Interview with Teresa Campbell, Portugal, 4 Jan. 1975.
21. Interview with Teresa Campbell, Portugal, 4 Jan. 1975.
22. Number 19, Via Donatello.
23. Unpublished postcard, RC to W. Lewis, [21 Oct. 1938] (CUL)
24. Unpublished letter, RC to E. du Plessis [Nov./Dec. 1938] (WHG)
25. Interview with Mary Campbell, Portugal, 5 Jan. 1975.
26. Unpublished letter, RC to his mother [May 1939]: quoted in B. Holt's unpublished *Outrageous Poet*, Chapter 6, p. 23. (BH)
27. Unpublished letter, RC to his mother [April 1939] (KCL)
28. Interview with Anna Cavero de Carondelet, Portugal, 2 Jan. 1975.
29. Interview with Mary Campbell, Portugal, 4 Jan. 1975.
30. Interview with Mary Campbell, Portugal, 5 Jan. 1975.
31. Unpublished letter, RC to E. Blunden, 30 May 1939. (HRC)
32. 'The Hoopoe' was completed after the World War.
33. Unpublished letter, RC to his mother [July 1939] (KCL)
34. Unpublished letter, RC to his mother, 17 Oct. 1939 [WHG], and interview with Mary Campbell, Portugal, 6 Jan. 1975.
35. Interview with Anna Cavero de Carondelet, Portugal, 2 Jan. 1975.
36. Interview with Teresa Campbell, Portugal, 4 Jan. 1975.
37. Unpublished Synopsis for Volume II of *Light on a Dark Horse*. (A)
38. Unpublished letter, RC to his mother [3 Oct. 1941] (WHG).
39. Unpublished letter, RC to C. W. Stewart, 28 July [1940] (F&F)
40. Interview with Mary Campbell, Portugal, 6 Jan. 1975.
41. Information taken from Campbell's passport, issued 10 September 1940.
42. 'Autobiography in Fifty Kicks'.
43. Interview with RC in Natal *Daily News*, 27 Aug. 1941.
44. Natal *Daily News*, 27 Aug. 1941.
45. Unpublished letter, RC to Mary Campbell [26 Sept. 1941.] (MC)
46. Unpublished letter, RC to Mary Campbell [26 Sept. 1941] (MC)
47. Unpublished letter, RC to Mary Campbell [26 Sept. 1941] (MC)
48. BBC Overseas Service broadcast, 2 March 1942.
49. *Light on a Dark Horse*, p. 226.
50. 'A Few Notes on RC' by Nancy Cunard, 25 Oct. 1958. (A)
51. RC's article in *Shenandoah*, Spring 1954: 'Dylan Thomas: The War Years', p. 26.
52. Harold Nicholson's Diary, 12 Sept. 1941: *Diaries and Letters*, Volume II, p. 186.
53. RC's article in *Shenandoah*, Spring 1954, p. 27.

54. Unpublished letter, RC to Mary Campbell [mid Oct. 1941] (MC)
55. Unpublished letter, RC to Mary Campbell [mid Oct. 1941] (MC)
56. Unpublished letter, RC to his mother, [3 Oct. 1941] (BH)
57. Unpublished letter, RC to his mother [3 Oct. 1941] (BH)

XIII. WAR

1. Date taken from RC's Army Discharge Certificate. (A)
2. Unpublished letter, A. Cruickshank to W. H. Gardner, 30 Sept. 1957. (HSRC)
3. Unpublished letter, A. Cruickshank to W. H. Gardner, 30 Sept. 1957. (HSRC)
4. King had commanded RC's air raid post.
5. RC to Mary Campbell [April 1943]. (MC)
6. Unpublished letter, A. Cruickshank to W. H. Gardner, 30 Sept. 1957. (HSRC)
7. Unpublished letter, RC to Mary Campbell [15 May 1942]. (HRC)
8. Unpublished letter, RC to Mary Campbell [late May 1942] (HRC), and *Light on a Dark Horse*, pp. 40–1.
9. Unpublished letter, RC to Mary Campbell [late May 1942]. (HRC)
10. Unpublished letter, RC to Mary Campbell [late May 1942]. (HRC)
11. Unpublished letter, A. Cruickshank to W. H. Gardner, 30 Sept. 1957. (HSRC)
12. Unpublished letter, RC to Mary Campbell [18 June 1942]. (HRC)
13. Unpublished letter, RC to Mary Campbell [6 Aug. 1942]. (WHG)
14. Rob Lyle's unpublished *Herdsman of Apollo*. (HSRC)
15. Unpublished letter, RC to Mary Campbell [Aug. 1942]. (MC)
16. Unpublished letter, RC to Mary Campbell [Nov. 1942]. (MC)
17. Interview with Mary Campbell, Portugal, 5 Jan. 1975.
18. Unpublished letter, RC to Mary Campbell [early Nov. 1942]. (MC)
19. Unpublished letter, RC to Mary Campbell [29 Nov. 1942]. (A)
20. Unpublished letter, RC to Mary Campbell [28 Dec. 1942]. (HRC)
21. Unpublished letter, RC to Mary Campbell [end Feb. 1943]. (MC)
22. Unpublished letter, RC to Mary Campbell, 24 March [1943]. (MC)
23. Unpublished letter, RC to Mary Campbell [April] 1943. (MC)
24. RC's unpublished *Synopsis* of Vol. II of *Light on a Dark Horse* (A), and unpublished letter to Mary Campbell, 12 May 1943. (A). But see RC's letter to Lady Duncan [20 April 1943] University of Cape Town Library, BC 294 E23 1.1.
25. Unpublished letter, RC to Mary Campbell [10 May 1943]. (MC)
26. Unpublished letter, RC to his mother [June 1943]. (HRC)
27. 'Snapshot of Nairobi' was first published in the military paper *Off Parade*.
28. Unpublished letter, RC to Mary Campbell, 12 May 1943. (A)
29. RC's talk on the African Service of the BBC, 15 July 1945 (BBC Archives).
30. In March 1944. Unpublished letter, RC to Mary Campbell, 2 April 1944. (A)
31. Unpublished letter, RC to Mary Campbell [mid Aug. 1943]. (MC)
32. Charles Mason's unpublished *Memoir* of RC. (HSRC)

33. Unpublished letter to Mary Campbell, 24 Aug. 1943. (HRC)
34. *New Statesman and Nation*, 11 March 1939.
35. Unpublished letter, RC to Mary Campbell [23 Oct. 1943]. (A)
36. Unpublished letter, RC to Teresa Campbell [12 Nov. 1943]. (HRC)
37. Unpublished letter, RC to his mother, 6 Jan. 1944. (HRC)
38. Unpublished letter, RC to Mary Campbell, 12 Jan. 1944. (WHG)
39. Unpublished letter, RC to Mary Campbell, 12 March [1944]. (HRC)
40. See for instance his unpublished letter to Mary Campbell, 17 March 1944. (MC)
41. Unpublished letter, RC to Mary Campbell [23 Feb. 1944]. (MC)
42. *Light on a Dark Horse*, pp. 1–3, and unpublished letters from RC to C. J. Sibbett and Mary Campbell [early May 1944]. (SANL and WHG)

XIV. LONDON

1. Unpublished letter, RC to Edmund Blunden [July/Aug. 1944]. (HRC)
2. Not to be confused with the earlier poem, 'Reflection', CP, I, 106.
3. Unpublished letter, RC to T. S. Eliot [Jan. 1946]. (VE)
4. Interview with Teresa Campbell, Portugal, 4 Jan. 1975.
5. Interview with Mary Campbell, Portugal, 5 Jan. 1975.
6. Unpublished letter, R. G. Townend to W. H. Gardner, 17 July 1961. (HSRC)
7. Unpublished letter, RC to his mother [12 December 1944]. (HRC)
8. Campbell called this preface 'A Yarn with Old Woodley', an allusion to the 1928 play *Young Woodley* by John Van Druten, portraying sex in a school setting.
9. Unpublished letter, T. S. Eliot to RC, 26 March 1945. (MC)
10. Unpublished letter, RC to T. S. Eliot [2 April 1945]. (VE)
11. Unpublished letter, RC to T. S. Eliot [Jan. 1946]. (VE)
12. Unpublished letter, RC to his mother [4 June 1945]. (HRC)
13. Unpublished letter, Geoffrey Grigson to the writer, 6 April 1978. (A)
14. Unpublished letter, RC to T. S. Eliot [Jan. 1946]. (VE)
15. David Wright, 'A Poet and His Dragons', *Telegraph Sunday Magazine*, May 1979.
16. Unpublished letter, RC to F. C. Slater [17 Dec. 1945]. (WHG)
17. David Wright, 'Roy Campbell: Portrait with Conversations', 1958. (A)
18. BBC files.
19. Unpublished letter, Mrs D. Collins (neé Chasmar) to the writer, 12 May 1978. (A)
20. Unpublished letter, Mrs D. Collins (neé Chasmar) to the writer, 12 May 1978. (A)
21. Unpublished letter, Mrs D. Collins to the writer, 12 May 1978. (A)
22. Unpublished letter, Mrs D. Collins to the writer, 12 May 1978. (A)
23. Unpublished letter, Geoffrey Grigson to the writer, 6 April 1978. (A)
24. *The Times*, 22 June 1946.
25. *New English Review*, July 1946.
26. *The Observer*, 30 June 1946.
27. *Poetry Review*, July 1946.

28. *The Listener*, 14 Nov. 1946.

29. *The Listener*, 28 Nov. 1946.

30. Unpublished letter, Stephen Spender to RC, 2 June [1946]. (WHG)

31. *Time and Tide*, 8 June 1946.

32. Unpublished letter, RC to Stephen Spender, 11 June 1946. (HRC)

33. *Tribune*, 28 June and 12, 19, and 26 July 1946.

34. *Tribune*, 26 July 1946.

35. Geoffrey Dutton, 'Roy Campbell', the *Bulletin*, 15 May 1957.

36. Interviews at the Catherine Wheel, London, 14 July 1977.

37. Campbell's annotations on his copy of Stephen Spender's letter to him, 2 June [1946]. (WHG)

38. David Wright, 'A Poet and His Dragons', *Telegraph Sunday Magazine*, May 1979.

39. Unpublished letter, Alister Kershaw to the writer, 30 March 1974. (A)

40. Unpublished letter, Mary Campbell to C. J. Sibbett, 15 Dec. 1947. (SANL)

41. Interview with Rob Lyle, Portugal, 7 Jan. 1975.

42. Interview with Rob Lyle, Portugal, 7 Jan. 1975.

43. Unpublished letter, RC to C. J. Sibbett [early 1948]. (SANL)

44. *TLS*, 24 March 1950.

45. Date taken from RC's passport. (A)

46. Unpublished statement, Rob Lyle to W. H. Gardner, June 1958. (HSRC)

47. Unpublished statement, Rob Lyle to W. H. Gardner, June 1958. (HSRC)

48. There are many versions of this incident; I have drawn chiefly on the memories of Rob Lyle, and on Robert Armstrong's account in the *Critic*, Feb./March 1962, pp. 18–21.

49. Unpublished letter, RC to Ross Nichols [May 1949]. (WHG)

50. Unpublished letter, Geoffrey Grigson to the writer, 6 April 1978. (A)

51. Interview with Rob Lyle, Portugal, 7 Jan. 1975.

52. Interview with Rob Lyle, Portugal, 7 Jan. 1975.

53. Interview with Rob Lyle, Portugal, 7 Jan. 1975.

54. *The Catacomb*, No. 11 (Feb. 1950): 'Fragments of Autobiography'.

55. *The Catacomb*, No. 10 (Jan. 1950): 'A Screw-tapey Letter'.

56. Unpublished letter, RC to Edith Sitwell [June 1949]. (HRC)

57. RC's passport. (A)

58. The Garage St Francois.

59. Unpublished letter, RC to Peter Russell (June 1950). (WHG)

60. Unpublished letters, Lewis Hastings to Tom Burns, 20 and 21 July 1950. (A)

61. Unpublished letter, Teresa Campbell to Tom Burns [24 July 1950]. (HSRC)

62. Unpublished letter, Augustus John to RC, 23 Aug. 1950. (A)

63. Unpublished letter, RC to F. C. Slater [Dec. 1950]. (SANL)

64. Interview with Professor Guy Butler, Cambridge, 10 April 1975.

65. RC's broadcast talk on St John of the Cross, BBC sound archives, 1952.

66. As Smith, *Lyric and Polemic*, amply demonstrates.

67. Unpublished letter, RC to F. C. Slater [end Jan. 1952]. (WHG)

68. Lyle's 'Statement' to W. H. Gardner, June 1958. (HSRC)

69. Dylan Thomas's review of *Light on a Dark Horse*, *The Observer*, 16 Dec. 1951.

70. Unpublished letter, Harold Nicolson to Christopher Hollis, 5 Feb. 1952. (A)

71. Unpublished letter, RC to Rob Lyle [2 Nov. 1951]. (WHG)

72. Unpublished letter, RC to Richard Aldington [late Feb. 1952]. (TC)
73. Unpublished letter, RC to C. J. Sibbett [April 1952]. (SANL)
74. *The Catacomb*, New Series, Vol 1, No. 1. (Summer 1950)
75. Unpublished letter, RC to Rob Lyle [May/June 1950]. (SUL)
76. Rob Lyle's unpublished *Herdsman of Apollo*, Chapter XV.
77. Rob Lyle's unpublished *Herdsman of Apollo*, Chapter XV.
78. Interview with Rob Lyle, Portugal, 7 Jan. 1975.
79. Unpublished letter, RC to Mary Campbell [May 1952]. (HRC)

XV. THE LAST YEARS

1. Unpublished letter, RC to John Sutherland [1 Dec. 1952]. (A)
2. Published at the end of 1952.
3. Published in 1952.
4. Campbell's excellent translations of Lorca have yet to appear.
5. Unpublished letter, RC to Richard Aldington [Nov. 1952]. (TC)
6. Rob Lyle's unpublished *Herdsman of Apollo*. (HSRC)
7. A portion of the typescript still exists. (A)
8. Lyle's 'Statement' to W. H. Gardner, June 1958. (HSRC)
9. Unpublished letter, RC to Richard Aldington [March 1953]. (TC)
10. Unpublished letter, RC to Rob Lyle [22 Oct. 1953]. (SUL)
11. Unpublished 'Impressions of Roy Campbell' by Professor L. A. Duchemin, 12 Oct. 1959. (A) I have drawn heavily on this excellent account of RC's visit to Mount Allison University, Sackville, N.B., on 22 Oct. 1953.
12. Unpublished letter, RC to John Sutherland [23 Oct. 1953]. (A) and Professor Duchemin's 'Impressions of Roy Campbell'. (A)
13. Unpublished letter, RC to John Sutherland [23 Oct. 1953]. (A)
14. Unpublished postcard, RC to Mary Campbell [15 Nov. 1953]. (MC)
15. Unpublished letter, S. Wofsy to W. H. Gardner, 12 Nov. 1959. (HSRC)
16. Unpublished letter, S. Wofsy to W. H. Gardner, 12 Nov. 1959. (HSRC)
17. Unpublished letter, Henry Regnery to W. H. Gardner, 3 Aug. 1959. (HSRC)
18. Quoted in Lyle's unpublished *Herdsman of Apollo*. (HSRC)
19. 'In Memoriam A. F. Tschiffely', from the manuscript in HRC.
20. Unpublished letter, John Sutherland to RC, 15 Dec. 1953. (WHG)
21. Unpublished letters, RC to Rob Lyle [March 1954]. (WHG)
22. Unpublished postcard, RC to Mary Campbell [11 March 1954]. (MC)
23. Unpublished postcard, RC to Mary Campbell [16 March 1954]. (SUL)
24. Unpublished letter, RC to Mary and Teresa Campbell [19 March 1954]. (SUL)
25. RC's annotated copy of an offprint from *Theoria* No. 6, (A), and Geoffrey Dutton, *Africa in Black and White*, p. 35.
26. Interview with George Campbell, Durban, 16 July 1975.
27. *Natal Witness*, editorial column, 22 March 1954. Subsequently printed versions of this speech are not reliable.
28. Unpublished letter, RC to Mary Campbell [21 March 1954]. (HRC)
29. Unpublished letter, RC to Edith and Osbert Sitwell [March 1954]. (HRC)

30. Unpublished letter, Mary Campbell to RC [March 1954]. (A)
31. Unpublished letter, RC to Mary Campbell [25 March 1954]. (SUL)
32. Unpublished postcard, RC to Teresa Campbell [April 1954]. (HRC)
33. Unpublished letter, RC to Mary Campbell, 4 May [1954]. (HRC)
34. The date of its composition is given in Lyle's *Herdsman of Apollo*, Chapter XV.
35. Interview with Teresa Campbell, 6 Jan. 1975.
36. They were broadcast in February, May, July and August 1955 (BBC Archives).
37. Unpublished letter, Richard Aldington to RC, 9 June 1954. (TC)
38. Unpublished letter, RC to Rob Lyle [Aug. 1954]. (WHG)
39. Unpublished letter, Henry Regnery to W. H. Gardner, 3 Aug. 1959. (HSRC)
40. Date taken from RC's passport. (A)
41. Unpublished letter, Henry Regnery to W. H. Gardner, 3 Aug. 1959. (HSRC)
42. Interview with Professor Guy Butler, Cambridge, 10 April 1975.
43. *New York Times* Book Review, 12 May 1955.
44. Quoted in RC's unpublished letter to Edith Sitwell [Aug. 1955]. (HRC)
45. Unpublished letter, RC to L. Whistler, 8 July 1955. (SUL)
46. RC's passport.
47. Unpublished letter, RC to Max Reinhardt [15 Sept. 1955]. (Bodley)
48. Unpublished letter, RC to Mary Campbell [17 Oct. 1955]. (MC)
49. Unpublished letter, RC to W. Payn [Feb. 1956]. (WHG)
50. Unpublished letter, RC to Mary Campbell [27 Oct. 1955]. (MC)
51. Unpublished letter, RC to W. Payn [Feb. 1956]. (WHG)
52. Unpublished letter, Sister Margaret Teresa to W. H. Gardner, 28 Oct. 1959. (HSRC)
53. It was published by Doubleday & Co.
54. Published by The Bodley Head, 23 Sept. 1957.
55. Unpublished letter, RC to Max Reinhardt [19 March 1956]. (Bodley)
56. Unpublished letter, RC to George Campbell [April 1956]. (A)
57. Unpublished fragment of letter to Edith Sitwell [June 1956]. (HRC)
58. Interview with Mary Campbell, Portugal, 5 Jan. 1975.
59. They had never lived in the small house they owned in London.
60. Unpublished letter to Edith Sitwell [Sept. 1956]. (HRC)
61. Unpublished letter, RC to Daphne Collins [Dec. 1956]. (DC) His letter to Reinhardt [Feb. 1957] is even more certain of death.
62. Published by Reinhardt, 1957.
63. Postcard [16 April 1957]. Published in *Poetry Society Bulletin*, May 1957.

POSTSCRIPT

1. Among them Count Robilac.

INDEX

RC = Roy Campbell